About this book

After the death of Syria's President Hafiz al-Asad in mid-2000, hopes were high that his son and successor, Bashar, might succeed in reforming a system that had become a byword for economic stagnation and the pitiless repression of dissent. For six months, and for the first time in decades, Syrians were able to speak freely, without fear of the hated secret police. Political discussion groups mushroomed. The press started carrying articles openly demanding democracy, and petitions were circulated insisting that democracy was essential not only for its own sake but as a condition for desperately needed investment and economic expansion.

Alarmed at the threat to their monopoly on power, regime hardliners struck back, closing down discussion groups and staging show trials at which pro-democracy activists were sentenced to years in jail. The regime cynically cited the need for 'national unity' at a time when Israel under Ariel Sharon and the United States under George W. Bush were subjecting the region to onslaughts that many Arabs saw as new manifestations of an old imperialism.

Based on the testimony of key players, *Syria: Neither Bread Nor Freedom* recounts the drama of the 'Damascus Spring' and its repression, and reveals what happens in a state like Syria to the institutions that occupy the political space between government and governed. From political parties to parliament, from the media to the judicial system and universities, this book lifts the veil of rhetoric and propaganda to reveal a system so demoralized and corrupt that power is wielded for no purpose but power itself. This is Bashar al-Asad's legacy and the system which, given time, he hopes to reform.

About the author

After graduating from Oxford University in 1970, Alan George gained his MA on Middle Eastern geography at Durham in 1972 and his PhD on Syria, also at Durham, in 1978. Since 1984 he has worked as a freelance journalist and researcher, contributing to a wide range of UK and international publications including the *Observer*, the *Independent* and *Private Eye* in the UK; *Profil* and *Der Standard* in Austria; *Panorama* in Italy; *Berlingske Tidende* in Denmark; and the London-based pan-Arab daily papers *Ash-Sharq al-Awsat* and *Al-Quds*. He frequently commentates on Middle Eastern affairs for radio and television. He is a former assistant director of the Council for the Advancement of Arab–British Understanding (CAABU), of whose Executive Committee he was a member for many years. He has visited Syria and the wider Arab region repeatedly since 1967.

SYRIA

Neither Bread nor Freedom

Alan George

Zed Books
LONDON AND NEW YORK

Syria: Neither Bread nor Freedom was first published by Zed Books Ltd, 7 Cynthia Street, London N1 9JF, UK and Room 400, 175 Fifth Avenue, New York, NY 10010, USA in 2003.

www.zedbooks.demon.co.uk

Cover designed by Andrew Corbett
Set in Monotype Dante by Ewan Smith, London
Printed and bound in Malta

Distributed in the USA exclusively by Palgrave, a division of St Martin's Press, LLC, 175 Fifth Avenue, New York, NY 10010.

A catalogue record for this book is available from the British Library

ISBN 1 84277 212 0 cased
ISBN 1 84277 213 9 limp
US CIP is available from the Library of Congress

Contents

Acknowledgements

It was MJ's idea to write this book, and it was a very good idea. Petra Stienen, first secretary at the Netherlands Embassy in Damascus, the acknowledged diplomatic specialist on Syria's civil society movement, gave generously of her time and her insights. I am greatly indebted to her. For his sagacious professional counsel and his steadfast friendship and encouragement, I thank profoundly George Joffé, visiting professor in geography at King's College, London University, and research fellow at Cambridge University's Centre of International Studies. Muntaha Sabah, who translated tapes and documents from Arabic, and who has been another good friend, also deserves special mention. I thank Albert Aji of the Orient Press Center in Damascus for his efficient and good-humoured assistance, without forgetting the contribution of his assistant, Salim Abraham. I also thank both Lotte Leicht, director of the Brussels office of Human Rights Watch, and Virginie Locussol, of the North Africa–Middle East desk of Reporters Sans Frontières, for their assistance and example. I am grateful to the writer Dr Rana Kabbani for her valuable comments on the final draft.

I thank those of my interviewees whom I am free to name (in no particular order): the philosopher Dr Sadiq al-Azm; his son, the archaeologist Dr Amr al-Azm; Dr Samir Altaqi, member of the politburo of the Syrian Communist Party faction headed by Yousef Faisal; the independent member of parliament and prisoner of conscience Riad Seif; his wife, Reem; Hussam Shehadeh, Riad Seif's office manager; the writer Michel Kilo; Professor Dr Hani Mourtada, president of Damascus University; 'Ali Sadr al-Din al-Bayanouni, superintendent-general of the Syrian Muslim Brotherhood; Professor Muhammad Aziz Shukri, chairman of Damascus University's Department of International Law; the late Mahmoud Salameh, editor-in-chief of *Ath-Thawra*; Hassan Abdul Azim, spokesman of the National Democratic Gathering; Ali Farzat, editor of *Ad-Dommari*; Haitham al-Maleh, president of the Syrian Human Rights Association; the writer and journalist Subhi Hadidi; the writer and journalist Dr Patrick Seale; *Al-Hayat*'s

Damascus correspondent, Ibrahim Hamidi; Abdul Qader al-Qaddura, the speaker of the Syrian parliament; the journalist and human rights campaigner Nizar Nayyouf; Dr Christian Berger, desk officer for Syria and subsequently political adviser in the Middle East Unit of the European Commission's External Relations Directorate-General; Muhammad Khair al-Wadei, former editor of *Tishreen*; Fua'd Mardood, editor of the *Syria Times*; Ghatfan Kandel, system administrator for the Syrian Telecommunications Establishment's Pilot Internet Project; the lawyer Da'ad Mousa; Ayman 'Abd an-Nur, adviser to President Bashar al-Asad; and Jerome Cassiers, deputy head of the European Commission's Mission to Damascus.

I am no less grateful to those interviewees and sources of information who, for obvious reasons, chose to request anonymity.

The Syrian authorities might not be pleased with my book, but I hope that H.E. Adnan Omran, the minister of information, will nevertheless accept my gratitude for his assistance and that of his officials. This applies equally to his predecessor, Dr Muhammad Salman, who always welcomed me to Damascus with much warmth. In the same spirit of personal goodwill, I thank Munir Ali, director of public relations and foreign media at the Information Ministry, and Ayman Alloush, formerly press attaché at the Syrian Embassy in London.

For their always reliable support and encouragement, I pay tribute to Z and our three children, Emily, Katherine and Michael.

To all the above, my thanks – although I alone bear responsibility for what follows.

Introduction

§ THE civil society movement (*harakat al-mujtama' al-madani*) which flourished in the months following the death of President Hafiz al-Asad in mid-2000 was one of the most exciting political developments in Syria in the nearly forty years since the 1963 coup which inaugurated authoritarian Ba'athist rule. Its values and objectives were not new; intellectuals and others had never ceased to express them in private. In the late 1970s they had momentarily dared to voice them publicly, before being silenced by Asad's iron fist. The 'Damascus Spring' was different. This time, reform appeared to have the blessing of Asad's successor, his son Bashar. Before, reformists had been isolated voices in a wilderness of oppression. In 2000–2001 they became a national movement whose vigour, spontaneity and courage put to shame the discredited system which was their target.

It was no surprise that the system hit back, deploying its habitual brute force rather than coherent argument. While reasserting the regime's power, however, the backlash also revealed a weakness at its core. As always in this Kafkaesque system, the details were hazy but Bashar plainly had been unable to withstand the demands of the regime's hardliners for whom reform, and especially political reform, was anathema. In a structure supposedly centred on the presidency, the President was evidently not the only centre and, on this issue, not the most important one. Whether and how quickly Bashar will be able to build his own support base and shrug off the hardliners are the central questions now facing Syria.

In suppressing the civil society movement, the regime sought to smear it as a treasonous 'tool of the Zionists and imperialists'. Another tack was to insist that Syria already had a civil society of clubs, charities and Muslim and church organisations; or even that it had a long-standing civil society comprising the extended family, clan, tribal, ethnic and religious groups. At worst, the regime's claims were downright lies. At best they were profoundly disingenuous, often involving deliberate confusion of the words 'civil' and 'civilian'.

Civil society has a long history and has meant different things to different people at different times and places.[1] In the United States it has come to mean local voluntary associations that can mediate between the state and the people. During the collapse of Eastern European communism in the late 1980s the dissidents wanted liberal democracy, the rule of law and respect for human rights, which they termed 'civil society'. Essential to both concepts, however, is the insistence on a tolerant, democratic political space *not dominated by the state*.

Certainly Syria has voluntary clubs and associations, but they must *all* be licensed by the government. They are allowed to function in peace only to the extent that they do not impinge on the prerogatives of the regime – which in this police state leaves them with only the smallest room for manoeuvre. To invoke primordial social groups such as family and clan as evidence of the existence of 'civil society' is nonsensical. By that token, any society since the dawn of history could be defined as one of 'civil society'.

Whatever their propaganda pronouncements, the Syrian authorities know that the country's civil society activists stand firmly in the tradition of the Eastern European reformers. They want multi-party democracy, the rule of law, respect for human rights and a free press. They demand an end to the State of Emergency which has been in effect for forty years and which gives virtually unlimited power to security agencies accountable only to their heads. They want an end to torture and 'disappearances'. They want to reclaim political territory that is no less occupied than is Syria's Golan Heights, seized by Israel in the 1967 Middle East war.

Syria's civil society activists explicitly argue that sweeping political reform is essential not only to improve the quality of life but also as a precondition for an end to their country's protracted economic crisis. Powerful support for their view came in *The Arab Human Development Report 2002*, a 178-page United Nations Development Programme (UNDP) study by a team of Arab intellectuals which explicitly linked the region's abysmal social and economic development record to the general absence of democracy, the marginalisation of women and the failure to invest in knowledge.[2] Some dispute this view, arguing that economic development can proceed within an authoritarian political context, citing Chile and South Korea as examples. What is beyond dispute is that the Syrian regime's policies have failed to deliver acceptable living standards for the majority.

Initially, Bashar al-Asad wanted both political and economic reform.

Under pressure from the hardliners, he opted for economic reform only. 'Man does not live on bread alone,' Hafiz al-Asad once commented. 'Man needs to live his humanity. He needs a moral meaning to his life. He needs freedom and dignity.'[3] In reality, he provided neither bread nor freedom. Riad Seif, a member of parliament imprisoned in 2001 for his part in the civil society movement, commented that Bashar had put 'bread before freedom'.[4] Whether and to what extent he can succeed are open questions.

Recording the 'Damascus Spring', when the civil rights movement flourished, and the subsequent 'Damascus Winter', when it was suppressed, was a main objective of this book. I also wanted to explore the 'occupied political territory' for which the movement is struggling: the realm of the omnipresent Ba'ath ('Renaissance') Party and the 'popular organisations'; of the rubber-stamp parliament, the corrupted legal system and the state-run media; of the over-stretched and underperforming universities: in short, the institutions of debate and ideas which in liberal democracies civilise the relationship between rulers and ruled. All this I have tried to set in a proper context by means of a lengthy introductory chapter that reviews the country and its political system as a whole. A concluding chapter assesses the first two years of Bashar al-Asad's presidency and examines his options as he wrestles with the demand for restraint from his regime's conservatives and with the clamour for reform from the people, and it suggests that he will try to steer a middle road – with no certainty of attaining his twin aims of regime stability and economic progress.

I have relied heavily on the testimony of interviewees who, although well placed, are relatively few. In my defence I would argue that sufficient interviews were conducted to say what needed saying; and that more officials would have been interviewed had they made themselves available. On successive visits to Damascus in 2001 and 2002 I formally requested meetings with senior Ba'ath Party functionaries. None was available. My conclusion was that the party, despite its ubiquity, either had nothing to say or nothing that it wanted to say. Another impediment was the Ministry of Information's failure to approve entry visas for planned visits in April and May 2002. In a manner that would have struck a chord with George Orwell or Franz Kafka, no reason was ever given. I was never formally blacklisted. The visas were never formally refused. It was just that, somehow, they were never issued.

This book will no doubt prompt the usual accusations from those in the Syrian regime who find it easier to flourish rhetoric than deal with reality. Some may denounce it as a malevolent assault from 'foreign enemies' intended to 'sow discord' within Syria and 'threaten national unity'. Others will merely claim that it is 'biased' and fails to highlight the 'glorious achievements' of the forty years of Ba'athist rule. To such critics, I would point out that nothing I have written will be news to the Syrians themselves who, whatever the official line may be, know very well that the system is as unpleasant as it is inefficient. Identifying and acknowledging problems are essential first steps towards solving them. Sticking one's head in the sand takes one nowhere.

The well-rehearsed excuses will be trotted out: that Syria faced constant threat from an aggressive Israel, and that this diverted national wealth into defence and necessitated a strong security apparatus; that human rights were put lower on the agenda than the need to guard against foreign plots aimed at exploiting Syria's patchwork of ethnic and religious groups to generate domestic strife which could escalate into civil war, as in neighbouring Lebanon. Of course such claims have a great deal of truth in them. Damascus *has* indeed been locked in deadly struggles with implacable enemies. The real question, however, is how Syria might have fared had it not been subjected to forty years of dictatorship.

Whatever the reasons and the excuses, the central reality is inescapable: that the system created by the Syrian Ba'athists – and especially Hafiz al-Asad – is cruel, capricious and venal. It has turned the country into a vast prison, and it has manifestly failed to deliver either acceptable standards of living or a credible military defence against Israel.

The depressing truth about the degenerate Syrian system is that it has become pointless. The echoes of totalitarian Oceania in George Orwell's classic parody of Stalinism, *Nineteen Eighty-Four*, are disturbing. In his Introduction to the Penguin edition, the historian Ben Pimlott noted: 'Where other ideologies have justified themselves in terms of a future goal, *Ingsoc*, the doctrine of the Party in Oceania, is aimless.' O'Brien, a Party functionary, explains to the book's hero, Winston Smith: 'We are interested solely in power. Not wealth or luxury or long life or happiness: only power, pure power.' It is, moreover, power to no end. 'The object of persecution is persecution,' says O'Brien. 'The object of torture is torture. The object of power is power.'[5] It's not quite that bad in Syria, but it comes pretty close.

En passant, I would note that the Syrian regime's most dangerous opponents have been the fundamentalist Muslim Brotherhood (Al-

Ikhwan al-Muslimoun). In *Nineteen Eighty-Four*, the Party's deadliest enemies are the Brotherhood, 'a vast shadowy army, an underground network of conspirators dedicated to the overthrow of the State'.[6]

If I criticise Syria's political system, I do so as a friend who has been captivated by the country ever since his first visit, as a long-haired hippie hitch-hiker in 1967. If I condemn the unwarranted assault on the civil society movement, I am in sympathetic company. The British writer and journalist Patrick Seale, whose books on Syria are an invaluable source for those wishing to understand the country, said: 'As a lifelong friend and student of Syria, I'm extremely sorry that hopes for President Bashar have not been realised. It's a tragedy that Syria has reverted to its former immobility on the domestic front.' He was 'saddened and alarmed' at the suppression of the civil society movement which 'serves no purpose except to anger opinion at home and blacken Syria's name abroad, thereby offering opportunities to Syria's enemies'.[7]

It is a tribute to the strength and vitality of the Syrian people that their spirit has not been entirely cowed by the dark decades of repression and the daily struggle to make ends meet. I am always struck by the decency, tolerance and solidarity with which Syrians treat each other. Nor has their humour deserted them; indeed, it is one of their most telling defences against the system. Consider the following local joke. A deep hole appeared in a Damascus street and there was nothing to warn drivers or pedestrians. As the accidents and injuries mounted, someone complained to the city authorities, demanding either that the hole be mended or that a warning sign be erected. Instead, a nurse was assigned to take care of the injured pending their transport to hospital by ambulance. There were more complaints, so the authorities put an ambulance on permanent standby near the hole to whisk the injured swiftly to hospital. This did not stop the flood of complaints, so the authorities ordered the construction of a hospital near the hole, and named it after Hafiz al-Asad's late son Basil. Still the complaints came in. At length, and following a meeting of the Ba'ath Party's highest executive body, the Regional Command, it was resolved to dig up the entire street and lower it to the depth of the hole. Problem solved.

The authorities have tried to smear the civil society activists as treasonous 'agents' of foreign enemies. This does not come well from a regime that has so signally betrayed its people's hopes and interests and whose over-riding preoccupation is power for power's sake. The real patriots and heroes of modern Syria are not the grasping heads of the intelligence agencies or the sloganeering Ba'ath Party functionaries. They are the civil society activists, of whom their country can be proud and to whom this book is dedicated.

London, September 2002

Notes

1. John Ehrenberg, *Civil Society: The Critical History of an Idea* (New York and London: New York University Press, 1999).

2. UNDP, *The Arab Human Development Report 2002* (New York: UNDP, July 2002).

3. People's Assembly, *The People's Assembly: One of the Great Achievements of the Glorious Correctionist Movement*, 2nd edn (Damascus, 1999), p. 8.

4. Interview with author, Damascus, 5 May 2000.

5. George Orwell, *Nineteen Eighty-Four* (London: Penguin Books, 2000), p. x.

6. Ibid., p. 15.

7. Interview with author, 7 July 2002.

Chronology

17 April 1946: Independence.

30 March 1949: Coup by Colonel Husni az-Za'im.

14 August 1949: Coup by Colonel Sami al-Hinnawi.

19 December 1949: Coup by Colonel Adib ash-Shishakli.

27 February 1954: Coup by Colonel Faisal al-Atassi restores parliamentary rule.

1 February 1958: Syria unites with Egypt to form the United Arab Republic (UAR).

28 September 1961: Coup led by Lieutenant-Colonel 'Abd al-Karim Nahlawi extricates Syria from the UAR and restores parliamentary rule.

8 March 1963: Ba'athist military coup.

23 February 1966: Coup by radical Ba'athists.

June 1967: War with Israel.

16 November 1970: Hafiz al-Asad's coup, or 'Corrective Movement'.

October 1973: War with Israel.

31 May–1 June 1976: Syrian forces enter Lebanon.

1976–82: Rebellion spearheaded by Muslim Brotherhood.

2 February–5 March 1982: Uprising in Hama.

1980–88: Syria sides with Iran in the Iraq–Iran War.

June 1982: Israel invades Lebanon.

November 1983–May 1984: The succession crisis.

1990–91: Syria sides with the anti-Iraq coalition in the Kuwait crisis.

October 1990: Lebanese civil war ends.

22 May 1991: Syria and Lebanon sign a Treaty of Brotherhood, Co-operation and Co-ordination.

October 1991: Arab–Israeli peace conference in Madrid.

21 January 1994: Basil al-Asad, heir apparent, dies in a speeding accident.

December 1999–January 2000: Abortive Israeli–Syrian peace talks.

24 May 2000: Israel withdraws from Lebanon.

10 June 2000: Death of Hafiz al-Asad.

17 June 2000: Bashar al-Asad becomes secretary-general of the Ba'ath Party.

17 July 2000: Bashar al-Asad becomes President.

January–February 2001: The regime counter-attacks against the civil society movement.

August–September 2001: Civil society activists arrested.

Vital Statistics

Population: 16.72 million (2001)[1]
Annual population growth rate: 2.5 per cent (2000)[4]
Urban population: 51.4 per cent (2000)[4]
Percentage of population aged under nineteen: 53.8 (2001)[1]
Life expectancy: 70.5 years (2000)[2]
Illiteracy rates:
 Adult (aged 15+) males: 11.7 per cent (2000)[4]
 Adult (aged 15+) females: 39.5 per cent (2000)[4]
Unemployment rate: 25–30 per cent (2001 estimate)[3]
Gross domestic product (GDP): $19.4 billion (2000)[1]
Per capita GDP: $1,186 (2000)[1]
Inflation rate: 0.54 per cent (2000)[1]
Exports: $4,670 million (2000)[1]
Imports: $4,033 million (2000)[1]
Trade balance: +$637million (2000)[1]
Land area: 185,200 square kilometres
Cultivable area: 5,905,000 hectares (2000)[1]
Cultivated area: 5,352,000 hectares (2000)[1]
Irrigated area: 1,210,500 hectares (2000)[1]
Per capita renewable water resources: 1,791 cubic metres (1995)[2]
Per capita annual water withdrawal: 1,017 cubic metres (1995)[2]
Per capita water balance: 774 cubic metres (1995)[2]

Sources

1. Office of the Prime Minister, *Statistical Abstract 2001*, Central Bureau of Statistics, Syrian Arab Republic.
2. UNDP, *The Arab Human Development Report 2002* (New York: UNDP, July 2002).
3. US Department of State, *Background Note: Syria* (Washington, DC: Bureau of Near Eastern Affairs, February 2002).
4. World Bank, *World Development Indicators Database* (Washington, DC: World Bank, April 2002).

TURKEY
Qamishli
Hassaka
Aleppo
Idlib
Balikh
Raqqa
Euphrates
Lake Asad
Orontes
Lattakia
Mediterranean Sea
Khabur
Deir az-Zor
Hama
Tartous
Homs
Tadmur
Abu Kamal
Tripoli
LEBANON
Beirut
IRAQ
Damascus
KEY
Israeli-occupied area
International boundary
Quneitra
ISRAEL
Sweida'
Der'a
JORDAN
0
50
100
150
Kilometres

Map of Syria

CHAPTER 1

'A Certain Equality of Misery': An Overview of Syria

§ IS Syria's new, young President, Bashar al-Asad, *really* less popular than his late father, Hafiz? In a 10 July 2000 referendum on his succession to the presidency – in which almost the entire electorate participated – 97.29 per cent of Syrians voted for Bashar. This was 2.64 per cent below the even more absurd 99.987 per cent achieved by his father on 10 February 1999, in a referendum on whether he should have a fifth seven-year term as Syria's leader. Cynics joked about who precisely were the 0.71 per cent who had voted against Bashar, not to mention the 219 voters (enumerated, incredibly, as precisely as that) who had spurned his father in 1999. Were they, perhaps, denizens of Syria's political prisons?

The outcome of these stage-managed events, accompanied by compulsory street parties and 'popular rallies' to demonstrate support for the sole candidate, is never in doubt. Asked to predict the result a week before Bashar's referendum, an Information Ministry official told me, entirely straight-faced: 'At least 99 per cent.' He was wrong, but only very marginally. By voting for Bashar, a British-trained ophthalmologist then aged thirty-four, Syrians had confirmed their wish for him 'to follow the march' of his father, explained the state-run Syrian Arab News Agency (SANA). 'Change within a framework of continuity' has since been the official theme in every sphere, domestic and foreign.

In Syria, however, politically charged words such as 'change' and 'continuity' do not necessarily carry their usual meanings. On the south side of Ibn Asaker Street in south-west Damascus, just before it enters Yarmouk Square, stands the headquarters of the Shurtat al-Murur (Traffic Police) – a hideously functional up-ended matchbox of a building. Above its entrance is a plasticised portrait of Hafiz al-Asad and the slogan of the ruling Ba'ath (Renaissance) Party: 'Unity, Freedom, Socialism'. Adjacent, also in plastic and in script half a metre high, is the declaration: *'Ash-Shurta fi Khidmat ash-Sha'ab'* ('The Police are in the Service of the People'). The slogan, with the rest of the political montage of which it is part, is backlit by night and derives from Article 12 of the Syrian Constitution proclaiming: 'The state is in the service of the people.'

Like much in Syria, it's eerily reminiscent of George Orwell's parody of Stalinism, *Nineteen Eighty-Four*, set in a totalitarian state where the ruling party and its head, Big Brother, watch everyone constantly, where dissent is ruthlessly eliminated and where power is wielded for its own sake under the slogans: 'War is Peace; Freedom is Slavery; Ignorance is Strength'. As Noam Chomsky has commented: 'The terms of political discourse typically have two meanings. One is the dictionary meaning, and the other is a meaning that is useful for serving power – the doctrinal meaning.'[1] In the Syrian police state, where the multiple and overlapping intelligence agencies – collectively known as the *mukhabarat* – employ perhaps 65,000 full-time officers plus several hundred thousand part-timers, occasional collaborators and informers,[2] the police are 'in the service of the people'. As the country's total population is 16.7 million (in 2001),[3] there is one full-time secret policeman per 257 Syrians. However, 59.5 per cent of Syrians are aged over fifteen years, and if only these adults are counted the ratio is one secret policeman per 153 Syrians. (If the United States had one secret agent per 257 Americans, its intelligence community would number well over one million.)

'Change within a framework of continuity' is nevertheless one of the regime's more honest slogans – albeit because it can mean everything and nothing. Some things have changed under Bashar al-Asad, but in its essentials the system has not. The country is still run by a president and a clique of surrounding strongmen. The Ba'ath remains the leading party, recognised as such in the Constitution (written in 1973, by the Ba'athists). The influence of the military and of the security agencies remains pervasive. Parliament remains a talking shop whose main task is to rubber-stamp presidential decisions. The judiciary – like every other professional and societal group – remains in thrall to the authorities, and ultimately the President. As before, the bloated, underpaid, ill-motivated and often corrupt bureaucracy – numbering around 500,000 of a total workforce of 4.9 million[4] – straddles society and the economy, stifling both efficiency and initiative and making the most mundane administrative task a Kafkaesque torment.

One of Bashar al-Asad's most valuable assets is precisely that he represents stability and continuity. Syria lies in a turbulent region and itself underwent a succession of regime changes, including several military coups (three in 1949 alone), in the twenty-five years between independence and Hafiz al-Asad's seizure of power in November 1970. According to the official terminology, of course, his was *not* a coup. It was a '*Corrective Movement*'.

'Under his father, there was a certain equality of misery. There was no endless fighting in the streets, which in this part of the world counts for a lot,' a senior Western diplomat in Damascus told me.

For all their grumbling at the system's manifest inability to deliver reasonable standards of living for more than a minority, at its almost complete absence of democratic accountability and at its related lack of respect for human rights, Syrians do credit the regime with bringing stability. They well know that their country is an inherently unstable patchwork of religious and ethnic communities. What happened in neighbouring Lebanon, which was torn apart by a vicious and catastrophic civil war in 1975–90, stands as a warning of what could befall them too. 'Confessionalism is like a fire under ashes,' said a woman from southern Syria who requested anonymity. 'It does not take much to kindle it. I'm sure of that.' She underlined the point with an anecdote: 'The other day I was buying a large collection of books of an Arab thinker. There was an old woman who said to me: "Excellent, my daughter, you are buying the Qur'an. Good for you!" As if all books are the Qur'an!'[5] Syrians also understand, however, that Syria's stability was achieved not so much for the public good as from the desire to perpetuate Asad's rule; that it was the result not of consensus, but of often savage repression.

The Religio/Ethnic Mix

Reliable detailed statistics on Syria's religious and ethnic composition do not exist but Arabic-speakers (broadly synonymous with 'Arabs') constitute some 90 per cent of the population. Seventy-four per cent of Syrians adhere to the majority Sunni branch of Islam.[6] Arabic-speaking Sunni Muslims account for around 63 per cent of the population. Of the Muslim minorities, the biggest are the Alawis, accounting for some 12 per cent of the population and concentrated in the north-western coastal mountains. The Druse, found mainly in the Jebel Druse uplands in the south, account for 3 per cent of the total population. Small communities of Yazidis, Imamis and Ismailis are found, respectively, near Aleppo; in the Ghouta oasis around

Damascus and in north central Syria; and in the Salamiya region of the central province of Hama and in the north-western coastal mountains.

The split between Sunni and Shi'a Islam arose from differences over the succession to and role of the Immamate (the supreme rulership over the Muslim community) and over the significance of the *Sunna* (the sayings of the Prophet Muhammad). Sunnis hold the *Sunna* to be a crucial body of religious teachings. They believe the succession to the Immamate is a matter for the Muslim community as a whole, and that a believer can settle his relationship with God by reference to the Qur'an without intermediaries. Shi'as more or less discount the *Sunna*; insist that only 'Ali bin Abi Talib, the Prophet's cousin, and his direct descendants through the Prophet's daughter Fatima, can hold the Immamate; and consider the Imams to be mediators with God. The majority of Shi'as are Imamis or 'Twelvers', so named because they acknowledge twelve rightful Imams, the last of whom is believed to have disappeared in 878.

To varying degrees, the Alawi, Druse, Ismaili and Yazidi sects are secret, with knowledge of key doctrinal elements being confined to religious elders. The Ismailis split from the main Shi'a community in the eighth century over the legitimacy of the sixth Imam. The Druse are an offshoot of the Ismailis and believe al-Hakim, the Fatimid caliph who ruled Egypt from 966 to 1021, to have been the human incarnation of God. The Alawi sect, founded in the tenth century, is a complex blend of Shi'a Islam and pre-Islamic paganism, with some Christian philosophy thrown in. The Kurdish-speaking Yazidis are the most rarefied of Syria's religious groups, having only 'the vaguest points of connection with Syria's other sects, even though they hold the Qur'an and the Bible in reverence'.[7]

Christians form 10 per cent of Syria's population and are concentrated in the main cities. The Greek Orthodox are by far the biggest Christian community while Syrian Orthodox and Greek Catholics are also significant. Other Christians include the Armenians, Syrian Catholics, Maronites, Chaldaean Catholics and Protestants.

The Kurds, almost all Sunni Muslim except for the small number of Yazidis, are the largest ethnic/linguistic minority, accounting for about 9 per cent of the population. They live mainly in the far north-east but are also found in the main cities. As non-Arabs in this explicitly Arab nationalist state and as members of a nation (divided between Turkey, Syria, Iraq and Iran) with dreams of independent statehood, the Kurds have been subject to much discrimination. As part of a programme to Arabise the north-east it was decreed in 1962 that Kurds who could not prove that they had lived in Syria since 1945 would stand to lose their citizenship. A special census identified about 120,000 people as 'alien infiltrators' who allegedly had arrived illegally from Turkish Kurdistan. At a stroke they were rendered stateless, losing their civil and political rights, including the ability to hold a passport, to own land, to work for the government and to be admitted to public hospitals. They and their descendants now number at least 200,000, although some estimates range as high as 360,000. The Armenians, who came as Christian refugees fleeing Ottoman pogroms during the First World War, are found mainly in Aleppo and Damascus. Syria also has small communities of Turcomans and Circassians. Both groups are Sunni Muslim, the former originating in Central Asia and the latter in the Caucasus. Syria also hosts a 400,000-strong Palestinian refugee community, mainly Sunni and mainly based in and around Damascus.

At the time of independence in 1946 there was a 30,000-strong Jewish community, mainly divided between Damascus and Aleppo although most emigrated in 1947–48 – a time of severe Arab–Jewish tension in neighbouring Palestine. For twenty-five years following Israel's creation in 1948 Syria's few remaining Jews (the 1957 total was 5,300) faced official discrimination stemming not so much from anti-Semitism as from suspicions about their loyalties to the state of Israel. Jews were forbidden from travelling more than four kilometres beyond their home towns without official permission and were often banned from travelling abroad at all. Their conditions improved under Hafiz al-Asad who lifted all remaining travel restrictions in 1992. By then, only 3,800 Jews were left and the number has since dwindled to about one hundred.

When I met him in Damascus in 1992 Syria's then Chief Rabbi, Ibrahim Hamra, was understandably keen to extol the virtues of Syria's leadership. 'We take the opportunity of your visit to offer greetings to the President,' he declared. 'We pray that God grants him good health and long life.' Just two years later Rabbi Hamra had emigrated to Israel, where he settled in the Tel Aviv satellite town of Holon. Interviewed on the day of Asad's funeral he offered a less effusive view: 'We had our ups and downs with him. I wouldn't say we exactly miss him, but there was a gradual improvement. We didn't go backwards.'[8]

Specifically religious and ethnic/tribal frictions are rare but not unknown in Syria. In November 2000 violent clashes erupted between semi-nomadic bedouin shepherds and Druse in the southern province of Sweida' as part of a long-running dispute over grazing and property rights. Some 5,000 troops were deployed and the area sealed off by military checkpoints. Several Druse, bedouin and soldiers were killed and about 200 were injured in the incidents.

The episode underlined the continuing importance of traditional loyalties to extended family or tribe and to confessional group. Political phenomena can often acquire a religio/ethnic dimension. The Ba'athist regime is secular and includes key figures from all Syria's main communities but its core, especially in the security and military services, is Alawi. Hafiz al-Asad himself was the son of a minor Alawi notable from the north-west mountain village of Qurdaha. Traditionally, the Alawis were an impoverished and marginalised group, many working as agricultural labourers for the Sunni landed gentry of the cities of Hama and Homs. The military was one of the few guaranteed ways in which the offspring of Alawi mountain peasants could secure a foothold in mainstream society. 'We are all Arabs' is the official line in Ba'athist Syria but the assertion is used to obscure the regime's Alawi origins – and the tendency for Alawis to receive preferment in the bureaucracy and military and the security services. Syria's rulers are highly sensitive to the charge – not wholly sustainable but not entirely without basis – that they are mainly an Alawi minority clique which has hijacked the state.

Ba'athist Rule

Placed under French Mandate after the First World War, Syria declared independence in 1943 but the last French troops did not depart until three years later. Although newly independent Syria was established as a Western-style democracy, the armed forces quickly moved to the fore, staging a succession of coups, starting in 1949, and wielding power in tandem with a political and economic elite centred on a relatively small number of land-owning and merchant families, most based in Damascus, Aleppo and Homs. These initial military regimes were more or less non-ideological but they came as the region was being swept by a tide of nationalism whose leaders were determined to rectify the mistakes and weaknesses which had led to the Arab defeat by the Zionists in the 1947–48 war in Palestine. In 1952 the Egyptian monarchy was toppled by young military officers headed by Gamal Abdul Nasser. The Iraqi monarchy fell in 1958. Ba'athism was one of the strongest currents in this tide. The Ba'ath Party itself was founded in Damascus in the 1940s by Michel Aflaq, a Greek

Orthodox Christian, and Salah ad-Din al-Bitar, a Sunni Muslim (see Chapter 4) and quickly developed into a pan-Arab movement. Its two key slogans were 'Unity, Freedom, Socialism' and 'One Arab Nation with an Eternal Mission'.

In 1958 Syria agreed a union with President Nasser's nationalist Egypt. The autocratic Nasser demanded, and it was agreed, that the Syrian Ba'ath Party should be dissolved as part of the unionist project but, unknown to civilian Ba'athists, a secret Ba'athist Military Committee was formed in 1959 by Syrian officers posted to Cairo, which included Hafiz al-Asad. The unionist marriage was unhappy and in September 1961 it ended with a rightist putsch in Damascus. After eighteen months of political turmoil in their country, the Ba'athists, in alliance with Nasserists and independent nationalists, seized power in a military coup on 8 March 1963 – just a month after a Ba'athist takeover in neighbouring Iraq. Ba'athist rule in Damascus was unstable, with leftists and centrists constantly at loggerheads. In 1966 the radicals staged an intra-party coup. Syria's resounding defeat by Israel in the June 1967 war, in which the Golan Heights were occupied, weakened the militant socialist regime and friction intensified between the radical civilian wing of the party and the more pragmatic military wing. The climax was another putsch staged by Asad, then defence minister, on 16 November 1970.

Although the initial Ba'athist coup of 1963 is celebrated to this day as a 'revolution', it was hardly worthy of the name. Banks and a limited number of industrial companies were nationalised and state monopolies were established for a range of basic commodities. An initial land reform had been implemented during the union with Egypt and this was extended in 1963. But these measures were largely *ad hoc* and reactive, designed (in the case of the nationalisations) to 'punish' the traditional elite following anti-regime disturbances in 1964 or (in the case of the land reform) to widen support from the better-off peasantry from whose ranks many of the Ba'athist coup-makers originated. Only after the 1966 coup by avowed leftists within the Ba'ath did ideology begin to play a major role, although even then it tended to come second to the messy imperatives of local power politics. A comprehensive development programme was elaborated in which state investment was to be the main driver of all economic sectors. Import substitution was the key industrial objective. Agricultural output was to be boosted by state-run irrigation schemes, particularly the giant Tabqa hydroelectric dam on the Euphrates. Modern services were to be brought to the countryside as part of a drive to raise rural living standards. Large sums were allocated for the construction of new roads and railways. The Soviet Union and other Eastern Bloc states became key partners in many of the new projects, underpinning the regime's close political and military links with Moscow.

Asad's Rule

The casual visitor to Damascus, unaccustomed to the contortions of Syrian rhetoric, might have imagined that Hafiz al-Asad's regime had a coherent and consistent 'revolutionary' political programme. There were (and still are) the posters of Asad and his two sons, Bashar and the late, lightly bearded Basil, often showing them in military uniform and sporting dark glasses, fixing steely gazes on the middle distance, for all the world like a militarised Sicilian mafia family. There were the cloth banners strung from lamp posts and flapping on the outside walls of shabby office blocks bearing slogans extolling the virtues of the leadership and proclaiming the loyalty of this or that state company or organ of the bureaucracy. Posters, usually tattered and often years old, carrying the same discredited slogans, disfigured the walls of Syria's towns and cities (and still do).

For the state-controlled media, the recurring page-one story was (and still is) whatever the President and his immediate circle happened to be doing. Take the execrably written English-language daily *Syria Times* on 28 April 2001. 'Ba'ath Vanguards Take Pride in President Al-Assad', is the banner headline. This over a catchy little story which begins: 'President Bashar al-Assad has received a cable of pride and appreciation sent by participants in the 26th Regional Festival of the country's Ba'ath Vanguards Organization.' The fare on television and radio was (and is) much the same and will be familiar to readers who have visited those other 'people's democracies' of the region, Iraq and Libya; or to those who knew the Egypt of the 1960s and 1970s and the old People's Democratic Republic of Yemen.

Such public signs of ideological coherence, however, were deceptive. Although Hafiz al-Asad wanted full control, and demanded total respect, pragmatism was his hallmark and people's private convictions were of little concern. As Volker Perthes, an acute analyst of Syrian affairs, commented:

> The state under Asad's regime has become authoritarian, not totalitarian. There is no all-encompassing ideology, which state and regime

> would offer or try to enforce on the population. Ba'athism and Arab nationalism have been watered down so as not to stand in the way of the pragmatic realpolitik of the regime. The personality cult around the President, including attempts at fabricating a charisma that extends to his offspring, does not make an ideology ... The regime demands that everyone pay respect to its symbols and refrain from questioning the absolute leadership of the President ... The regime does not, however, prescribe what people should believe.[9]

Riad Seif, the self-made industrialist and independent member of parliament for Damascus who at the time of writing was languishing in prison for his leading role in the civil society movement, put it more pithily: 'There is no ideology except that they made the revolution and want to benefit for ever.'[10]

Ideology was less a preoccupation for Asad than it had been for his predecessors. Power was far more important. Asad launched his Corrective Movement (or *Correctionist* Movement, as it is often termed in official literature) first because had he not, he would have been ousted himself; and then because he favoured more pragmatic economic policies, including a bigger role for the private sector, looser links with the Eastern Bloc and closer ties with the wealthy Arab Gulf states and the West. Certainly the state continued as the central player in the economy after Asad's November 1970 coup, but the aim was more to boost production than to attain an egalitarian society. In Asad's view, increased national income meant increased political weight for Syria in its regional dealings, while he doubtless calculated that, at home, higher living standards would erode anti-regime sentiment. Pragmatism was the hallmark of *all* domestic policies under Hafiz al-Asad, and not just economic policies, and this has persisted into his son's presidency. The over-riding, all-pervading objective has been the maintenance of the regime: not out of any particular sense of responsibility to the populace at large, not in the service of any particular grand vision, but simply as an end in itself.

Restructuring the State

Hafiz al-Asad nevertheless revolutionised Syria, although not in the way that official rhetoric cares to acknowledge. Previous regimes had perched atop the country, enforcing their writ as best they could and tackling problems essentially *ad hoc*. From the start, Asad understood that to ensure real security for his regime every niche of society would have to be brought firmly under his control. The formal structures of the state were key arenas for his programme. In 1971 a tame People's Assembly, or parliament, was created (see Chapter 5). The following year saw the formation of the Progressive National Front (PNF) linking the Ba'ath Party and five other parties deemed to be 'progressive' and 'patriotic'. In 1973 a new Constitution was promulgated guaranteeing the leading role of the Ba'ath Party in both state and society and granting the President ultimate power in all fields. In 1971 the party itself was restructured (see Chapter 4). Its collective leadership was relinquished in favour of Asad personally, and lower leadership appointments were henceforth made from above rather than being subject to election by the membership. Party membership, bringing with it petty privileges and access to the power system, was encouraged. Membership stood at just over 400 at the time of the 1963 coup;[11] by 1971 it had reached 65,398. Ten years later it stood at 374,332 and by mid-1992 it had jumped to 1,008,243.[12]

At the same time there was a massive expansion of the state bureaucracy and of the military and intelligence services, bringing tens of thousands of Syrians and their families within the direct purview of the Asad-controlled state. In 1970 the public sector workforce, including military and security personnel, numbered only 236,000; by 1980 the total had more than tripled to 757,000; and by 1991 it had reached 1.215 million. The civilian workforce grew more rapidly than its military/security counterpart: 136,000 civilians worked in public administration and for state-run institutions and companies in 1970; by 1991 the figure had almost quintupled, to 685,000. Military and security personnel increased from 100,000 in 1970 to 530,000 in 1991. In the same period, the national workforce as a whole did little more than double, from 1.7 million to 3.7 million.[13]

As part of the restructuring of the state, Asad breathed new life into a process, originally launched after the 1963 Ba'athist takeover, in which society was to be organised into a series of regime-controlled, functional associations or 'popular organisations' (see Chapter 4). Foremost among them were the trades unions – some originally created as long ago as the 1930s – and the Peasants' Union, formed in 1964. In the same category belong professional associations for lawyers, engineers, doctors and journalists, for example, which have all been brought under regime control and whose leaders are appointed by the state rather than elected by their members.

'To the extent that the participation of societal interests was considered necessary', observed Perthes, Asad moulded the system according to 'a model of authoritarian-corporatist group representation'. The model 'conceives of society as an organic body whose different functional groups fulfil specific tasks under the leadership of the government ... the functional groups ... should be organised in compulsory, non-competitive, functionally differentiated, hierarchic associations exclusively representing the members of that functional group and their legitimate interests *vis-à-vis* the state'.[14] While this system allows input by the groups into the national decision-making process, each group supinely accepts the government's role as the mediating, organising 'brain', and each group functions not only as an association for its members but also as a government agency and an instrument of government control over its members. As Perthes further remarked: 'All these organisations and institutions which the regime euphemistically depicts as participatory have a somewhat ambivalent nature – serving as instruments of social control, and even political repression, as well as, to varying degrees, channels of interest representation.'[15]

Ask most Syrian officials and you will be told that Syria is a popular democracy in which all citizens may participate via parliament, the PNF and the popular organisations. The reality is that democracy and democratic accountability are nowhere to be found. 'Syria became a monopoly for a certain group leading the country,' said Riad Seif. 'Even the Ba'ath Party became just a tool. After they had a monopoly in politics and they had full power, this monopoly was extended to the economy, to culture, to the media.'

Within a few years of seizing control, Hafiz al-Asad, perched at the pinnacle of every interlocking pyramid of state power, was unassailable. He was the supreme commander of the armed forces, secretary-general of both the Regional (Syrian) Command and National (pan-Arab) Command of the Ba'ath Party, and head of the executive branch of government. He was personally responsible for appointing his vice presidents, the prime minister, government ministers and their deputies, military officers, senior civil servants and judges. The government was answerable not to parliament or the people, but to Asad himself, who had the right to dissolve parliament at will. Crucially and unsurprisingly, Asad also controlled the succession to the presidency. Under the 1973 Constitution, Syria's presidents are elected by referenda, with the sole candidates being nominated by the party's Regional Command – itself headed by Asad. No wonder that the Information Ministry can predict the outcome of presidential elections with such accuracy! Just in case, Asad even empowered himself to propose amendments to the Constitution, although such amendments must be approved by a two-thirds majority of parliament. However, parliamentary approval can be trumped by a presidential veto.

Despite this extraordinary concentration of power in the hands of one man, Article 2 (2) of the Constitution intones: 'Sovereignty is vested in the people.' And Article 12 – source of the Traffic Police HQ's slogan – affirms: 'The state is in the people's service. Its establishments seek to protect the fundamental rights of the citizens and develop their lives.' Article 25 (1) declares that 'freedom is a sacred right. The state protects the personal freedom of the citizens and safeguards their dignity and security'; while, incredibly, Article 28 (2) stipulates: 'No one may be kept under surveillance or detained except in accordance with the law.'

The problem is that 'the law' includes Decree 51 of 9 March 1963 – one day after the first Ba'athist coup – which declared a State of Emergency ostensibly in response to the military threat from Israel but in reality to give the regime a free hand to crush its domestic opponents. This law, which established special security courts (see Chapter 6), gives virtually untrammelled powers to the security agencies and makes a complete nonsense of the purported guarantees of human and civil rights in the 1973 Constitution. Anyone whose loyalty is suspect may be arrested, interrogated and detained on the flimsiest of pretexts, with no recourse to legal representation and with no avenue of appeal or complaint. Especially in the 1980s, torture was routine and death in custody not uncommon – although these aspects of the system have improved markedly since the late 1990s.

Torture

Chilling and detailed accounts of the Asad regime's apparatus of repression have been produced by respected human rights bodies including Human Rights Watch and Amnesty International. 'The Asad regime has been a gross violator of human rights [and] its practices remain repugnant,' said Middle East Watch, a division of Human Rights Watch, in a major report in 1991. 'Having killed at least ten thousand of its citizens in the past twenty years, the Asad regime continues to kill through summary executions and violent treatment in prison. It routinely tortures prisoners and arrests and holds thousands without charge or trial.'[16] In 1984 Amnesty International listed thirty-eight types of torture used in Hafiz al-Asad's Syria. As well as such mundane practices as 'extracting finger and toe nails' and 'applying electricity to sensitive parts of the body', the list included: '*Al-'Abd al-Aswad* (the Black Slave): strapping the victim onto a device which, when switched on, inserts a heated metal skewer into the anus'; and '*Al-Farruj* (the Chicken): strapping the victim to a revolving wooden bar resembling a roasting spit and subjecting him or her to beating with sticks'.[17]

In the last decade of Asad's rule, when the regime felt more secure, the situation improved, although prisoner releases were partially offset by new arrests. In June 2000, following Hafiz al-Asad's death, Amnesty International reported that Syria's jails still held at least 1,500 political prisoners and that thousands of people detained in earlier years had 'disappeared' and had probably been murdered.[18] In November that year 600 prisoners were freed (see Chapter 2), giving a total political prisoner population of about 900 by year's end.

Corruption

In addition to the direct control it exerts through its near total takeover of the state apparatus and of the institutions usually belonging to the realm of civil society, the regime also uses corruption and favouritism on a grand scale as a means of control. From top to bottom the system is riddled with informal clientelist networks, often based on ties of family, tribe, region and religion. At one extreme, the President's immediate circle appropriates enormous wealth by dint of its ability to 'broker' major business deals (i.e. block them unless substantial kickbacks are paid) and oversee illicit trade and smuggling. During the 1980s, when Syria was suffering acute foreign exchange shortages which caused a fierce imports squeeze, illicit goods – everything from large electricity generators to cigarettes and whisky – were pouring into the country from Lebanon. Much of this unrecorded trade was organised by the army, which had intervened in Lebanon's civil war in 1976 and remains there to this day. At the other end of the scale, a lowly customs official might expect a modest tip for expediting documentation. A ministry clerk might expect payment for progressing a petty administrative matter. Public sector pay is so paltry that it is widely understood and accepted that civil servants cannot survive without an illicit income or a second job. Eighty per cent of government officials earn between $40 and $120 per month, nothing like the amount needed to begin to support a family.[19]

So labyrinthine is Syria's bureaucracy that the scope, indeed the need, for such transactions is vast. 'Wherever a deal is struck with the state, where licences are needed, or where jobs can be provided, illicit gains can be made,' said Perthes. 'Where high-ranking military or civilian officials make sure that a public-sector contract is won by a particular foreign company, kickbacks of millions of dollars may be in play; where a custom official closes his eyes to some illicit private import, he might be rewarded with a *baqshish* of no more than a dollar's equivalent. Bribery is ubiquitous.'[20] The healthcare, educational and judicial systems are not exempt (see Chapters 6 and 8). At a price, students can gain university degrees without reaching the required academic standard, patients can jump the queue for operations and litigants can assure themselves of victory. Only the presidency itself stands above it all. But, as a Syrian journalist once said to me of Hafiz al-Asad: 'He owns the entire country, so why should he trouble himself with a few million dollars?'

Periodically, the regime launches high-profile anti-corruption drives but these are deeply cynical exercises. Corruption is not only tolerated but is encouraged as a crucial element in the informal system of patronage networks which are an important means of political control. It may well be that one aim of the clean-up campaigns is to prevent corruption from reaching such uncontrollable levels as to cause the entire system to implode. Certainly another objective is to mollify a public disgusted by high-level greed. But a third objective is to neutralise individuals who have irritated the regime or who may do so in future. Hafiz's late son Basil, while being groomed for the presidency in the early 1990s before his sudden death in a car crash in January 1994, headed a major anti-corruption drive. In the first half of 2000, prior to his becoming President, Bashar headed a similar drive which, although presented as a general clean-up, was plainly used to ease out individuals who might hinder Bashar's rise to the presidency or destabilise him thereafter.

In March 2000, amid the anti-corruption campaign, a new government – the first in thirteen years – was appointed. Dr Bashar, as he is known in Syria, explained that the new team's priorities would be 'to modernise the administration and reduce the level of corruption'.[21] The former prime minister, Mahmoud Zu'bi, had been targeted in the anti-corruption drive and eventually committed suicide. Salim Yassin, formerly deputy prime minister for economic affairs, and Mufeed Abdul Karim, formerly transport minister, were detained pending the outcome of inquiries into Syrian Arab Airlines' purchase of European-built Airbus aircraft. In December 2001 both were sentenced to ten years' imprisonment. Riad Seif and his fellow member of parliament Ma'moun al-Homsi, both jailed in 2001 for their vociferous criticism of the regime, have been accused of tax evasion – although this allegation was not raised as part of the formal cases against them (see Chapter 3). As if corruption was something unusual in their country, many Syrian officials (including individuals of whose petty financial indiscretions I have first-hand knowledge) now lose no opportunity to smear Al-Homsi and Seif. 'We would prefer that you did not interview him,' one Information Ministry official told me when I expressed an interest in meeting Seif. 'He is a corrupt man,' he explained, asking, 'Who does such a person represent?'

Islamist Rebellion

Those officials defending Asad's record never fail to invoke the stability he brought to the country as one of his greatest achievements. For a period in the late 1970s and early 1980s, however, stability was the last word one might use to describe the Syrian situation. Deprived of all legitimate outlets for political activity, conservative Islamist opponents of a regime which was avowedly secular, and which was regarded by many traditional Sunnis as a clique of socially inferior and heretical Alawis, turned to violence. The lead role was played by the Syrian branch of the Muslim Brotherhood (Al-Ikhwan al-Muslimoun), a fundamentalist Sunni organisation which was founded in Egypt in 1928 and has a considerable regional following. In 1976 Ikhwan militants launched a campaign of assassinations of senior Alawi and regime figures and bombings of regime symbols such as *mukhabarat* offices and military headquarters. The campaign escalated and the attacks became more daring and spectacular. In June 1979, for example, 200 Alawi cadets were killed in an assault on the Aleppo Artillery Academy.

The Islamists were not the only aggrieved section of society. The Syrian army's intervention in Lebanon against a Muslim/Palestinian/leftist alliance fighting a rightist, Maronite Christian-dominated establishment supported by Israel was deeply unpopular in Syria. So too were the ostentatious corruption of Asad's elite, the favouritism enjoyed by Alawis in official appointments and the capricious and pervasive powers of the *mukhabarat*. In addition, the economy, which had grown rapidly in the early 1970s, was now stagnating (see below) and spiralling inflation was causing serious hardship to the lower-paid. Parallel to Islamist terrorism, the regime faced increasingly fierce criticism from intellectuals, professionals and activists from secular opposition parties. Protest strikes were organised by those professional associations, such as the doctors' and engineers' associations, that had managed to retain their independence from the state. While responding to the Islamists' terrorism with mounting brutality of its own, the regime also moved to crush its non-violent and non-Islamist opponents. The lawyers', engineers' and doctors' associations were disbanded in 1980 and their leaderships imprisoned (see Chapters 4 and 6). Thousands of Islamist suspects were detained but so too were hundreds of intellectuals and activists from secular opposition parties.

The climax of what was almost a national rebellion against the Ba'athists was a three-week uprising in the central city of Hama in February and March 1982, to which the regime responded ferociously. The city was pounded by artillery and much of its historic centre, including its Great Mosque, was flattened. Between 5,000 and 10,000 people were killed. It is hard to over-state the fear that such brutality instilled in Syrians. Until the end of the 1980s, Hama remained a taboo subject in conversations with foreigners. Visiting Hama in 1986, when reconstruction was in full swing, I asked an elderly passer-by directions to the Great Mosque, which had been in the epicentre of hostilities. 'There's no such mosque here,' he replied. I persisted, saying that I had visited the magnificent mosque in 1967. The man would not relent: 'No. There is no such mosque.' Behind him were the remains of old stone-built houses, their walls pockmarked by bullets and shrapnel. Nearby stood a determined-looking plain-clothes security man, a machine-gun draped across his chest – one of hundreds who were still stationed in and around the city four years after the carnage.

Rif'at Challenges His Brother

By 1983 the Ba'athist regime again seemed secure but, having survived the challenge from its domestic opponents, it was next threatened from within. In November that year Hafiz al-Asad collapsed, either from exhaustion or from a heart attack depending on differing accounts, and he vested responsibility for managing state affairs in a six-man committee of trusted associates. Not included in the committee was his younger brother, Rif'at, who after Hafiz was the second most powerful member of the Ba'ath Party's, and hence the country's, highest executive body, the Regional (i.e. Syrian) Command. The key to Rif'at's power were the Defence Companies, a 55,000-strong praetorian guard which had played a crucial and ferocious part in defeating the Ikhwan. The Alawi generals at the regime's core were dissatisfied with the six-man committee and instigated a meeting of the Regional Command which resolved to substitute itself for the committee, thereby placing Rif'at at centre-stage. In early 1984 Hafiz al-Asad recovered and was furious at the disloyalty of his brother and of the generals, some of whom quickly withdrew their support from Rif'at.

The antagonism between the brothers 'split the army, the party and the higher echelons of the regime: everyone had to take sides'.[22] In late February 1984 military units of the opposing sides came close to conflict in Damascus. A bloody showdown was averted after the Regional Command agreed a compromise under which Rif'at would become one of three vice-presidents. His duties remained unspecified, however, while he was relieved of his command of the Defence Companies. Refusing to accept marginalisation, on 30 March 1984 Rif'at ordered his forces to move on the capital and seize power. Intervening in person, Hafiz al-Asad managed to persuade his brother to back off. In May of that year, seventy officers, including Rif'at, were banished abroad. All but Rif'at were soon recalled. Never again would he play anything more than a bit-part in Syrian politics.

Foreign Affairs

Hafiz al-Asad was far more interested in foreign policy than in domestic affairs – an interest that might partly explain the torpor and chaos which afflicted his country at home. Even Syrians deeply critical of his fiercely authoritarian system readily concede that he was a master player in the regional and international arenas, skilfully extracting the maximum returns from often unpromising circumstances. Before, Syria had been punching below its weight, a weak and fractious state staggering from coup to coup. Albeit at terrible human and economic cost, Asad turned it into a stable country with a military and security apparatus which opponents ignored at their peril. His postures echoed themes evident long before he seized power. Regionally, Syria's outlook has been deeply coloured by its history as a geographical entity embracing all the Levant which was divided between the French and the British after the First World War, and then further divided under the French Mandate. To the south, the British took control of Palestine and Transjordan. In 1920 the French detached large parts of western Syria to create the state of Lebanon. In 1939 they ceded the Alexandretta province, north-west of Aleppo, to Turkey, which renamed it Hatay. Damascus consistently sought hegemony over its immediate neighbours in this area of Greater Syria, and even when unable to prevail it has been sufficiently powerful to block the plans of others. In the wider region, Syria has sought ties with the oil-rich Gulf states which have been important sources of aid; and with Egypt, the region's most populous and powerful state, although relations with Cairo were resumed only in November 1989, a decade after Damascus severed ties because of Egyptian President Anwar Sadat's 1979 peace treaty with Israel, which Syria rightly saw as a major breach of Arab solidarity that would allow Israel to pick off its other enemies one by one. With Iraq, ruled by rival Ba'athists, relations have generally been on a scale from strained to poisonous, while relations with Turkey have been uneasy. Since the 1979 Islamic Revolution in Iran, Syria has enjoyed a remarkably close relationship with Tehran, underpinned by common hostility towards Iraq and Israel and common suspicion of the West.

Beyond the region, Syria's stance had been closely linked to its regional priorities. Until the collapse of communism in the late 1980s, Syria enjoyed close ties with the Soviet Union as a means of countering the West's apparently open-ended support for Israel, whose creation in 1948 involved the seizure and ethnic cleansing of Palestine. Damascus played host to thousands of Soviet and Eastern European military and civilian advisers and in 1987 the relationship was formalised in a twenty-year Treaty of Friendship and Co-operation. Although the Soviet Union became Syria's main military supplier, Damascus never became a puppet of Moscow, never allowed the USSR bases on its territory, and always kept lines open to the United States and to Europe. The collapse of the Soviet Bloc in the late 1980s was a watershed for Syria, depriving it of its key allies. Asad responded by improving links with the United States although he understood that Washington's usefulness would be limited because of its intimate support for the Israelis. At the same time, Syria moved to develop its relations with Europe and the European Union (EU) which it saw as a crucial source of financial aid and, potentially, as a mediator in the conflict with Israel which would be less biased than the USA. Damascus is part of the so-called Barcelona Process which was launched at a meeting of European and Mediterranean foreign ministers in the Spanish city in 1995 and which involves comprehensive political and economic collaboration. Bilateral association agreements have a central place in the process. These provide for mutual reductions of trade tariffs and require Mediterranean littoral states to open their economies to market forces and respect human rights in exchange for EU assistance. The agreements are the basic building blocks in a process leading to the establishment by the target date of 2010 of a Euro-Mediterranean Free Trade Area. Syria – about two-thirds of whose exports go to the EU and one-third of whose imports come from the EU – confirmed its desire to negotiate an association agreement in 1997. At that stage it did not appear to grasp the full implications of such an agreement either for its ramshackle, state-directed economy or for its abysmal conduct on human rights. Indeed, serious negotiations were begun only after Bashar al-Asad had succeeded his father.

'I think there was a change with the swearing-in of the new President, and that there is [now] a real commitment to proceed with this,' said Jerome Cassiers, the well-informed Belgian deputy head of the European Commission's Mission to Damascus. 'The first rounds were essentially general discussions, giving the impression that they subscribed to the idea but had no immediate interest in concluding an agreement.'[23]

Often – and routinely in the 1980s – Syria has used terrorism as a foreign policy tool and, although it has paid a price in terms of Western political and economic sanctions, this undoubtedly boosted the international perception of Syria as a state which could not be ignored. Care must be taken with definitions. Israel and the United States foolishly smear as 'terrorist' Palestinian and Lebanese groups which are genuine liberation movements. Nevertheless, at one time or another, Damascus has hosted and/or materially supported the late Abu Nidal's Fatah Revolutionary Council, a Palestinian faction which certainly deserves the terrorist label; and Abdullah Ocalan's Kurdish Workers Party (PKK), which has perpetrated numerous terrorist outrages in its fight with Turkey. Nor has Syria shrunk from mounting its own terrorist operations, in Lebanon, Iraq, Jordan and further afield. A striking example was an abortive attempt in April 1986 to bomb an Israeli El Al jumbo jet departing from London's Heathrow airport, an operation that caused the United Kingdom to sever diplomatic ties with Damascus.

Israel and the fate of the Palestinians have been Syria's over-riding foreign policy priorities since independence, reflecting the close personal interest that ordinary Syrians take in these subjects. Indeed, successive Syrian regimes have linked their legitimacy to their ability to defend Palestinian and Arab rights against the Israelis. The first Syrian coups in 1949 were sparked by the ineffectual response of the initial post-independence government to the Zionist takeover of Palestine. Liberating Palestine was central to the rhetoric of the Ba'athists who took power in Damascus in 1963, although their actual performance was dismal. Syria stumbled into the catastrophic June 1967 war with Israel at a time when its armed forces, poorly equipped and fatally weakened by political purges of officers, were ill-prepared for conflict. For the Israelis it was a walkover. The defeat, in which Syria lost the Golan Heights, spelled the end for the radical civilian wing of the Ba'ath, which had ruled in Damascus since 1966. Asad – who had been defence minister at the time of the 1967 defeat – staged his Corrective Movement in November 1970.

Recovering both the Golan and Arab pride were the limited aims of the October 1973 war that Syria launched in concert with Egypt, which had lost the Sinai Peninsula in 1967. No territory was recovered by either, but both the Egyptian and Syrian forces, transformed since 1967 by major Soviet military aid programmes, performed creditably, inflicting serious losses on the Israelis. Arab self-respect was restored, and the war was hailed as a triumph in the region, boosting Asad's popularity. It ended with UN Security Council Resolution 338, itself incorporating Resolution 242, which had ended the 1967 war and which affirmed the right of 'every state in the area' to live in peace. Previously, Syria had rejected 242. By accepting 338 it formally accepted for the first time Israel's right to exist. Since then, Damascus has tried to recover the Golan by diplomacy, offering full peace for a full Israeli withdrawal. An Israel which for most of the period since the late 1970s has been ruled by extreme nationalist governments has preferred to cling to a territory which many Israelis claim as part of their divine patrimony.

Syria has always portrayed itself as a champion of the Palestinians but it has worked ceaselessly to gain hegemony over the Palestinian guerrilla movement which arose in the mid-1960s after the abject failure of Arab governments to secure any restitution of Palestinian lands or rights. In 1983 Syria encouraged dissident Palestinian factions in Lebanon to rebel against the mainstream Palestine Liberation Organisation (PLO), and its chairman, Yasser Arafat. What became a bitter Palestinian civil war ended with Arafat's loyalists' expulsion from Lebanon. 'For many years,' Eyal Zisser commented, 'Syria regarded the Palestinian issue as too important to leave in the hands of Arafat.'[24] Syria was determined not to be isolated by any PLO–Israeli accommodation and it was therefore aghast at the ill-fated peace agreement known as the Oslo Accords, negotiated in secret and signed in Washington in September 1993.

Asad may have been unable to recover the Golan Heights or block an Israeli–Palestinian peace which left him out in the cold but he did succeed in expelling the Israelis and their influence from Lebanon and in making Syria the key arbiter of its neighbour's affairs. In Lebanon an unwritten National Pact, agreed at the time of independence from France in 1943, had institutionalised the political and, in this region where politics and money are deeply intertwined, economic dominance of the Maronite Christians, on the now shaky grounds that they had been the majority during the French Mandate. The Lebanese Muslims – as in Syria a patchwork of Sunnis, Shi'as and Druse – had a much higher birth rate than the Christians and by the 1960s had become the majority. The Maronite Christians, however, refused to relinquish any of their privileges and monopolies. This fossilised confessional system has been at the heart of Lebanon's protracted tensions. The Muslim–Christian population balance was further tipped in the Muslims' favour after the 1970 defeat of the Palestinian guerrillas in Jordan (see below). Thousands of guerrillas fled to Lebanon with their families, where the Palestinians were already antagonising the Beirut authorities by establishing the sort of 'state-within-a-state' which had been partly to blame for the hostilities in Jordan.

In 1975 civil war erupted in Lebanon, pitting a Christian/rightist alliance, increasingly backed by Israel, against a Muslim/Palestinian/leftist coalition loosely backed by Damascus. But apparently fearing the emergence of a radical leftist state on his flank, and the potential that this might create for Israeli intervention, Asad sent his troops into Lebanon in June 1976 at the request of the Beirut government to help reverse Muslim gains, which they did. They have remained there ever since. This is not the place to detail one of modern history's most complex wars. Suffice it to say that, increasingly, it became a conflict between Syria and Israel, acting through their proxies in Lebanon. Israeli influence climaxed in 1982 with a full-scale invasion and the installation of a Maronite regime in Beirut. Slowly and doggedly, Syria and its local allies – notably including the formidable Iranian-backed Shi'a Hizbollah ('Party of God') militia – managed to turn the tide. In September 1990 a new political settlement was imposed giving greater representation to the Muslims, and in October the last Christian military resistance was crushed. Syrian hegemony over Lebanon was enshrined in a Treaty of Brotherhood, Co-operation and Co-ordination signed by Asad and his then Lebanese counterpart Elias Hrawi on 22 May 1991. In May 2000 the Israelis, smarting from their losses in a sustained guerrilla campaign, finally pulled their occupying troops out of Lebanon.

Syria's relations with its southern neighbour, Jordan, have been unstable, with periods of amity interrupted by episodes of deep tension. In part, this reflected the contrasting perspectives of radical Arab nationalist Syria and a conservative, pro-Western monarchy with strong (if secretive) ties to Israel. Even more it stemmed from Damascus's determination to impose its writ on a key part of its Greater Syrian backyard, particularly at times when facing the danger of regional isolation. The Palestine/Israel issue has been a particular fount of Syrian–Jordanian friction. In September 1970 Syrian armour briefly crossed into Jordan to help Palestinian guerrillas who were facing defeat by the Jordanian army. Having secured US and even Israeli pledges of assistance, the Jordanians engaged the Syrians, who swiftly withdrew. In 1980 Syrian troops again massed on the Jordanian frontier amid tension over Jordanian support for the Muslim Brotherhood which was causing havoc within Syria. During the 1980s the atmosphere was chilled by Jordan's stalwart support for Syria's long-time rival Iraq, then at war with Syria's ally Iran. Damascus has always worked to harmonise Arab positions towards Israel albeit while insisting that Syria should define what those positions should be. Syrian–Jordanian relations thus nose-dived following the October 1994 signature of an Israeli–Jordanian peace treaty. With King Hussain's death in 1999 and the succession of his son Abdullah, the Jordanian–Syrian climate improved and has since remained relatively warm.

Relations with Turkey have been unsettled by a protracted dispute over sharing the water of the Euphrates river, by Syrian support for anti-Turkish Kurdish guerrillas of the PKK organisation (see above) and by Israeli–Turkish military co-operation which was intensified in the mid-1990s. A constant undercurrent has been Syria's continued claim to Turkey's Hatay district, carved from Syria by the French during their Mandate. Twice, in 1996 and 1998, the two states came to the brink of war. The climate has improved since late 1998 when, in a move to avert armed conflict with Turkey, Syria expelled PKK leader Abdullah Ocalan from Damascus and closed PKK camps in Lebanon's Bekaa Valley. In mid-2002, as part of a campaign to improve ties with its neighbours at a time when it was under mounting US pressure over its relationship with Iraq (see below), Syria signed its own military co-operation agreements with Ankara.

Syria and Iraq inaugurated cordial relations in 1997 which warmed to the point in 2002 where Syria was buying 150,000–200,000 barrels per day of Iraqi oil in violation of UN sanctions and warning the USA against a possible invasion of Iraq aimed at toppling Saddam Hussain's regime. Although Arab unity nominally lies at the core of Ba'athism, such closing of ranks between the Middle East's two Ba'athist regimes has been the exception rather than the rule. For most of the period since 1963, when different wings of the party seized power in Damascus and Baghdad, the two regimes have been at loggerheads, each claiming to be the sole heir to authentic Ba'athist ideals, each supporting the other's domestic opponents and each sometimes conducting terrorist attacks against the other.[25] They have differed over virtually every regional and international issue. The schism was underlined by Hafiz al-Asad's close alliance with Iraq's Gulf War enemy, Iran, and by Syria's decision to play an active military role in the coalition which expelled the Iraqis from Kuwait in 1991. Syria's support for Kuwait also ended its long estrangement from the Gulf states, which had strongly supported Iraq in its 1980–88 war against Iran and had been infuriated by the 'defection' of a key Arab state like Syria to the Iranian camp. Gulf aid to Damascus, which had dried up in 1980–88, resumed at generous levels in the early 1990s.

The Economy

Syria remains essentially an agricultural country. Although 65 per cent of its land area is desert or semi-desert, a crescent extending from Damascus in the south through Homs and Hama to Aleppo in the north and thence eastwards parallel to the Turkish border receives sufficient rain for agriculture. The main crops are cotton (mainly in the Euphrates Valley) wheat and barley (in the central and southern plains) and fruit and vegetables (especially in the Damascus Ghouta and the north-western mountains). Sheep- and goat-raising are important in semi-desert areas. Despite several decades of large-scale rural–urban migration, especially to Damascus and Aleppo, half the 16.7 million Syrians in 2001 were rural dwellers, and in 2000 agriculture accounted for 32 per cent of the labour force and 25 per cent of gross domestic product (GDP).[26] Efforts to stabilise agricultural production and rural incomes by expanding irrigation systems have been only partially successful and the agricultural economy remains highly vulnerable to drought.

Reflecting Syria's agricultural wealth and diversity, textile and food processing plants have long been the main sectors of Syrian manufacturing. Considerable effort has been put into developing import-substitution industries but progress has been limited and in 2000 industry and mining (data for the two being combined in official statistics) provided jobs for only 13.1 per cent of the labour force but accounted for 30 per cent of GDP. Outside the crucially important oil sector (see below), the most significant mineral extraction activity is phosphate mining, which started in 1971 at Khneifis in the desert near Tadmur – the site of ancient Palmyra – east of Homs. Echoing the traditional importance of trade in this country at the crossroads between Europe, Asia and Africa, 14.5 per cent of the labour force in 2000 worked in trade establishments and hotels and restaurants. Wholesale and retail trade contributed 15 per cent of GDP while transport and communications accounted for 13 per cent of GDP and 5.3 per cent of the labour force. Building and construction accounted for 12.4 per cent of the workforce in 2000, underlining the continuing pace of urban expansion, although this sector contributed only 3 per cent of GDP; and 22.7 of the labour force was engaged in activities officially defined as 'other services' – essentially the public sector bureaucracy,[27] although the share of 'government services' in GDP was a mere 8 per cent, underlining this sector's inherently unproductive and over-expanded nature.

By far the most significant recent structural change in the economy – other than the enormous growth of public administration under Hafiz al-Asad – has been the expansion of oil output following the development of major new oilfields in the Euphrates Valley in the 1980s. In the early 1970s Syria was producing 120,000 barrels per day (b/d) of low quality oil from fields in the north-east. By 1983 output was 580,000 b/d, most of it high quality crude from new fields. More recently oil production has eased to about 530,000 b/d. Oil revenues in recent years have accounted for 60–70 per cent of exports and 40–50 per cent of the state budget.

Remittances from Syrians working abroad – mainly in the Gulf and in neighbouring Lebanon – are also important for the economy although subject to shifting economic cycles in countries hosting Syrian expatriates (see below).

Considerable economic and financial benefits have flowed from Syria's regional influence and its confrontation with Israel. On the 'Arab street', as they say in the region, Asad won kudos for his refusal to acquiesce in any unjust settlement with Israel and for his insistence on building a military machine which, while never able remotely to threaten Israel with defeat, was sufficiently credible to be taken seriously by Tel Aviv and which was certainly capable of imposing Syria's writ in Lebanon. Trading on this military and hence political influence, Damascus received billions of dollars' worth of military equipment from the old Soviet Bloc and hundreds of millions of dollars in grants and soft loans from the Gulf states. A problem was that the aid, essentially political, was subject to the vagaries of regional and international relations. Since the collapse of communism, Russia has been pressing Damascus for repayment of some of the estimated $11–12 billion in military debt Syria owes Moscow and which Damascus never expected to have to repay. Aid from the Gulf declined after Syria's initial intervention in Lebanon in 1976 and fell even further when Asad sided with Iran in the 1980–88 Iran–Iraq war. The Gulf aid tap was opened again following Syria's participation in the anti-Iraq coalition formed after Baghdad invaded Kuwait in 1990. Foreign aid – like the revenues from the newly developed Euphrates Valley oilfields – was never sufficient to kick-start self-sustained growth in the Syrian economy. It merely enabled the regime to avert economic collapse while lurching from one crisis to the next.

Most of Syria's economic gains in recent decades have been nullified by rapid population growth. In 1970–80 the economy expanded more rapidly than the population and per capita GDP (expressed in constant prices of 1995 to eliminate the effect of inflation) reached 42,853 Syrian Pounds in 1980.[28] Thereafter, the economy stagnated and by 1990 real per capita GDP had fallen to 32,145 Syrian Pounds. A recovery in the first half of the 1990s brought the figure to 41,779 Syrian Pounds in 1996. A slowdown followed and in 2000 real per capita GDP was down to 40,844 Syrian Pounds, nearly 5 per cent lower than two decades earlier. In current prices, per capita GDP in 2000 stood at 54,941 Syrian Pounds ($1,186).

The discontent in the late 1970s (see above) was fuelled by the start of the economic downturn which intensified in the 1980s. It had several causes. In the 1980s world oil prices collapsed, leading to a slump in aid from the oil states (aggravated by the political factors as described above) and a steep decline in workers' remittances as expatriate workers in the Gulf were laid off. Western aid dried up because of Syrian involvement in international terrorism. Syria was meanwhile hit by a series of droughts which devastated the crucial agricultural sector and required large-scale and costly food imports, further squeezing its depleted hard currency resources. The situation was gravely aggravated by the centrally controlled economic system. Agricultural produce had to be sold to state marketing companies at unrealistically low prices, thus discouraging production. State-run industries were overstaffed and inefficient and unable to sell their frequently shoddy products outside Syria, where they often enjoyed monopolies. Their operations were plagued by bottlenecks in the supply of raw materials and other inputs, including finance. Managers often were politically loyal but otherwise untrained and ill-suited to their posts. Overseeing the entire shambles was the vast, under-paid and under-motivated bureaucracy in which the safest course was to do as little as possible and where initiative could be positively dangerous.

For Hafiz al-Asad, the economy was always a secondary consideration. Of far greater moment were matters of 'high policy': the conflict with Israel; Lebanon; relations with regional states; and, above all, regime stability. Even he, however, could not ignore the 1980s recession and the discontent it spawned. The immediate response was swingeing spending cuts and import restrictions, whose impact was eased by massive smuggling, largely organised by key government figures. In 1985 a Ministry of Supply official was quoted as expressing the 'belief that the Customs Department is in possession of data which indicate that there are about 50,000 smugglers in this country. It is probable that through the contraband traffic no fewer than 10,000 have become millionaires.'[29] A report prepared by economists in 1987 said that the unofficial economy 'is believed to exceed – and possibly by much – 30 per cent of the Gross Domestic Product'.[30] Unrecorded transactions on such a scale mean that official economic data (including those cited in this book) must be treated as indicative only. The Arab historian Hanna Batatu recorded that 'when a delegate to the 1985 Ba'ath Regional Congress raised the issue of outlawing the Lebanese black market, a Ba'athist lady reportedly stood up and boldly wondered how could it be proscribed when "all present" thrived on it, "drawing a hearty laugh from Asad"'.[31]

Pragmatic as ever, however, the regime also responded to the 1980s recession by taking cautious steps towards eliminating some of the more bizarre aspects of the command economy, and towards economic and fiscal liberalisation, including some encouragement of the private sector. Agricultural prices were raised and incentives were offered to encourage private investment, initially in tourism and agriculture and later even in such 'strategic' sectors as power generation. A system whereby the Syrian Pound was subject to three separate exchange rates (none of them bearing much relation to the actual value of the currency, as expressed on the outlawed but booming black market), depending on the type of transaction, was gradually scrapped. Only as late as 2000, however, were the first steps taken to create a modern banking system (see Chapter 9). This cautious, halting *infitah* ('opening'), forced by circumstance and not part of any grand strategy, has not entailed any diminution of the state's guiding role. Even private entrepreneurs – some of whom have grown immensely wealthy – owe their success to their patronage by key figures in the regime. This is no great victory for market forces. Rather, it is a process by which private business is being used to clear up the system's worst messes. The economic situation in the 1990s remained strained but was a far cry from the dark days of the previous decade. The *infitah* played its part, as did the rapid expansion of oil output and an influx of Arab aid in the early 1990s following Syria's participation in the military coalition against Iraq during the 1990–91 Kuwait crisis. Now, the debate is about how far and how fast the economic liberalisation should go.

The drive to recover the Israeli-occupied Golan Heights has headed Syria's political agenda since their loss in 1967. The regime's refusal to contemplate a peace treaty with Israel without a full withdrawal is widely supported by Syrians. So too is the success with which the country's political and economic independence has been maintained. Many a US and Israeli political and military project in the region has foundered on Damascus's opposition. Not for Syria the austerity and restructuring programmes of the International Monetary Fund (although in actual impact the gradual *infitah* of the past decade has not been markedly dissimilar). For most Syrians, however, as for people the world over, everyday living standards are the top priority. Although Damascus has benefited materially from its strategic stances, an independent foreign policy is scant comfort to an unskilled manual labourer struggling on the bread-line. The lowly clerk in a state company who has to hold down a second job in the evenings to make ends meet is not over-impressed by Syria's victorious management of the Lebanese civil war. For the vast majority of Syrians, everyday life is a harsh struggle; and nationalist sentiment does not pay the bills.

Economic reform is by far the biggest challenge facing Bashar al-Asad, and the situation becomes ever more critical. The population growth rate has slowed from well over 3 per cent per annum to 2.6 per cent per year in 1996 and 2.5 per cent per year in 2000.[32] At least 200,000–250,000 job seekers nevertheless each year enter a labour market in which unemployment is officially put at 11.2 per cent[33] but is actually 25–30 per cent. The authorities' nightmare is that the disaffected unemployed, many of them Islamist in outlook, might turn to violent street protest which could rock the regime. A fundamental dilemma is that the economy is at the same time a system of political control and patronage. So deep is the economic malaise that mere tinkering will be ineffectual. But radical reform, which would certainly entail the laying-off of tens of thousands of bureaucrats and other public sector workers, would effectively mean dismantling a system that has for decades been part and parcel of the regime. Any such project would be fiercely opposed by key figures in the military–security establishment who would want to defend their privileges in the same manner that they acquired them in the first place: through brute force. Syria's much-vaunted stability would be at stake. It is exactly the dilemma that faced the former Eastern Bloc states with the collapse of communism.

Bashar al-Asad's accession to the presidency in July 2000 brought a change in the political climate which emboldened Syria's intellectuals to demand root-and-branch reform, and their analysis explicitly linked the economic crisis to the absence of democracy, human rights and the rule of law. This *harakat al-mujtama' al-madani* (civil society movement) was reminiscent of similar movements in the Eastern Bloc in the dying days of communism. Although it posed no immediate challenge to the system, which after initial hesitation cracked down hard, it at least reminded Syrians that there are alternatives to brute force and fear as the basis of political life. With its tolerance, liberalism and sheer humanity, the movement was far more 'in the service of the people' than anything the regime had to offer.

Notes

1. Noam Chomsky, *What Uncle Sam Really Wants* (Tucson, AZ: Odonian Press, 1992), p. 86.
2. Volker Perthes, *The Political Economy of Syria under Asad* (London: I.B. Tauris), 1995, p. 193.
3. Office of the Prime Minister, *Statistical Abstract 2001*, Central Bureau of Statistics, Syrian Arab Republic.
4. Ibid.
5. Interview with author, Damascus, spring 2001.
6. US Department of State, *Background Note: Syria* (Washington, DC: Bureau of Near Eastern Affairs, February 2002).
7. Hanna Batatu, *Syria's Peasantry, the Descendants of Its Lesser Rural Notables, and Their Politics* (Princeton, NJ: Princeton University Press, 1990), p. 15.
8. Eric Silver, 'After Asad', *www.jewishjournal.com*, 16 June 2000.
9. Perthes, *Political Economy*, p. 189.
10. Interview with author, Damascus, 5 May 2001.
11. Batatu, *Syria's Peasantry*, p. 161.
12. Ibid., p. 177.

13. Perthes, *Political Economy*, p. 141.

14. Ibid., p. 134.

15. Ibid., p. 162.

16. Middle East Watch, *Syria Unmasked: The Suppression of Human Rights by the Asad Regime* (New Haven and London: Yale University Press, 1991), p. 146.

17. Amnesty International, *Syria: Torture by the Security Forces* (September 1984).

18. Amnesty International, *Syria: Amnesty International Calls for Release or Fair Retrial of All Political Detainees*, Press Release, 27 June 2000.

19. Office of the Prime Minister, *Statistical Abstract 2001*.

20. Perthes, *Political Economy*, pp. 185–6.

21. *Al-Hayat*, 7 March 2000.

22. Patrick Seale, *Asad: The Struggle for Power in the Middle East* (Berkeley and Los Angeles: University of California Press, 1995), p. 429.

23. Interview with author, Damascus, 31 April 2001.

24. Eyal Zisser, *Asad's Legacy: Syria in Transition* (London: Hurst and Co., 2001), p. 88.

25. Eberhard Kienle, *Ba'ath v. Ba'ath* (London and New York: I.B.Tauris, 1990).

26. Office of the Prime Minister, *Statistical Abstract 2001*.

27. Ibid.

28. Ibid.

29. *Tishreen*, 29 June 1985.

30. Batatu, *Syria's Peasantry*, pp. 212–13.

31. Ibid., p. 214.

32. World Bank, *World Development Indicators Database* (Washington, DC: World Bank, April 2002).

33. 'CBS Releases Latest Statistics on Syria's Labour Force', *The Syria Report*, 9 September 2002.

CHAPTER 2

'Damascus Spring': The Rise of the Civil Society Movement

§ RIAD Seif looked younger than his fifty-six years, but the stress still showed. His deep brown eyes were red-rimmed, glazed and slightly haunted. Throughout our interview in his central Damascus office he sat uneasily on the edge of his chair and chain-smoked determinedly. 'We are all the same,' he insisted, drawing deeply on his *Hamra'*, a popular local brand of cigarettes. 'As a minimum, we want to create a state of rights and laws, where every Syrian has equal rights, and where every Syrian has the chance to compete fairly and equally. To attain that, we need the *badihiyat* [fundamentals], the basic elements of democracy: free elections, an independent parliament, independent courts of law, a free media and a civil society with non-governmental organisations (NGOs).'[1] Seif, who had become one of the biggest thorns in the regime's side, insisted that the new Syria should be 'according to Syria's culture. I don't want a copy of any other democracy.' He was adamant, however, that 'these rules are universal. Free elections, for example. No one can say that democracy does not involve free elections.'

A once wealthy self-made businessman (whose local industries had produced high-quality goods of a standard rare in the country) whom the government had already punished with bankruptcy, Seif would be arrested shortly after I met him. He had been elected to parliament as an independent on the list for Damascus in 1994 and re-elected for another four-year term in 1998, despite a determined smear campaign against him by the authorities. I mentioned that the Ministry of Information had tried to persuade me not to meet him, on the grounds that he was corrupt and represented no one but himself. 'I am Enemy Number One,' he laughed. 'They want to isolate me as much as they can.' The son of a carpenter from the working-class Midan district of

Damascus, Seif took a part-time job at a clothing factory in 1959. In 1963 he and his brothers established a small clothing workshop which expanded until it became one of the country's biggest clothes factories, with 1,400 workers and with the Adidas multinational as its major client. On entering parliament, however, Seif showed none of the customary deference to the regime, repeatedly condemning its economic mismanagement and other manifest deficiencies. The response was a formal accusation that Seif owed millions of Syrian Pounds in back-taxes. The outcome of this witch-hunt was his bankruptcy. Armed with the claim – laughable from a system so venal – that Seif was corrupt, the authorities tried and failed to prevent his re-election to parliament in 1998.

New President, New Mood

In the last months of Hafiz al-Asad's presidency, at a time when Bashar increasingly publicly was being groomed for the succession, the political climate in Syria had already lightened: the regime moved to counter public cynicism by allowing wider debate, albeit clearly circumscribed. The fundamentals of the system were still taboo but aspects of how it functioned – for example the inefficiencies of the bureaucracy – became permitted areas of discussion in the media and elsewhere. The economy and moves towards its liberalisation became a particularly large area of acceptable debate.

Bashar, whose only formal title before 2000 was chairman of the Syrian Computer Society – like his late brother Basil when he was being prepared to take over from his father – was fully identified with the new mood, bringing forward younger, more dynamic individuals and spearheading an (admittedly somewhat cynical) anti-corruption campaign, again as Basil had done. 'Modernisation' and 'technology' became his buzz-words. 'We need change,' he told the pan-Arab daily *Al-Hayat* in March that year. 'We need it more today than at any other time.'[2]

At the time of the President's death on 10 June 2000, hopes were already high that Syria might be on the brink of a major political as well as economic liberalisation. In his inaugural speech to parliament on 17 July Bashar did not dim those hopes – although at the same time he offered little of substance and stressed that his task was the continuation of the policies of the late 'Immortal Leader'. His father, he affirmed, had 'prepared for us a strong ground, a firm foundation and a great tradition of principles and values which he defended and upheld until his death, not to mention the infrastructure that he built and the great achievements he made possible in all walks of life throughout the homeland, which enables us to head for the desired future strongly and confidently'. Bashar nevertheless called for the application of 'creative thinking' to Syria's problems, and pointed to 'the dire need for constructive criticism'. He expressed his support for 'transparency' and 'accountability', and highlighted the need for 'social, economic, scientific and other strategies that promote development and steadfastness'.

At the same time he indicated that he was no liberal democrat and that the most he was prepared to contemplate was some sort of 'reactivation' of the moribund Progressive National Front (PNF). 'To what extent are we democratic?' he asked. 'Is it in elections, freedom of the press or freedom of speech, or in other freedoms and rights? I would say it is none of the above.' Averring that such 'rights' were 'not democracy; they are merely democratic practices and results of democracy', Bashar argued, somewhat opaquely, that 'all these are built on democratic thinking, and this thinking is based on accepting other views'. It was, he continued, 'a two-way street ... what is a right for myself is a right for others ... Accordingly, democracy is a duty we should perform towards others before it is a right to which we are entitled.' In a clear rejection of Western-style democracy, Bashar declared: 'We should not apply to ourselves the democracy of others. Western democracies are the outcome of a long history ... We must have our own democratic experience which springs from our own history, culture and personality.' He went on to describe the PNF as 'a democratic model developed through our own experience' and to assert that it had 'become necessary to develop the Front's working formula in a manner that responds to the needs of development'.

Some Syrians remained deeply sceptical. The Paris-based political analyst and writer Subhi Hadidi, an erudite Marxist from the north-eastern town of Qamishli who went into exile in 1987, but only after having suffered the heavy hand of the regime's prisons, castigated Bashar for instituting a 'Corrective Movement Mark II'. If Syria appeared to be stable, it was because 'nothing moves, nothing changes ... There are no attacks on the dinosaur, so there is no resistance from the dinosaur.'[3] Ridiculing the plans for the PNF, Hadidi said that the new President had 'conveniently ignored what every adult Syrian knows: that this Front was a dead body when it was first set up and has continued to decompose with an unbearable stench ever since'. He noted, moreover, that the need to reactivate the PNF was 'exactly what Asad Senior used to say in every re-election speech in the thirty years he was in power'.

Most of those wanting change, however, were much encouraged by Bashar's inaugural speech. While disappointed by his failure to offer more than mere tinkering with the existing system, they understood that his hands were tied by the imperatives of the system itself; by the need to ensure the loyalty of the key military and security figures upon whom his presidency would depend. There was a widespread feeling – encouraged by the image that Bashar had cultivated prior to his father's death – that he personally favoured far more radical changes. With his accession to the presidency – or, more accurately, with his father's death – civil rights activists seized the initiative.

The Civil Society Movement

'It started hours after Asad's death,' said Subhi Hadidi. 'It was not only in Syria. It encouraged people to talk loudly, in Lebanon and elsewhere in the Middle East, wherever there was a link to Syria. People felt: "The strong man is dead. Now we have a chance."'[4]

The first seed of Syria's civil society movement (*harakat al-mujtama' al-madani*) was planted even earlier, at a 28 May 2000 meeting at the Damascus home of film director Nabil al-Maleh. The meeting was organised by the sixty-year-old writer and long-standing dissident Michel Kilo who had been jailed in 1980–83 at the height of the country-wide rebellion against the regime. Also present were the poet and writer Adel Mahmoud and the film director Muhammad Qa'arisili. 'The subject of the meeting was: "How could we revive the cultural and democratic movement in Syria?"' recalled Kilo. 'This was, if you want, the inaugural meeting of the civil society movement in Syria.'[5] The group continued to meet informally but subsequently established itself formally as a Constituent Board for the movement, which was named the Committees for the Revival of Civil Society in Syria (*Lijan Ihya' al-Mujtama' al-Madani fi Suriya*).

'We had two choices,' recalled Kilo, speaking in his book-lined apartment in east Damascus, near Sarhat at-Tahrir (Freedom Roundabout) and close both to the Masjid al-Firdous (Paradise Mosque) and to the ugly headquarters of Air Force Intelligence. 'Either we could work as an elite and found a new political party. Or we could work in a different way, offering knowledge, ideas, experiences, reflections and emotions to [that part of] society which is now outside politics: to help society restore itself politically through a cultural project that we offered. This was the project with which the civil society movement started.'

Class models of political analysis appropriate in industrialised states did not apply in Syria, Kilo explained. There was no real bourgeoisie and no mass working class. 'The only social force able to implement a political project is the middle class,' he said. The Ba'athist movement had first arisen from parts of the middle class but it had been taken over by the army (see Chapter 4), which had then excluded the middle classes from any effective political role. 'If the middle classes do not play an active role in political life, our society [as a whole] will not [either],' said Kilo. 'Any political project to confront the present regime should arise from the middle classes, or from certain groups of the middle class who are particularly sensitive to the issues of democracy.' The emphasis should be on activating these groups, such as lawyers, intellectuals and students, 'because it is they who can transmit the ideas of democracy and freedom to society'. The Kilo group envisaged the creation of 'committees on all levels, professional and other, which would link the particular problems of each sector with the general political problem. The lawyers, for example, would integrate the problems they face – the interference of the security apparatus in the courts, the injustice of certain laws – into a comprehensive, democratic programme.'

Kilo, who hails originally from the port city of Lattakia, rightly reminded me that while the 'Damascus Spring' in the second half of 2000 had been exceptional, the struggle for democracy and human rights by Syria's intellectuals had pre-dated it by many years. An earlier 'spring' had occurred in the late 1970s, parallel to the armed uprising against the regime by the Muslim Brotherhood. Many of those prominent in 2000 had also played key roles in the earlier surge of agitation. Kilo himself was a prime example. That older 'spring' had been crushed along with the Muslim Brotherhood's rebellion. Kilo was in prison in 1980–83 and then went into forced exile. The same point was made by *Al-Hayat*'s well-informed Damascus bureau chief, Ibrahim Hamidi: 'In the late 1970s and early 1980s we had something very similar, with a dialogue between the authorities and the opposition. [Vice President Abdul Halim] Khaddam himself had meetings with intellectuals at Damascus University. We tried to activate civil society, and there were tough articles in the official press against the intellectuals. [In the end] the whole movement was just shut down.'[6]

Riad Seif, who already had a well-deserved reputation as an outspoken critic of the regime, had close links with Kilo's group and attended their meetings in August and September 2000. While Kilo and his associates envisaged a politico-cultural movement, however, Seif favoured a more overtly political campaign which might attract support from reformers within the regime. Several groups of intellectuals had met informally and intermittently over the years for guarded discussions of quasi-political subjects. In July 200, however, Seif launched an explicitly political discussion group, or forum, in his offices in a slightly shabby block near Victoria Bridge in central Damascus, just a stone's throw from the Interior Ministry. 'From the start of July 2000, we gathered about twenty intellectuals here in my office every Sunday. We met here until the end of August,' recalled Seif. 'This was the first civil society forum in Syria.'[7]

In late August 2000 he and his associates issued a statement outlining a proposal for the formation of an association to be named 'Friends of Civil Society in Syria'. The statement affirmed the need 'to revive the institutions of civil society and achieve balance between their role and that of the state in the context of a real partnership between them in the higher national interest'. It stressed 'the importance of freedom of opinion and expression, respect for opposing views, active and positive individual participation in public life and the adoption of dialogue, positive criticism and peaceful development to resolve differences, as being among the most important foundations of civil society'. The statement added: 'The rule of law, the independence of the judiciary and the abolition of special courts, martial law and emergency legislation also constitute a solid basis for civil society.'

Syria's Law of Association, No. 39 of 1958, requires every civil association to secure a licence from the Ministry of Social Affairs. 'I knew that to give us permission would be a very important decision that someone at a very high level would take,' said Seif. 'So I telephoned the Vice President, Abdul Halim Khaddam. I said: "We have to talk about an important issue."'[8] A meeting with Khaddam, who is one of the regime's traditionalist 'old guard', did not go well. 'I presented him with our statement of objectives,' recalled Seif. 'His reaction was very, very negative. He said: "It's a coup. You want to destroy the system and take over, and this is Communiqué Number One."' Seif explained: 'It's very well known in Syria, when someone stages a coup, immediately on the radio comes *Al-Bayan Raqam Wahad* [Communiqué Number One].' He added that Khaddam's reaction 'had also been the reaction of an important general in the secret police who was the one responsible for this issue', whom he had met the same day. Seif himself preferred not to identify him but other sources say that he was Bahjat Suleiman, the Alawi head of the internal branch of one of the main *mukhabarat* agencies, the General Intelligence Directorate and *de facto* head of the organisation in Damascus.

According to *Al-Hayat*'s Ibrahim Hamidi, both Khaddam and Suleiman suggested that Seif delay the formation of his planned association because 'Syria was entering a period of reforms and openings in all fields and in the near future there would be a law on political parties. Then [they said to Seif], instead of establishing a civil society association or committee, you can establish a political party, and now you can start discussing publicly all the principles and priorities of this party.'[9] Hamidi added that despite their deep misgivings about Seif's plans, both Khaddam and Suleiman indicated that they had only 'two red lines: no relations with Westerners; and no secrets'.

The unease felt by some parts of the regime at the growing calls for democratisation was also underlined by the response to an open letter to Bashar al-Asad from the eminent Syrian philosopher Antoun al-Maqdisi published in *Al-Hayat* on 14 August and demanding similar reforms. The status of the Syrian people, he wrote, should be changed 'from one of subjects to one of citizens'. The official response was swift. Al-Maqdisi's contract with the Ministry of Culture was terminated.

In December 2001 Al-Maqdisi would receive a Prince Claus Award from the Netherlands' Prince Claus Fund for Culture and Development. Named after the husband of Holland's Queen Beatrix and established to mark his seventieth birthday, the fund works to enhance the understanding of cultures and promotes interaction between culture and development. Al-Maqdisi, born in 1915 while Syria was still an Ottoman province, had been honoured because 'in the past he has plotted new paths for thought in the Arab world' and because 'today he continues to advocate freedom, democracy and human rights – a position that has shaped and inspired generations of intellectuals'. Al-Maqdisi was 'for many in his country a major point of reference and an oracle'. It was such a man that the Ministry of Culture deemed fit to dismiss.

Encouraged by Khaddam and Suleiman to believe that his plans were not too far removed from those of the regime, Seif pressed on. 'I decided at once to open a forum in my home, benefiting from my immunity as a member of parliament. We invited people to study every Wednesday the subject of civil society. Each week a renowned professor gave a one-hour lecture, and then we discussed this lecture for another two hours. The first, in early September, was by Antoun al-Maqdisi. Each week, 200 to 250 people attended.' Syria's uniformly state-controlled media resolutely ignored these developments. 'They behaved as if we did not exist,' said Riad Seif. Crucially, however, Seif's so-called National Dialogue Forum was reported intensively by the Arab media and most importantly by the Qatar-based *Al-Jazeera* satellite station which has a wide regional following. 'All Syrians were thus informed about what was going on in that forum. And after about November other forums started appearing in Damascus and then in other cities,' Seif recalled.

'Suddenly the civil society forums (*muntadayat al-mujtama' al-madani*) were everywhere in Syria, not just in Damascus,' said Subhi Hadidi. 'There was a sense that the movement was getting larger and larger.'[10] Within six months of Bashar taking office hundreds had appeared, most of them hosted in private houses and with those attending knowing full well that a brutal response from the authorities could not be ruled out. 'By January [2001] it was like a fashion,' said Seif. 'Every week you heard an announcement of the opening of a new forum.'

Civil Society's Pedigree

For an exposition of what 'civil society' means to Syrians, I turned to Sadiq Jalal al-Azm, one of his country's leading thinkers who was also an intellectual who publicly supported Salman Rushdie against Iranian Ayatollah Khomeini's *fatwa*. In a meeting at his home in the well-heeled Damascus neighbourhood of West Malki, near the old presidential palace on the slopes of Jabal Qasioun which dominates the city, Al-Azm explained: 'When civil society is mentioned in the West, what primarily comes to mind are things like clubs, churches, civil associations, trade unions etc.'[11] This was 'certainly part of the meaning of civil society and, given the extreme – what we would regard from our perspective as extreme – atomisation of current capitalist society in the West, it seems natural that the meaning of civil society there should concentrate on things like clubs and NGOs that bring the social atoms together, that bring people together'. In Syria, by contrast, there was no shortage of such traditional clubs and associations, continued Al-Azm. Even in countries like Syria, where the state sought to control all aspects of the life of societies, many independent charities and organisations could be found. 'What we lack are the other aspects of what in the West would be called civil society: things like civil liberties; independence of the judiciary; some measure of the democratic process; some autonomy for the individual; the idea of equality before the law,' he explained.

As well as linking with European democratic ideals, Syria's civil society movement also had a strong local pedigree, stressed Al-Azm. The first sustained programme to introduce concepts of citizenship transcending traditional ethnic, familial and religious allegiances and loyalties was implemented by the Ottoman Turks during the nineteenth century, a process which had started, under the ruler of Egypt, Muhammad Ali, around 1830. The motive was a desire to modernise in the face of commercial, technical and military challenges and pressures from Europe. 'This is a line that goes back to the Ottoman *perestroika* – the *tanzimat*. I call what Gorbachev did the Russian *tanzimat*, and what the Ottomans did starting from about 1830, I call the Ottoman *perestroika*,' said Al-Azm. 'I think these are the beginnings of something called civil society, compared to something which in Arabic I and others call *ahli* [communal] society, where links are organic, where allegiances are familial, tribal and so on.'

In Europe, civil society was created as the result of demands from below. 'In the case of the Ottoman reforms and modernisation, the leadership came from the state – which was also regarded as the Muslim system – and from the elites that ran the state,' explained Al-Azm. 'Muhammad Ali is the prime example. In most Arab countries – and especially the central Arab countries such as Syria, Iraq and Egypt – the state persisted as a force for modernisation, which necessarily meant greater and greater disintegration of the *ahli* society and the rise of the idea of citizenship, of nationalism and so on. The difference between us and Europe is that this was led by the state, with the intent of modernising as a survival strategy, while in Europe, it came from below.' In a sense, the state had been almost too successful: 'Now, I think, at least in Syria, enough of the elements of the idea of citizenship and civil society have formed that society is reacting against this patronage by the state. It's like the state going out and teaching everybody how to read and write. It does a good job, but then the people start saying: please stop dictating to us what we're supposed to read. So they rebel against the state because the state taught them how to read but it also imposes on them what to read.'

Al-Azm is well aware that the traditional allegiances of *ahli* society remain potent and that there is a danger of these exploding into violence if states relax their iron grip on their subjects. 'This is a point of implicit debate and contention in Syria,' he affirmed. 'The authorities remind those who are working for the ideas of a civil society, democracy, human rights and so on, of the fact that these allegiances could again assert themselves and could lead to situations like Sudan, Algeria or Lebanon. They use this fear as a stick to beat the civil society movement and more or less to freeze the situation – to perpetuate themselves in power.' He explained: 'Our argument is that there is no question about the strength of these pre-civil society allegiances, and about the concern that they could take over. But our purpose is to transcend them by trying to reinforce those aspects of our lives that have become something of a civil society, in the modern sense of the term – in other words, aspects where citizenship is decisive, rather than religious or tribal affiliation.' Al-Azm declared: 'If we don't try – with the co-operation of the authorities – to transcend these pre-civil society allegiances, then there is no hope for us. We'll always end up being a society torn by tribalism, by clannishness and so on. The only way to save the situation is to work hard to build as much of a civil society as possible.'

Part of the official reaction to the civil society movement has been to insist that Syria already has a civil society embracing a range of bodies such as political parties, trade unions, youth and women's organisations and Islamic and Christian associations – although many of these bodies are state-controlled. Al-Azm condemned this as 'deliberate obfuscation', pointing out: 'The way they argue, tribal society would be civil society. A slave society could be civil society. They are blunting the cutting edge of the concept: that we want to push forward the movement we have made already from pre-civil society to something like a civil society. If you say all society is, in the end, civil society then you have blunted the cutting edge of the concept and the movement.'

The Statement of 99

A major landmark in Syria's civil society movement came on 27 September 2000 when the daily *Al-Hayat* carried a statement signed by ninety-nine Syrian intellectuals, artists and professionals demanding an end to the State of Emergency which had been in effect since 1963; a public pardon for all political detainees and exiles; the establishment of 'a state of law' that would recognise 'political and intellectual pluralism', freedom of assembly and freedom of expression and the press; and the liberation of public life from 'the [restrictive] laws, constraints and [various] forms of censorship imposed on it' (see Appendix 1). The Statement of 99, as it became known, affirmed that 'no reform, be it economic, administrative or legal, will achieve tranquillity and stability in the country unless fully accompanied by the desired political reform'. Signatories included Michel Kilo; Antoun al-Maqdisi; Adonis (one of the Arab world's leading poets); Sadiq Jalal al-Azm; Fares al-Hellou, a popular comedian living in Damascus; Abdullah Hannah, a historian living in Damascus who is an expert on Syrian nationalists of the French Mandate period; Khalid Taja, a well-known television actor based in Damascus; and Sarab al-Atassi, an academic and the daughter of the late Jamal al-Atassi, a former senior Ba'athist who had split from the party to head a faction of the Arab Socialist Union (see Chapter 5).

The Statement was carefully crafted to minimise annoyance to the regime. There was no demand for the wholesale democratisation of Syrian institutions; no ideological flavour; no attack on the manner in which Bashar al-Asad had come to power. None of the signatories had significant histories of anti-regime activism and the authorities were thereby denied the chance to condemn them as 'well-known enemies of the state' or 'agents of Israel'. The official response was simply to ignore the Statement. Nowhere was it mentioned in the state-run media, and foreign newspapers reporting it were banned.

In the second half of 2000, however, the authorities took a series of steps which were seen as a response to the rising clamour for reform. In June and July dozens of Islamists and leftists were freed from prison. Most were members of the outlawed Muslim Brotherhood that had openly confronted the regime in the early 1980s, and of the Communist Action Party. On 15 November Asad issued a decree releasing 600 political prisoners, of whom 380 were Muslim Brotherhood members and most of the rest were leftists, including twenty-two from the Communist Action Party. 'We hope that this is just the start,' said Amnesty International, 'and the release of all prisoners of conscience and political prisoners who have been detained for years without trial will follow.' The amnesty was reported in Syria's official media – ironically, the first time that the regime had actually acknowledged that it imprisoned people for political reasons. Four days later Asad decreed the closure of the notorious Mezzeh prison in western Damascus, an ugly two-storey structure on a barbed-wire-fenced hilltop built by the French in the 1920s. Sceptics noted, however, that there remained plenty of other political prisons in Syria, and that one reason for Mezzeh's closure was that it had become an anachronism and an eyesore in an upper-income district of the capital where many top cadres lived. On 22 November a sweeping general pardon for non-political prisoners was announced to mark the thirtieth anniversary of Hafiz al-Asad's Corrective Movement. The beneficiaries included people sentenced for violating the military service law, for smuggling and for fraud (the amnesty for the latter being conditional on their repaying their victims within one year). Announcing the pardon, the Syrian Arab News Agency (SANA) explained: 'This great offering by the great heart will instil happiness, joy, thanks and gratitude in the hearts of children, spouses, brothers, fathers and sons. It proves the leader's love for the masses and his concern for the needs and requirements of the homeland and citizens.' In December, meanwhile, fifty-four Lebanese political prisoners were transferred from Syrian to Lebanese jails. The move was hailed by Amnesty International as 'a step forward in redressing human rights violations committed by the Syrian forces operating in Lebanon over two decades'.

The months following Bashar al-Asad's taking office also saw the re-emergence of one unofficial human rights organisation, the Committees for the Defence of Democratic Freedoms and Human Rights in Syria (CDF), and the creation of another, the Syrian Human Rights Association (SHRA). Formed in July 2000, the SHRA was headed by lawyer Haitham al-Maleh who had been imprisoned for seven years in the 1980s (see Chapter 6). The CDF had been created in 1989 but suppressed in 1991 when its chairman, Aktham Nu'aisah, and other key figures were arrested. In September 2000 the CDF met and elected a new board of trustees, eight of whom live within Syria. In December it publicly urged a general amnesty for all political prisoners, explaining that it had 'emerged once again to work in the open' because of 'the positive political developments in Syria'.

In August, shortly after taking office, Bashar al-Asad met with the leaders of the parties allied to the Ba'ath in the Progressive National Front (PNF) to discuss ways to invigorate the grouping. In December it was reported that the Ba'ath Party command had decided to allow the six PNF parties to open provincial offices and issue newspapers publicly. A decision was also made to abandon the appointment of Ba'ath Party officials from above and instead to elect them, as of the start of 2001, in a process to be completed by early 2002. The mood was further lightened in January 2001 by the issue of a licence for the publication of *Ad-Dommari* (*The Lamplighter*), the country's first privately owned newspaper (see Chapter 7).

Sceptics viewed all these steps as half-measures aimed merely at blunting criticism of the system, and certainly hardliners such as Vice President Abdul Halim Khaddam opposed meaningful concessions to a civil society movement which they saw as a threat to the entire edifice and to their personal privileges. Clearly, however, there were those at the top of the system – apparently including Bashar – who felt that greater freedom could be introduced without a general collapse.

The Statement of 1,000

This duality was mirrored within the civil society movement. Some felt that the best strategy was a tacit alliance with reformers within the regime, and that to demand too much too quickly would alienate those, including Bashar, upon whom ultimate success would depend. Others were uncompromising and insisted that the system was incapable of reforming itself and that the movement should therefore press on regardless of the regime's attitude. Some observers identified Michel Kilo's group with the first, more cautious, current, and Riad Seif's with the second current; while others asserted precisely the opposite. Some reports claimed, moreover, that the two factions had fallen out badly over the direction the civil society movement should take.

Certainly Kilo felt that Seif was over-optimistic. 'He [Seif] thought that he was Lech Walesa [leader of the Solidarity trade union that had led Poland's pro-democracy movement in the 1980s] and that Syria was Poland and that the Syrian regime was about to fall,' claimed Kilo.[12] 'We told him that the regime in Syria should be dismantled piece by piece and could not be toppled by a popular movement.' Kilo attributed Seif's approach to his 'inexperience in politics'. On the other hand, Seif had demonstrated considerable caution by meeting Khaddam and Suleiman, and the allegation of inexperience would appear misplaced when applied to a man who had maintained his integrity in the face of a sustained official campaign of harassment leading to bankruptcy.

The reports of a significant cleavage between Kilo and Seif appear greatly exaggerated. In reality, they were engaged in separate but complementary projects. Certainly they had their differences but these seem to have been more personal than political and did not extend to any freezing of relations. 'People thought that Riad and the others [Kilo's group] had disagreed, and newspapers wrote about that disagreement, which did not exist,' said Hussam Shehadeh, Seif's office manager. 'Riad and Michel stayed in touch with each other. They used to phone each other. Michel attended the last lecture, by Burhan Ghalyoun [a sociologist at the Sorbonne who was introducing a five-hour discussion on the establishment of a multi-party system and the ending of the State of Emergency Law], in Riad's house. This was one day before Riad's arrest' (see Chapter 3).[13]

By December 2000 Kilo's organisation, the Committees for the Revival of Civil Society, was drafting a second major declaration, to be signed by 1,000 people, as the sequel to the Statement of 99. The drafting process was tortuous, reflecting the different tendencies within Kilo's group. 'There was a disagreement,' explained *Al-Hayat*'s Ibrahim Hamidi. 'I have all the documents [and] there were three versions. There was disagreement not about having it but about the language.'[14]

A draft of the Statement was leaked before the 1,000 signatures had been collected and an article quoting extensively from the document appeared in the Beirut daily *As-Safir* on 11 January 2001. Shortly after, the entire text was reproduced in the Arab press (see Appendix 2). The lengthy document affirmed that Syria urgently needed to 'draw lessons from the last decades' and plan its future 'following the deterioration of its social, political, economic and cultural conditions, and in response to the challenges of globalisation and economic integration and the challenges of the Arab–Israeli conflict'. Syria today required 'the efforts of all its citizens to revive civil society' whose weakness had 'deprived the country's development and construction process of crucial national capacities'. The Statement – also known as the Basic Document – stressed that civil society had existed in Syria before 'revolutionary legitimacy' had usurped 'constitutional legitimacy'. Civil society had been marginalised through the establishment of a state with 'one party, one colour and one opinion ... a state for one part of society ... which ... portrayed itself as representing the people' and where 'citizenship was reduced to the narrow concept of belonging to one party and to personal loyalty'. Those controlling the state 'considered the rest of the population as a mere herd' while 'the wealth of the state and of its institutions, the country's resources and those of the institutions of civil society, became like feudal estates which were distributed to followers and loyalists', continued the Statement of 1,000.

Marginalising civil society had caused the marginalisation of the state itself, it argued, as the two were interlinked: 'Civil society constitutes the very substance of the modern state, while the state is civil society's political expression. Together, they constitute the democratic system of government.' The Statement expressed confidence that Syria was 'still capable of rebuilding its social and political life; of rebuilding its economy and culture' and could 'overcome the relationships and structures that produced tyranny'. In a reference to the demise of the Soviet system – very much a model for Syria's Ba'athist dictatorship – the Statement affirmed that 'the consequences of coups against political democracy in the name of socialism are now plain.' Equally obvious were the consequences of failing to acknowledge the reality of social, cultural and political diversity; and of failing to recognise the law as an expression of what citizens have in common, as an 'historic compromise' between different interests and groups.

There was 'a great need today to revive societal and social institutions free of domination by the executive authority and by the security apparatus, which usurped full powers' and 'free of all traditional forms of social ties, relationships and structures, such as those of tribalism and sectarianism'. This was required in order 'to re-establish politics in society' as a means 'to achieve the crucial balance between society and state, co-ordinating their activities, and thus achieving liberty, equality and justice'. The Statement asserted: 'National unity is thus bolstered, as is the dignity and sovereignty of the state' and 'the rule of law becomes the final arbiter for all'. Affirming that 'no social or political group has the right to decide by itself where the country's national interests lie, and what means should be pursued to achieve those interests', the Statement called on 'all groups – including the present ruling power' to set out their programmes 'for discussion and dialogue'. It declared that 'No dialogue is possible without freedom of opinion and expression, free political parties and trade unions, a free press, free social organisations and a legislature that genuinely and effectively represents the people.' The Statement stressed that economic reforms would fail unless 'preceded and accompanied by a comprehensive package of political and constitutional reforms'.

It listed eight urgent measures:

- ending the State of Emergency, special courts, martial law and related laws; the release of all political prisoners and correction of the status of those stripped of civil rights and the right to work under emergency legislation; and the repatriation of political exiles
- granting political freedoms, and notably freedom of opinion and expression; enacting legislation to regulate the activities of political parties, associations, clubs and NGOs
- restoring a media law guaranteeing freedom of journalism and publication
- enacting a 'democratic election law' to regulate elections 'at all

levels' under the supervision of 'an independent judiciary', with parliament becoming 'a genuine legislative and supervisory institution, truly representing the will of the people'

- ensuring the 'independence and integrity' of the judiciary and applying laws 'equally to rulers and ruled'
- granting citizens their economic rights, 'most of which are stated in the Constitution', and in particular their right to 'a fair share of national wealth' and to 'suitable employment'; and protecting the right of future generations 'to their fair share of the country's wealth and to a clean environment'
- acknowledging that the claim that the PNF represented 'the most vibrant of forces' in Syrian society and that the country needed nothing more than the reinvigoration of the PNF would 'perpetuate further the social and economic stagnation and political paralysis'. It was therefore imperative, said the Statement, to reconsider the Front's relationship with the government and to 'reconsider the concept of [the Ba'ath Party as] "the leading party in society and the state"'
- the abolition of 'legal discrimination against women'

The Statement concluded by calling for 'the establishment of committees for reviving civil society in all sectors of Syrian life' with the aim of ending the 'stagnation that doubles our backwardness in relation to the pace of international development' and of taking 'the step to a free, independent and democratic society'.

The Statement of 1,000 was a devastating and unprecedented assault on the fundamentals of Ba'athist rule. Unlike the Statement of 99, it explicitly demanded a multi-party political system and it explicitly questioned the lead role of the Ba'ath Party. Even more clearly than the Statement of 99, it insisted that the economic reform programme upon which the regime was engaged would fail without sweeping – indeed revolutionary – political change. Three days after its publication, Kilo expressed his appreciation that the authorities had not censored the Arab newspapers that had published it and had not taken action against potential signatories or against journalists who had commented on the Statement. He told *Al-Hayat*: 'We are very grateful for the broad-mindedness of the leadership – represented by President Bashar Al-Asad – which dealt with the document positively.'[15]

On 23 January Muhammad Sawwan, a former member of the Arab Socialist Union (a Nasserist party belonging to the PNF), announced a project to form a Coalition for Democracy and Unity (CDU). The new group, attracting the support of leftist and Arab nationalist figures, aimed to 'strengthen national unity through democratic dialogue', said Sawwan.[16] A week later, the focus switched again to Riad Seif who during a 31 January meeting of his National Dialogue Forum announced plans for the formation of an independent political party to be named the Movement for Social Peace. 'We will concentrate on the young generation, which is entitled actively to take part in building the future without having trustees who underwent political experiences,' Seif told *Al-Hayat*'s Ibrahim Hamidi.[17] He added that his party would not be under the 'trusteeship of political trends that committed mistakes and did not practise, when they were politically active, the democracy they are now preaching'. Many of the key civil society activists have leftist/Marxist backgrounds and Seif's jibe was an apparent reference to his rivals in the Constituent Board of the Committees for the Revival of Civil Society.

For the regime hardliners, these tentative moves towards the unauthorised creation of political parties proved the final straw.

Notes

1. Interview with author, Damascus, 5 May 2001.
2. *Al-Hayat*, 7 March 2000.
3. *Al-Quds al-Arabi*, 25 July 2000.
4. Interview with author, Paris, 17 June 2001.
5. Interview with author, Damascus, 4 December 2001.
6. Interview with author, Damascus, 17 February 2002.
7. Interview with author, Damascus, 5 May 2001.
8. Ibid.
9. Interview with author, Damascus, 17 February 2002.
10. Interview with author, Paris, 17 June 2001.
11. Interview with author, Damascus, 5 May 2001.
12. Interview with author, Damascus, 4 December 2001.
13. Interview with author, Damascus, 2 December 2001.
14. Interview with author, Damascus, 17 February 2002.
15. *Al-Hayat*, 14 January 2001.
16. Gary C. Gambill, 'Dark Days Ahead for Syria's Liberal Reformers', *Middle East Intelligence Bulletin*, 3 (2), February 2001, p. 3.
17. *Al-Hayat*, 26 January 2001.

CHAPTER 3

'Damascus Winter': The Suppression of the Civil Society Movement

§ CIVIL society was 'an American term' which had been given 'additional meanings' by 'groups that seek to become [political] parties', asserted Information Minister Adnan Omran, a former ambassador to London and former deputy secretary-general of the Arab League.[1] Speaking to journalists in Damascus on 29 January 2001, he opined that civil society groups in developing countries were backed by foreign embassies which 'provided financial benefits and privileges' to the pro-democracy activists.

It marked the start of a concerted campaign by the government to confront the dissidents head-on which would culminate later in the year with the arrests of the two independent members of parliament, Riad Seif and Ma'moun al-Homsi, of Riad at-Turk, head of the outlawed Syrian Communist Party-Political Bureau, the economist Aref Dalila and several other leading civil society activists. The official *volte face* signified that Bashar al-Asad was losing ground to regime hard-liners centred on Vice President Abdul Halim Khaddam. Their real fear was the challenge to their power and interests posed by the civil society movement but this was cynically cloaked in protestations of the need for national unity and stability in the face of an Israel which, always aggressive, had become even more dangerous following the February 2001 election of a right-wing Likud government headed by the extremist Ariel Sharon.

Information Minister Omran declared that the well-respected Egyptian human rights activist, Professor Sa'adeddin Ibrahim, who at that time was on trial in Cairo, was 'an [activist] in civil society institutions, and he is accused of receiving money from foreign countries and of [conducting] security missions at the behest of foreign parties'. Omran explained that 'neo-colonialism no longer relies on armies'. On 21

May 2001 Professor Ibrahim and twenty-eight of his colleagues at his Ibn Khaldoun Center for Developmental Studies in Cairo (named after the celebrated medieval Muslim historian) were found guilty of a range of alleged crimes such as 'spreading false rumours to tarnish Egypt's image abroad' and 'receiving unauthorised donations' (from the European Commission). His sentence was seven years' hard labour, while six of his colleagues received from two to five years' hard labour. Twenty-one others were given one-year suspended sentences and released. Both the Ibn Khaldoun Center and an associated body promoting women's voting rights were closed down. The Center was established by Ibrahim, who teaches sociology at the American University of Cairo, to promote civil society in Egypt. In February 2002 an appeal court ordered a retrial and this concluded on 29 July by confirming the sentence on Dr Ibrahim and twenty-three of his colleagues and reducing the prison terms of four others. On 3 December 2002 Dr Ibrahim and four co-defendants won an appeal in Egypt's Court of Cassation, which ordered a final retrial, scheduled to start in January 2003.

Omran explained: 'This does not mean that we do not believe in freedom as a major demand for all society. But not absolute, blind freedom. Each society has its red lines. Political freedom has red lines. Social freedom has red lines. Cultural freedom has red lines.' In Syria, the 'political red lines' were defined by the Constitution which stated that 'any talk that undermines the unity of society is a threat to society as a whole', he said. 'We want responsible freedom which allows the citizen to express his ideas and views in keeping with the Constitution.' Asked what was the official attitude towards the civil society movement, Omran said it was one of 'respect for the other view, so long as this is done within the framework of the Constitution, national responsibility and the unity and laws of the land'. Omran said that the 1963 State of Emergency had effectively been frozen but he noted that Syria faced Israeli 'occupation and aggression and is in a state of war that could turn into an active war at any time because the enemy's policy is based on aggression'.

Less than twenty-four hours later the novelist Nabil Suleiman was attacked and severely beaten by two men who had waited for him outside his home in the north-western port of Lattakia. Suleiman had inaugurated a Cultural Forum in the city on 15 January whose first event had been a lecture on civil society and political reform. Afterwards, he had been called for questioning by local security officials. On 25 January, meanwhile, the novelist's car had been vandalised.

Suleiman's attackers were never identified but official involvement was widely suspected by civil society activists. The next day a group of intellectuals went to the headquarters of the Writers' Union to express solidarity with Suleiman against 'the forces of darkness, whoever they may be'.

Riad Seif became a special target for the authorities. Five Ba'athist academics attended a 31 January meeting of his National Dialogue Forum at his home in Sehnaya, 15 kilometres south of Damascus, at which Seif announced further details of his plans for a political party. As he read out a statement of principles which stressed the uniquely Syrian character of the country – in stark contrast to the pan-Arab ideology of the Ba'ath Party – the loyalists interrupted and denounced Seif as a 'foreign agent' and an 'anti-nationalist'.

During February 2001 the regime's campaign, apparently masterminded by Abdul Halim Khaddam, intensified. A watershed was an interview given by President Bashar al-Asad to the pan-Arab daily *Ash-Sharq al-Awsat* on 9 February. Syria's intellectuals, he averred, were 'a small group which portrays itself as an elite'. It was 'entirely unnatural' for them to be 'truly representative of the majority'. It was 'only natural' for him 'not to be swayed by what is said by a few people here or there', continued Bashar. 'It is obvious that there are great differences between the priorities of most of our people and what this group is advocating.' The President thus dismissed the civil rights activists as an insignificant minority representing no one but themselves and as being (unlike himself) out of touch with the people as a whole. But he did not leave it at that. 'When the consequences of an action affect the stability of the homeland, there are two possibilities,' intoned Bashar. 'Either the perpetrator is a foreign agent acting on behalf of an outside power, or else he is a simple person acting unintentionally. But in both cases a service is being done to the country's enemies and consequently both are dealt with in a similar fashion, irrespective of their intentions or motives.' The civil society movement was thus denounced by the highest authority in the land as a collection of spies, fools or both, serving the malevolent interests of foreign states – for which read Israel and America.

Asked how far he would go down the road of political liberalisation, Bashar replied that there were 'two levels: a horizontal level limited by the nation's borders and a vertical level limited by the security and stability of the homeland. Within these limits, everything is permissible, while any attempt to overstep them would be met with a stern response.' Later in the interview he insisted that 'economic reform is the main subject of discussion in Syria today. Within this sphere, there are no limits.'

In mid-February the Ba'ath Party sent seventeen members of its highest executive body, the twenty-one-member Regional Command, to all governorates and to the country's four universities to address meetings where they tried to counter the activists' arguments. On 18 February Khaddam himself told a meeting of teaching staff at Damascus University: 'Before raising this slogan [about civil society], we must study its significance. There might be flaws in some institutions. We should discuss these but not blow up the existing structure, because no one has a substitute. We will not in any way allow Syria to become another Algeria or Yugoslavia. This should be clear to everybody.'[2]

The activists were far from being cowed. In late January, seventy lawyers issued a statement demanding wide-ranging political reforms and the abolition of the State of Emergency. They called for the enactment of a law on political parties that would guarantee political pluralism and ensure the neutrality of state agencies during elections. The lawyers insisted that the rule of law meant that laws should apply to all state officials, regardless of rank. It was a brave move bearing in mind what Asad senior had done to the lawyers' association in 1980 (see Chapter 6).

The same month parliamentary Speaker Abdul Qader al-Qaddura ordered Riad Seif to close his forum. Recalled Seif: 'It was verbal, and was done in the name of the President. I said [that] without a written order I would not comply.'[3] A few days later charges were filed against him accusing him of having 'violated the Constitution' by floating his plan for a political party. Afterwards, 'the number of participants [in the forum] dropped from 350 to around seventy, and then many secret police attended', said Seif. The parliamentarian was questioned for two hours before an investigating judge at the civil court in the Palace of Justice, near the historic Hamidiya *suq* in Damascus. 'It was just to intimidate me. I've heard nothing since,' Seif told me in May 2001, four months before he was jailed.

Closing the Civil Society Forums

The biggest blow to the civil society movement was a mid-February order stipulating that forums could meet only with the formal permission of the Ministry of Social Affairs. Organisers were required to apply for permission to meet at least fifteen days in advance, detailing the venue and time of the meeting, the topics to be discussed, the speakers and those who would attend. It was a demand designed so that it could not be met. How could a forum organiser know in advance who would be attending?

Within a few weeks, virtually all Syria's civil society forums had closed. Sometimes, they ceased functioning because of sheer uncertainty about their status and the accompanying fear of police action. Often, however, organisers applied for permission but were refused. Some activists continued to hold private meetings in their homes, which they characterised as 'gatherings of friends', but the movement had lost its momentum. 'They were a bit afraid,' explained Subhi Hadidi. 'And they were right to be. They could not gauge the moment when the regime might just decide to go back to the old style of repression.'[4]

The Jamal al-Atassi Forum in Damascus, which meets in a large, modern apartment in the Mezzeh district overlooking the main highway to Beirut, fared better than the others. The authorities handled this forum with more care than the others because it represented the National Democratic Gathering (At-Tajammu' al-Watani ad-Dimuqrati), which had been formed in January 1980 at the height of the Islamist-led rebellion against the regime and which had since operated semi-legally. The Gathering links leftist parties which are not members of the PNF, including a wing of the Arab Socialist Union (ASU) and Riad at-Turk's Syrian Communist Party Political Bureau (see Chapter 5). The ASU faction in the Gathering had been headed by Jamal al-Atassi, a founder member and later senior official of the Ba'ath Party. The authorities were reluctant to move against groups that they perceived as representing a significant body of opinion which, while not allied to the regime, was not overtly hostile. 'Bashar Al-Asad thought that this forum might be an organ for the whole National Democratic Gathering, and should be allowed to debate,' said Subhi Hadidi. 'But even this margin was not tolerated by the hardliners.'[5]

The Atassi Forum, one of those that had pre-dated the 'Damascus Spring', was refused the requisite permission to function although it openly defied the authorities and continued to meet publicly. On 2 December 2001, I attended one of its meetings, at which the speaker was the Syrian journalist and film-maker Muhammad Ali al-Atassi. It was an extraordinary event, underlining the distance that Syria had travelled since the fierce repression of the 1980s when no one would have dared to attend and any attendees would have been arrested outright and whisked off to prison. Four hundred participants – many, but not all, young people and including headscarved girls – packed the premises, overflowing down the stairs and into an entrance courtyard. On the pavement outside, plain-clothed *mukhabarat* officers kept watch, none too discreetly. The lecture lasted one hour and was followed by a lively and sometimes heated debate lasting some two hours in which the regime's policies were defended by Ba'athist academics who made a point of attending all forum meetings. Attendees told me how the secret police at earlier gatherings had stood at the door taking the names of those entering.

As of December 2001, the Atassi Forum's programme of monthly meetings extended until April 2002. The topics were: 'The rule of law and the independence of the judiciary'; 'The world after 11 September'; 'The Syrian–Egyptian union: the future of the nationalist project'; 'Opinion and the opinion of the other'; and 'Readings on the nationalist and democratic thinking of Dr Jamal al-Atassi, on the eighth anniversary of his death'. Plainly, the organisers of this forum at least were not expecting closure and as of September 2002 it was still functioning.

While moving to counter the civil society movement by banning its discussion forums and by vilifying it in the official media, the regime also sought to stiffen morale within loyalist institutions. A seven-page memorandum, Circular No. 1075, issued on 17 February 2001 and published in the Ba'ath Party journal *Al-Munadil* (*The Struggler*), hailed Bashar's programme of 'development and modernisation', conceded that mistakes had been made in the past and went on to claim that 'whether deliberately or not' the civil society activists 'harm their country because they serve the country's enemies'. Party members were urged to intensify their efforts to rebut the activists' arguments (see Chapter 4). One of the more bizarre attacks came from the Defence Minister General Mustafa Tlass, well known for his off-beat utterings. In early April he told Abu Dhabi television that he had 'evidence' that intellectuals who had signed the Statement of 1,000 were agents of the US Central Intelligence Agency (CIA). He could provide the passport numbers of those concerned, he explained, along with the dates of their visits to the USA and the amounts of money they had been paid by the CIA to sign the document.[6]

The National Social Contract

Undaunted, and with hopes that reformers within the system might gain the upper hand having largely evaporated, Michel Kilo and his colleagues in the Committees for the Revival of Civil Society on 14 April issued another major policy document, *Towards a National Social*

Contract in Syria (see Appendix 3). The preamble to the nine-point document explained that it presented 'broad guidelines' as a 'foundation for a comprehensive national dialogue' and 'as a basis for a new social, political and moral covenant grounded in the honour and freedom of the individual, human rights linked to the law and a sense of responsibility, equality of opportunity, social justice and equality before the law'. It affirmed that:

- 'Citizens shall be treated as free subjects … Free citizens should be the building blocks for our social and political system'
- 'The people shall be treated only as a unitary entity of free citizens and not as a body of diverse religious and economic groups and sects'
- 'The independence, freedom, dignity, strength and unity of our country are common goals in a continuing battle that also targets domestic greed and, abroad, the Zionist enemy and forces of plunder and hegemony'; and 'Democracy is our most potent weapon for winning this battle'
- 'The state shall be based on justice and the rule of law'
- 'The Syrian economic system is in need of profound reform' and 'Democracy, which embraces transparency, political and media pluralism, civil society, the rule of law, separation of authorities and free elections held under independent supervision, is a necessary condition for the success of economic reform'
- 'Occupied Arab lands cannot be liberated without an Arab democratic system that can activate the necessary potential and effort'
- 'Work should be undertaken towards rebuilding Arab solidarity and strengthening ties between Arab states to a level where they can face the threats confronting the Arab nation'
- 'The people shall not be held in trusteeship. The people's right to choose the social, political and economic system they want for themselves shall not be usurped, since they are the source of all authority and the sole font of legitimacy'; and 'Our country shall not revert to the days of chaos and military coups. The continuation of the state of unemployment and stagnation threatens us all with serious ramifications and can only be reversed through an enlargement of democracy and through liberating civil society from the tyranny of political and ideological exclusivity'
- 'Dialogue and consensus' were the 'way to settle problems in our country' and 'Oppression and coercion should be abandoned as a way to run our national life'.

The Contract met the authorities' main arguments head-on. The regime had denounced the activists as unpatriotic. The document affirmed the importance of national unity, the recovery of Israeli-occupied Arab territories and pan-Arab solidarity. It raised the stakes, moreover, by affirming that democracy and the rule of law were key elements in achieving these nationalist objectives. The regime had accused the activists of pursuing political change when economic development was the key challenge. Like the earlier declarations, the Contract stressed that economic development could succeed *only* via democracy.

The National Social Contract had far less impact than it could have had, appearing as it did at a time when the civil society movement was already in deep trouble; the same was true of a major and innovative statement issued by the Muslim Brotherhood on 3 May committing the movement to democracy, political pluralism and the rule of law (see Chapter 5). By July and the first anniversary of Bashar al-Asad's accession to the presidency, the 'Damascus Spring' was virtually moribund. 'I'm really pessimistic,' the exiled Syrian writer and political analyst Subhi Hadidi told me in June 2001. 'Certainly things will eventually change in Syria. But the price will be very high. At best we might see a series of half-measures that are mostly cosmetic, nothing else. Now, things are exactly the same as they were six months before the death of Asad. No policy. No movement. People are just waiting for something to come, which will not come. It's really tragic.'[7]

Sadiq Jalal al-Azm, a leading intellectual and a member of the civil society movement, was slightly less gloomy. 'An important concept which the Palestinians gave the world is the concept of the pessoptimist,' he told me in May 2001, referring to Emile Habiby's book *The Secret Life of Saeed, the Ill-Fated Pessoptimist: A Palestinian Who Became a Citizen of Israel*. 'Habiby created a new word in Arabic. It's a combination of the two. He can't lose hope – he's an optimist. But the current conditions are so lousy that it makes him a pessimist. Pessoptimism means that we act as if we do have some hope.'[8] Al-Azm (speaking, it must be emphasised, before the arrests started) drew some comfort from the authorities' use of administrative measures to hit the civil society movement. 'For us, the fact that they went about it in the way they did is already a very significant piece of progress,' he said. 'It's not a Prague Spring and it's not Jaruzelski's repression yet. We are neither here nor there. We're in the middle, in this grey area.'

Bashar Chooses Bread Before Freedom

Bashar al-Asad had always stressed the importance of economic reform and a series of fiscal and economic measures were taken in the months after he took power. On 2 December 2000, for example, the Ba'ath Party's Regional Command announced its approval of plans to establish the country's first private banks and a stock market and to float the local currency, marking the end of a forty-year state monopoly on banking and foreign exchange transactions. With the crackdown on the civil society movement came a significant new twist: that economic reform should take priority over political reform – a position heralded by the President in his 8 February interview in *Ash-Sharq al-Awsat*.

'In my opinion, in the beginning the new President believed it might be possible to start reforming in parallel in the political and economic spheres,' said Riad Seif. 'But this movement for democracy grew so quickly that it was out of control. That's why there was a sudden decision to stop it, under the pretext that reforming the economy and improving life for the people should come first.' He summed up the regime's argument thus: 'bread before freedom'; and he firmly rejected it, insisting that successful economic reform depended on effective political reform.[9] Sadiq al-Azm agreed. 'I'm an old Marxist,' he told me. 'I think the economy is decisive. But tinkering with the economy without at the same time making the adjustments that even the tinkering requires, I think, will not yield any results.'[10] He elaborated: 'Syria has decided to permit private banks. That automatically implies that you need an independent judiciary, because when the banks quarrel with their clients or amongst themselves or with the government, if they don't trust a minimum of independence of the judiciary, then they will leave, or they will close or the whole thing will collapse. To say that you can start banks and not do something about the judiciary is very simplistic thinking.'

Al-Azm felt that the 'economy first' argument stemmed from a mistaken belief that painful disruptions of the type suffered by the former Soviet Bloc after the collapse of communism could be avoided by embracing the Chinese model. 'It's not true that the Chinese are simply making changes in the economy and not making changes at a lot of other levels. The entire ruling *équipe* has changed in China, while in Syria it's still the same. The "old guard" is there. Secondly, in China you can delay the political changes and concentrate on the economy because there is a very high rate of economic growth. When people feel that they are advancing, that there are opportunities, they swallow the deal: "You organise the economy and we'll keep quiet now about all the other aspects." This doesn't apply to Syria at all. There is no flourishing economy that will bribe people into keeping quiet about the needed political, social and judicial reforms.'

What of the suggestions that Syria's civil society movement was somehow linked to foreign, 'alien' powers? 'It's a knee-jerk reaction,' said Al-Azm. 'Particularly now, with the crisis in the Middle East – with Sharon in Israel, the siege of Iraq – popular feelings are running very high against the USA and the West in general, so using this argument now may find some appeal at the emotional level, but it's also so discredited. They haven't come up with new arguments, new tools. They still rely on their old tool box.' Another line of official argument was to portray the intellectuals as an unimportant minority but Al-Azm was convinced that this was mere posturing. 'They know better than that. Many of them, when they were in opposition in an earlier period, were led and influenced by intellectuals. So they know from their own experience that you cannot dismiss the intellectuals.' He insisted that the 3,000 or 4,000 intellectuals who had been directly involved in Syria's civil society movement accurately reflected mainstream opinion. 'The intelligentsia is trained to conceptualise much more fluid and foggy attitudes, emotions, feelings that are widespread in society. That's why it's always very bad policy simply to dismiss what the intelligentsia is saying and doing. Look at the Eastern European countries. There too the system treated the intellectuals like dirt, and they turned out to be the vanguard that saw early the catastrophe that was coming.'

It is not hard to find evidence to support Al-Azm's contention. In late April 2001 I arrived at midnight at Damascus Airport and took a yellow taxi into the city. How was life in Syria, almost one year after Bashar took power? The driver raised his eyes, shrugged his shoulders and declared: 'Worse than ever.'

Arrests

By late spring 2001 the civil society activists already had good reason for pessimism – or at least 'pessoptimism' – but worse was in store. By late summer Bashar al-Asad and his immediate circle of cautious reformers within the regime appeared powerless to resist hardliners demanding more than administrative action against the activists. The first arrest, on 9 August 2001, was of MP Ma'moun al-Homsi, who had started a hunger strike in support of a ten-point manifesto he had issued demanding reform and who had earlier irritated the hardliners by establishing a parliamentary human rights commission. The authorities had already accused Al-Homsi of tax evasion – a charge the regime has often made against its opponents. On 20 August, thirty-five intellectuals including Michel Kilo and the philosopher Antoun al-Maqdisi issued a statement demanding Al-Homsi's release and calling for 'those who violated the law of the country and the constitution, regardless of their posts and positions' to be put on trial.

Next, on 1 September, it was the turn of veteran communist leader Riad at-Turk, who in 1998 had been released after serving seventeen years in jail, almost all of it in unspeakable conditions in solitary confinement. Accused of defaming the regime and the late and 'immortal' leader, Hafiz al-Asad, his presumed 'crimes' were a sharply critical interview he had given to *Al-Jazeera* television in mid-August and a forthright address he had given at the Atassi Forum on 5 August in which he had condemned the country's 'hereditary republic' and called for a change from 'dictatorship to democracy'. Seventy-one-year-old At-Turk was arrested while at a doctor's clinic in the coastal town of Tartous, where he was being treated for a heart ailment. In a written statement protesting against his arrest, 216 academics, journalists, film-makers and writers condemned 'this arbitrary and illegal measure' and demanded that he be 'freed immediately and that those responsible for his arrest be prosecuted'.[11]

Despite the growing political chill, on 5 September MP Riad Seif relaunched his National Dialogue Forum at his home, where over 400 people heard Burhan Ghalyoun, a sociologist at the Sorbonne, lecture on the need for a multi-party political system and an end to the emergency laws. Seif had suspended his forum in February 2001 and he convened the meeting even though he had failed in his attempt to obtain the requisite licence. The following day he was summoned to the Interior Ministry where he was arrested by *mukhabarat* officers and taken off to join Al-Homsi and At-Turk in 'Adra prison, north-east of Damascus. Five hours before his arrest Seif told the *Financial Times* of his determination to continue his political work despite the arrests of Al-Homsi and At-Turk who had been arrested 'because the authorities want to frighten people' and 'want citizens to know they will not tolerate any kind of democracy'.[12]

On 8 September, Kamal al-Labwani and Walid al-Bunni, both doctors who had attended Seif's forum, were seized. Al-Labwani was on the executive committee of the Committees for the Defence of

Democratic Freedoms and Human Rights (CDF; see Chapters 2 and 7). The day after came the arrests of economist Aref Dalila – a leading figure in the civil society movement – businessman Habib Saleh and retired schoolteacher Hassan Sa'adoun, all three of whom had also attended Seif's forum. On 12 September Seif's lawyer, Habib Issa, a former journalist and the spokesman for the Jamal al-Atassi Forum, was arrested after he had defended his client during an interview with *Al-Jazeera* TV. Arrested the same day was Fawaz Tello who, with Issa, had been a founding member of the Syrian Human Rights Association (see Chapter 6).

The arrests were accompanied by a virulent campaign in the state-run media denigrating the activists, especially At-Turk, Al-Homsi and Seif. Incredibly, the daily *Ath-Thawra* (*The Revolution*) actually had the gall to allege that the detainees had 'interfered with the national dialogue and atmosphere of freedom that is spreading through Syria'.[13]

Trials

Of the ten arrested, only Seif and Al-Homsi were tried in open court. It was something of an innovation in Syria, where political dissidents have usually either been held without trial (often for many years) or have been tried by special security courts (see Chapter 6). Both were charged with 'seeking to change the Constitution by illegal means', 'hindering the authorities in the exercise of their duties', 'insulting the authorities' and 'incitement to confessional strife'. Seif was also accused of establishing a 'secret association'.

High drama surrounded their court appearances. For his first hearing on 30 October 2001, Al-Homsi was escorted from 'Adra prison to the Palace of Justice by thirty armed police officers. Declaring his innocence, Al-Homsi affirmed, 'I repeat the demands made earlier' (which had prompted his arrest). When a lawyer claimed that the presence of journalists proved the existence of democracy in Syria, the MP shouted from the steel cage which acted as the dock: 'Had there been democracy in Syria I wouldn't be standing here. We went to prison for the sake of freedom.'

Riad Seif's first hearing, on 31 October, was entirely overshadowed in the international media by the simultaneous joint press conference on terrorism being given at the Sheraton Hotel on the other side of town by Bashar al-Asad and British Prime Minister Tony Blair. Seif, too, vehemently denied the allegations against him, declaring: 'I'm certain that he who wrote and filed the accusations against me is himself convinced of their falsehood.' Demanding 'a fundamental and not a general explanation of why I'm here', he said: 'The existing regime in Syria does not accept any opposition or argument other than its own ... I did not violate the Constitution. I am here because I demanded a break of the political, cultural, economic, social and media monopoly in Syria.' Several times the judge tried to interrupt his speech but Seif persisted, sometimes in a raised voice.

An estimated 3,000 supporters gathered outside the Palace of Justice for Ma'moun al-Homsi's second hearing on 13 November, bringing traffic to a halt in central Damascus. Underlining their continued belief in the President's basic goodwill towards the civil society movement, the demonstrators chanted: 'With our blood, with our lives, we sacrifice for you, Oh Bashar.' Present in court were journalists, and diplomats from the missions of the European Union, the United States, Norway, France, Japan and Italy, and a representative from the Cairo-based Arab Human Rights Commission. Al-Homsi, dressed in a smart black business suit, entered court with a Syrian flag draped over his shoulders. When he tried to speak the judge silenced him. The MP retorted: 'I've spent four months in jail and I believe I'm entitled to four minutes of speaking. This is not justice.' Addressing the courtroom at large, he declared: 'They accuse us of violating the Constitution and yet they violate it themselves.' As he was escorted out, Al-Homsi shouted: 'We will sacrifice everything for Syria! Long live Syria! Long live freedom and justice!'

The following day Riad Seif was escorted from his cell at 'Adra for his second hearing. The court was packed with friends and family members and diplomats from the United States, Norway, the Netherlands, Switzerland, Belgium and Germany. As he entered after a five-hour delay he was given a standing ovation. Shortly after, his wife Reem, declaring that she was 'proud of him', told me that Riad 'feels optimistic. He doesn't care what will happen.'[14] Conditions at the 'Adra prison were good. Her husband and Ma'moun al-Homsi each had a cell to themselves while the other eight were divided between two cells. Riad was allowed out of his cell for exercise for one hour per day, during which he ran, except on Fridays (the Muslim day of rest). Visitors were permitted only on Sundays, 'but I asked the head of the prison and sometimes he allows me to visit him at other times', said Mrs Seif.

Incongruously, while giving no quarter to the civil society activists, the regime marked the thirty-first anniversary of Hafiz al-Asad's accession to power in November 2001 by releasing over one hundred Islamist and other political prisoners, some of whom had been held since 1987. Despite the discouraging political climate, on 15 January 2002 a group of Syrian lawyers announced the formation of a new National Committee for the Defence of Freedom of Opinion which would campaign for the institution of the rule of law. The following day the Committees for the Revival of Civil Society issued another lengthy declaration which denounced the activists' arrests but otherwise added little to the earlier *Towards a National Social Contract in Syria*.

After a protracted delay, Ma'moun al-Homsi was sentenced on 19 March 2002 to five years in prison for 'seeking to change the Constitution by illegal means', for 'insulting the authorities' and for 'hindering the authorities in the exercise of their duties'. He was acquitted of the charge of 'incitement to confessional strife'. Reiterating his innocence, Al-Homsi declared: 'Liberty and dignity have a price ... Prison has no fear for me.' Five Western diplomats were among those in court. On 4 April 2002, Riad Seif was also handed a five-year prison term for 'seeking to change the Constitution by illegal means' and for creating a 'secret association'. He too was acquitted of the charge of 'incitement to confessional strife'. Seif reacted with characteristic aplomb, declaring the verdict to be an honour and shouting: 'Long live the people! Freedom! Freedom!' Again, Western diplomats were present during the hearing.

Riad at-Turk was charged with inciting armed insurrection, trying to change the Constitution by illegal means and harming the state's image and its financial position. His trial before the Supreme State Security Court in Damascus opened with a fifteen-minute hearing on 28 April 2002 – eight months after his detention – at which the judge agreed a postponement until 19 May to give the defence an opportunity to consider the evidence, which had not yet been made available to them. Diplomats from the European Union and journalists were among those present. At the second hearing on 19 May the court postponed At-Turk's trial until 27 May. This hearing was closed to the public – excepting a single journalist from the state-run Syrian Arab News Agency, SANA – although about one hundred supporters, journalists and Western diplomats were present outside the court. At-Turk told the court that he would refuse to answer any questions unless his trial was opened to the public. A month later, on 26 June, he was sentenced to two and a half years in prison.

Journalists and others – again excepting a single SANA journalist – were also barred from the Supreme State Security Court trials of the other detained civil society activists. On 24 June Habib Saleh received a three-year sentence for 'opposing the objectives of the revolution' and 'inciting ethnic and sectarian strife'. Arif Dalila and Walid al-Bunni received ten-year and five-year sentences, respectively, on 31 July and Habib Issa received five years on 20 August. The other three detainees were sentenced on 28 August. Fawaz Tello received five years, Kamal al-Labwani three years and Hassan Sa'adoun two years.

The arrests and political trials deeply dented Bashar al-Asad's carefully nurtured image as a vigorous, reforming leader who would pull his country into the modern world and the global economy after its decades of isolation. Observers speculated that the long delays in bringing the activists to trial reflected uncertainty within the regime. Certainly, some regime insiders felt that the arrests, whatever their moral dimensions, had been a counter-productive mistake. Ayman 'Abd an-Nur, one of Bashar's inner circle of advisers, told me that in his opinion it had been foolish to detain the activists because by doing so the regime had unwittingly adopted the activists' own agenda. He opined that they had engineered their own arrests by deliberate provocation: 'My opinion – it's an official opinion – [is that] they wanted to push us to make a wrong step, and they succeeded because of the narrow-mindedness of some [*mukhabarat*] officers.'[15]

Possibly, such thinking influenced the surprise release of Riad at-Turk on 16 November 2002, officially for humanitarian reasons. The move, however, was not expected to herald any wider relaxation. Almost certainly it signalled only that the regime felt that its point had been made: that it, rather than the civil society activists, called the shots in Syria.

A Bleak Outlook

By autumn 2002 the immediate outlook for the civil society movement was bleak indeed. Key activists were in prison. Such forums as continued to meet did so semi- or entirely clandestinely. While the old atmosphere of fear that had characterised the country during Hafiz al-Asad's rule had not returned, dissidents were far more cautious than during the heady days of the 'Damascus Spring' when, fleetingly, anything had seemed possible. Despite the crackdown, however, the leaders of the civil society movement were undismayed, seeing their project as a long-term venture which would eventually succeed. 'I am neither optimistic nor pessimistic,' said Michel Kilo, insisting that 'the intellectual does not work according to the balance of power but according to convictions and ideals'.[16] The civil society movement had not failed. On the contrary, it had encouraged the creation of a broad alliance of opposition tendencies – including the crucially important Muslim Brotherhood (see Chapter 5) – based on democracy. 'Now we have a democratic Islamic trend, a democratic secular trend, [namely] the National Democratic Gathering, the democratic intellectuals and the civil society movement,' explained Kilo. 'A bloc has been formed whose basis – for the first time [in Syria] – is democracy, although its member-tendencies are Islamic, nationalist, communist, liberal.' Syria had two blocs: 'the bloc based on democracy; and the bloc which is the regime, which knows that it has failed and that it has no real programme of reform.'

Haitham al-Maleh, the courageous head of the Syrian Human Rights Association (SHRA), agreed, pointing out that the regime's indiscriminate repression had been a crucial factor in forging this mixed alliance of democrats and encouraging the mutual toleration upon which it depended. 'I thank Hafiz al-Asad because he put me in jail,' he said to me in London in May 2002. 'All ideologies in Syria were in jail. Now we have a new understanding.'[17] Before travelling to London, he had hosted a barbecue at his house. 'The guests were from all political shades – communists, Ba'athists, Islamists. I said: "We have to thank Hafiz al-Asad. If we had not been in jail, we would not be here together."' Soon after, in late August 2002, Al-Maleh and three colleagues from the SHRA would also become the subjects of arrest warrants (see Chapter 6).

Reform was urgently needed and inescapable although the actual reform was a long-term goal, said Michel Kilo. 'It is our duty to work on different levels. We should not forget our original project: the revival of society and the re-establishment of politics as an activity of society. But we also must present a vision of the reform that puts pressure on the regime and which at the same time mobilises society. That will not take a long time.'

He insisted: 'Our movement froze but it never died; and we are determined to pursue our project.'[18]

Notes

1. *Al-Hayat*, 30 January 2001.
2. *Al-Hayat*, 10 July 2001.
3. Interview with author, Damascus, 5 May 2001.
4. Interview with author, Paris, 17 June 2001.
5. Ibid.

6. *Al-Quds al-Arabi,* 11 April 2001.
7. Interview with author, Paris, 17 June 2001.
8. Interview with author, Damascus, 5 May 2001.
9. Ibid.
10. Ibid.
11. 'Syria Pressed Over Dissident's Arrest', *BBC News website*, 3 September 2001.
12. *Financial Times*, 8 September 2001.
13. Roger Hardy, 'Syrian Old Guard Fights Back', *BBC News website*, 8 September 2001.
14. Interview with author, Damascus, 2 December 2001.
15. Interview with author, Damascus, 4 December 2001.
16. Ibid.
17. Interview with author, London, 16 May 2002.
18. Interview with author, Damascus, 4 December 2001.

CHAPTER 4

'The Leading Party in Society and the State': The Ba'ath Party

§ 'COMRADES, there are solemn missions waiting and grand challenges facing [*sic*],' Bashar al-Asad told the Arab Ba'ath Socialist Party's Ninth Regional Congress on 20 June 2000, as reported by the state news agency, SANA, in its fractured English. 'We shall confront [these] challenges and will go together, through your trust, love and support, for the sake of accomplishing these missions and surpassing those challenges.'

Bashar had just been unanimously elected secretary-general of the Regional Command, a position held by his father until his death ten days earlier. His elevation was the most important item on the agenda of the party's four-day Congress. The Ba'ath had been born in the 1940s amid a pan-Arab ferment of idealism and hope that the region could unite, shed its colonial tutelage and achieve a fairer division of wealth between rulers and ruled. Under Hafiz al-Asad, it had been reduced to a machine for the generation of loyalty to the President. Bereft of any coherent ideology, it had nothing to say beyond empty slogans, above all, 'Unity, Freedom, Socialism'. No wonder that Bashar's response to becoming secretary-general was to mouth sweet nothings.

That the June 2000 Regional Congress was the first for fifteen years spoke volumes about the state of the party. 'The Ba'ath is in complete disarray,' said the exiled Syrian writer Subhi Hadidi. 'It's like a dead body. It's no longer a party in any normal sense of the word'.[1] Hanna Batatu, the leading chronicler of the Ba'ath Party and its social origins and development, confirms:

> Under Asad the character of the Ba'ath changed ... Whatever independence of opinion its members enjoyed in the past was now curtailed, a premium being placed on conformity and internal discipline. The party became in effect another instrument by which the

regime sought to control the community at large or to rally it behind its policies. The party's cadres turned more and more into bureaucrats and careerists, and were no longer as vibrantly alive ideologically as in the 1950s and 1960s, unconditional fidelity to Asad having ultimately overridden fidelity to the old beliefs.[2]

Early Days

At the beginning it was all very different. Syria was under a hated French mandatory regime that had blatantly exploited the country's ethnic patchwork to divide and rule. It had created a semi-autonomous Alawi state in the north-west and a similar Druse state in the south. In 1920 Lebanon had been created from Syria's western areas, and in 1938 the northern province of Alexandretta had been ceded to Turkey. To the south and south-west, the British ruled Trans-Jordan and Palestine. Under the terms of their Mandate over Palestine they were committed to creating a 'Jewish National Home' – a euphemism for a Jewish state so far as the Zionist movement was concerned – and Jewish immigrants were pouring in, to the dismay of the Palestinian Arabs who rightly feared dispossession. To the east, the British also held Iraq. Within Syria, meanwhile, the colonial occupiers were able to rely on an urban-based elite of landed and mercantile families that had been equally dominant under the Ottoman Turks. While this minority enjoyed great privileges and extreme wealth, the mass of the people lived in poverty, many as sharecroppers or as landless agricultural labourers.

This political and social ignominy fuelled nationalist movements, one of which – ultimately ineffectual – was headed by Zaki al-Arsuzi, an Alawi secondary school teacher from Antioch who in 1936–38 had led the anti-Turkish movement in his home province and who claimed to have been the first to use the word *ba'ath* ('renaissance') in the name of a political faction. A graduate of the Sorbonne, Al-Arsuzi was among the thousands of Arabs who fled southwards when Alexandretta, whose Turkish population constituted a minority, was handed to Turkey, which renamed it Hatay. Al-Arsuzi settled in Damascus where he lived in penury because the French authorities had banned him from teaching in either public or private schools. In 1939 Al-Arsuzi divided his supporters into a political group named the Arab Nationalist Party and a cultural group named the Arab Ba'ath.[3] Al-Arsuzi's group atrophied, however, and he himself became disillusioned with politics, moving to Lattakia and then Tartous, both on the coast, and concentrating instead on philology. Today, his memory is honoured in the name of a public park in the Syrian capital, just behind the Central Bank.

Another group, headed by Michel Aflaq and Salah ad-Din al-Bitar, two teachers at the influential *Tajhiz* in Damascus, the country's leading secondary school, would prove far more successful. Both graduates of the Sorbonne, Al-Bitar was a Sunni Muslim who taught physics while Aflaq was a Greek Othodox Christian who taught history. Their group, initially named Harakat al-Ihya' al-'Arabi (Movement of Arab Revival), issued its first communiqué in 1941 and from 1943 used the appellation Harakat al-Ba'ath al-'Arabi. In the mid-1940s the term *haraka* ('movement') increasingly gave way to *hizb* ('party') and in 1945 the group's first executive bureau was formed. Although not legally constituted, the Ba'ath was already functioning as a party and it was formally constituted at a congress held in April 1947 at the Rasheed coffee shop, adjacent to what was then an open-air cinema and garden known as the Luna Park and what today is the site of the Russian Cultural Centre. Most of Zaki al-Arsuzi's followers joined the Ba'ath Party. He himself did not even attend the inaugural congress. By all accounts he never forgave Aflaq and Al-Bitar for 'stealing' the name Ba'ath from him.

In its early years the Ba'ath Party, advocating Arab unity and social justice as the way to an Arab revival, was hardly a mass movement. It had only a few hundred members, most of them students from rural backgrounds – a reflection of the high proportion of teachers in the party's leadership. By the early 1950s the membership totalled only about 4,500. They included a high school student in Lattakia named Hafiz al-Asad, and another named Abdul Halim Khaddam (later to become their country's president and vice president).

A landmark in the Ba'ath's development came in 1952 when it merged with the Arab Socialist Party (ASP) of Akram al-Hawrani, a step which gave the party its first mass peasant constituency. Al-Hawrani, a lawyer from the city of Hama (whose centre would be razed by Ba'athist forces quelling an Islamist revolt in 1982), had earned a reputation as an Arab nationalist during the French Mandate and, following Syrian independence in 1946, as a champion of his region's oppressed peasant farmers. Disparities of wealth in his region were breathtaking. Of the 113 villages in the Hama district, ninety-one were owned by just four families.[4]

In 1950 Al-Hawrani organised his followers into the ASP, whose headquarters were in Hama. Under the dictatorship of Adib ash-

Shishakli, who had seized power in December 1949 (in the third coup of that year), Al-Hawrani, Al-Bitar and Aflaq all took refuge in neighbouring Lebanon where they agreed to merge their parties into an Arab Ba'ath Socialist Party. It was, said Patrick Seale, 'a coalition of the white-collar urban class, schoolteachers, government employees and the like, with revolutionary peasants'.[5] Batatu noted, however, that the merger was 'little more than a loose arrangement' with only some eighty leading ASP members actually adhering to the merged party. Ordinary ASP members 'remained passionately loyal to Hawrani's person. In fact, the two constituent forces retained their distinctive character.'[6]

During the 1950s, a period when Arab nationalism was convulsing the region, support for the Ba'ath grew rapidly and was given new impetus after the party's decision in 1955 to support Gamal Abdul Nasser, the nationalist army officer who had toppled Egypt's monarchy in 1952 and who was riding the crest of a pan-Arab wave of popularity. By 1958, however, when Syria united with Egypt to form the United Arab Republic, the Ba'ath Party was in considerable difficulty. An internal party report in 1957 pointed to a 'breakdown of discipline' and to 'chaos' and asserted that the party had become 'an alien social institution'. A 'profound chasm' had opened between a demoralised membership and the leaders who 'act in isolation from the party and view it as a heavy burden and a hindrance to their freedom'.[7]

This inner turmoil perhaps made it easier for the Syrian Ba'athists to agree to dissolve the party on Syria's entry into its 1958–61 union with Egypt, which Nasser had made a condition of the unionist project. Pan-Arabist icon he may have been but Nasser was no liberal democrat and he brooked no opposition, especially not from rival nationalist groups such as the Syrian Ba'ath. For him, Syria was very much the junior partner in the union: merely the 'Northern Province' of the United Arab Republic (UAR). Syrians had their first real taste of life in a police state where the *mukhabarat*, or secret police, were used routinely to root out and eliminate dissent. Syrian liberals often date the start of their country's present travails to the period under Nasser.

The Ba'ath in Transition

Whatever its failings, this original Ba'ath – what Batatu terms the 'Old Ba'ath' – was at least an authentic political party with policies (or at least ideals and aspirations) and a membership, and it had enjoyed some success in elections. It was succeeded by something very different: a clandestine Military Committee founded in 1959 by Syrian officers who had been posted to Cairo (among them Hafiz al-Asad) and who were increasingly antagonistic towards the union. The committee, which was dominated by members of Syria's minority religious communities, especially the Alawis and Druse, 'acted with such circumspection that until 1964 the Ba'ath old-line leaders remained utterly in the dark about its existence and true purpose'.[8]

The UAR disintegrated not because of the Ba'athists but because of a rightist military coup in Damascus on 28 September 1961, staged by Lt-Col. 'Abd al-Karim Nahlawi. The putsch was backed by Saudi Arabia and Jordan, and by a well-to-do Syrian business community jolted by the nationalisation decrees of July 1961. The coup marked a short-lived return of the urban elite which had presided over Syria's affairs for centuries. Within days of the coup, sixteen leading politicians signed a manifesto thanking the army for extricating Syria from Nasser's clutches. The signatories included both Salah ad-Din al-Bitar and Akram al-Hawrani. Two of the greatest Syrian champions of Arab unity were denouncing the Arab world's first unity project. They were doing so, moreover, in support of a secessionist regime representing the most conservative elements in Syria: the wealthy urban notables whose greed and political incompetence they had lambasted as key causes of the country's weakness. Al-Bitar later withdrew his name from the manifesto but too late to save his reputation. It was an early demonstration of an ideological ambivalence that lies at the heart of Ba'athism and that perhaps made its ultimate failure inevitable.

In spring 1962 the other Ba'athist leader, Michel Aflaq, convened a congress in the central city of Homs that resolved to re-establish the party. The Ba'ath Military Committee watched carefully but did not show its hand. Its members were not overly concerned about the size or nature of the civilian party. Their aim was to seize power directly, by a military coup, and this they executed in alliance with Nasserist and independent nationalist officers on the night of 7–8 March 1963. At that time, the re-created civilian party had just over four hundred members. A recruitment drive brought the figure to about 2,500 by mid-1963, and by late 1967 the membership had grown to about 5,000 full members and perhaps 40,000 candidate members.[9] A party that had been launched amid optimism and idealism had captured the state, but the price was high and is still being paid today by the Syrian people. 'Almost from the start', noted Patrick Seale,

> they had to govern by force rather than consent. They were a fraction of what was itself a minority, a military splinter group of a semi-defunct party without a popular base. The experience of those early days affected their attitudes for years to come: even when the party grew strong and secure, it never rid itself of habits of wariness and repression.[10]

This is not the place to review in detail the complex feuds and power struggles that convulsed what Hanna Batatu has termed the 'Transitional Ba'ath' of 1963–70. Suffice it to say that there was constant tension between the party's radical and socialist civilian wing and its more pragmatic military wing, and that each wing was riven by its own tensions and rivalries. The period also saw the Ba'ath's Regional Command (responsible for the Syrian region of the Arab world) take clear precedence over its National Command (responsible for the Arab world as a whole). A watershed was yet another military coup, staged on 23 February 1966 by a faction headed by Salah Jadid, an Alawi member of the Military Committee who had served as army chief of staff since 1963, and backed by Hafiz al-Asad, also an Alawi, who was then the air force commander. Before, the regime had been essentially pragmatic despite its revolutionary socialist rhetoric. The coup marked a sharp leftwards lurch – and it brought Asad the defence portfolio, greatly improving his chances of ultimate power.

Despite the ideological issues, at base it was all about raw power. 'The history of the Ba'ath of the 1960s is the history of factions,' explained Batatu:

> The internal party discords were never purely sectarian or purely regional in character ... Often personal factors or aspirations for sheer power were at play. Ideological affinities had some role but do not appear to have been decisive. To be sure, the labels 'leftists' and 'rightists' were freely tossed about. But the political conduct of the period's central figure, Salah Jadid, did not point to a clear or consistent ideological commitment.[11]

Soon, and especially after the disastrous Syrian defeat in the June 1967 war with Israel, Asad and Jadid were at odds. After the 1966 coup, Jadid had resigned as chief of staff and ruled Syria through his position as the party's assistant secretary-general. Essentially, the power struggle was between Asad and the armed forces and Jadid and the party. The protracted turbulence included a partial coup on 25 February 1969 in which armoured forces under Asad's command occupied strategic points, including media establishments, in Damascus. The climax came at the Tenth Extraordinary National Ba'ath Party Congress, held in Damascus from 30 October to 12 November 1970. The proceedings were unusually acrimonious, with Jadid denouncing Asad as a 'fascist' who had created a 'duality of power' in Syria. The Congress ended by passing a resolution stripping Asad of his defence portfolio and removing his key ally, the Sunni Muslim Mustafa Tlass, an ex-member of the Military Committee who had become chief of staff in early 1968.

Asad did not delay. On the night of 12–13 November his men arrested Jadid and his closest associates and on 16 November came the official announcement of what Asad termed a 'Corrective Movement' but which was in reality a military coup. Finally, Asad had risen to the top, having prevailed against all his ex-colleagues in the old Military Committee (which itself had been superseded in August 1965 by the party's Military Bureau). His triumph marked the end of the Ba'ath Party as an autonomous force, and even as a forum for serious debate.

Asad and the Cult of the Leader

After his November 1970 seizure of power, Hafiz al-Asad is said to have considered abolishing the Ba'ath altogether.[12] Instead, he chose to mould it into a powerful institution of political control that at the same time could confer an appearance of legitimacy upon his presidency. That said, as a guarantor of regime existence the party has never rivalled the *mukhabarat* and the elite, regime-shielding military formations such as the Presidential Guard and the Special Forces. Under Asad, the Ba'ath was 'transformed', noted Volker Perthes. 'It was further inflated such as to neutralise those who had supported the overthrown leftish leadership, it was de-ideologised; and it was restructured so as to fit into the authoritarian format of Asad's system, lose its avant-garde character and become an instrument for generating mass support and political control. It was also to become the regime's main patronage network.'[13]

The flavour of the new Syria was underlined in May 1971 when the Ba'ath Party's new Regional Command saluted Asad as 'the Leader of the [Nation's] March'. Syria's people 'lay emphasis on the need for a leader … and have begun to see Comrade Hafez al-Assad in this role', asserted the Command. The Eighth Regional Congress in January 1985 – following Asad's triumph over the Islamist revolt and over the challenge from his brother Rif'at (see Chapter 1) – went further, hailing Asad as 'Our Leader Forever, the Faithful Hafez al-Assad'. The Congress asserted that 'loyalty to him is loyalty to the party and to the people and their cause' and that disloyalty 'in whatever form … constitutes a grave deviation'.[14]

Aflaq and Al-Bitar had seen the Ba'ath as a vanguard party, akin in that respect at least to the Soviet Union's Communist Party, to which entry should be carefully controlled. Under Asad, the entry criteria were relaxed. Asad spelled out his contrary view within a few weeks of seizing power: 'After this day the Ba'ath will not be the party of the elect, as some have envisaged … Syria does not belong to the Ba'athists alone.'[15] The party's membership has since expanded dramatically. In 1971 there were 65,398 members (i.e. full members aged eighteen and over plus 'supporting members' aged between fourteen and seventeen). By 1981 the figure had jumped to 374,332 and by mid-1992 to 1,008,243 – an astonishing 14.5 per cent of all Syrians aged fourteen and over.[16] Today, party membership is put at 1.8 million – 18 per cent of the fourteen-plus age group.[17] The membership drive paralleled a major expansion in the size of the public sector. Many tens of thousands were becoming directly dependent on the regime for their livelihood (see Chapter 1). It was natural that they should seek the added security of party membership.

The party's expansion has not been entirely smooth. A party Organisational Report in 1985 noted that thousands of 'supporters' had been recruited without adequate regard for rules and standards in the period before the Seventh Regional Congress of January 1980. It said that 'indiscipline amongst the ranks of the supporters' had resulted from 'a policy of expansion in which quantity became more important than quality'. The resultant 'indiscipline' had 'heavily burdened and confused successive party leaderships, forcing them into taking collective dismissal decisions and dismissing thousands of people'.[18]

In Asad's Syria a high premium was placed on political loyalty, and loyalty could bring material and other benefits. There was, affirmed Batatu, 'a widespread feeling that the party was one of the more accessible means for moving upward in society'.[19] It was therefore no surprise that what the party termed 'opportunism' had become widespread, and was another cause for the expulsions. The 1985 Organisational Report was remarkably candid:

> When quantity became more important than quality, opportunists infiltrated into the party ranks and constituted a dangerous phenomenon. These people never miss meetings and are never late in settling their subscription fees. They proclaim obedience, loyalty and commit-

> ment. They are mercurial types, with no personal opinions, whether right or wrong. Their main concern is to attain leading and responsible positions in order to realise moral and material gains and to reap the fruit at the cost of the party's reputation and its combatants … They seize opportunities to make illegitimate profits by purchasing houses, precious objects and agricultural lands, speculating in real estate, acting as stockbrokers, smuggling and exploiting the party and state mechanisms for their own personal purposes, without any consideration for the party's revolutionary and combat principles.[20]

The report disclosed that no fewer than 133,580 supporter-members (almost one-third of all such members) had been expelled in 1980–84. This compared with the expulsion of 3,242 full members (just over 4 per cent of the total full membership) in the same period.

In line with its corporatist view of the state, in which the President guides a seamlessly unified populace, the regime constantly suggests that there is no real difference between the party and the populace as a whole; and that party membership amounts to a manifestation of patriotism. 'Let me tell you', insisted Ayman 'Abd an-Nur, one of Bashar al-Asad's inner circle of advisers, '[the Ba'ath Party] is not a party brought in from outside. It started here. It wasn't imported. It reflects the people … And let me tell you this. Because of families, each [party member] reflects [represents] four or five people. That means that the real membership is nine million – more than 55 per cent of our people.'[21] 'Abd an-Nur was reiterating an old theme. Asad had told the party's Thirteenth National Congress in July 1980 how, after his coup, 'we asserted that the party should attract into its ranks all the citizens, all the strugglers, who in principle are the whole people … all the people are at bottom good people … and believe in their homeland … and must within the bounds of possibility be drawn into the party'.[22]

Michel Kilo, a Damascus-based writer who has played a leading role in the civil society movement which flourished after Bashar al-Asad became President and who was jailed in 1980 after demanding political reforms, puts it more succinctly: 'The Ba'ath does not recognise society. It considers itself [to be] society.'[23]

If the party was capable of representing the great majority of the Syrian people, it was unsurprising that it should be defined in the new Constitution of March 1973 as 'the leading party in society and the state' and that its historic slogan 'Unity, Freedom, Socialism' should be enshrined in the Constitution's preamble as the very essence of 'the Arab nation's aspirations'. The Ba'ath, which is funded from the public purse, was further institutionalised in 1979 by the passage of Law 53 covering party security. This prescribes lengthy prison terms for a range of offences including parallel membership of another party, infiltration of the Ba'ath Party on behalf of another party, attacking party offices, obstructing party activities and attempting to obtain confidential information. For offenders acting on behalf of foreign interests, the penalty for such transgressions is death.

While expanding its membership, the post-Corrective Movement party also became more rigidly hierarchical. Before, party members were able to elect their local leaderships. After Asad's coup these were appointed by the twenty-one-member Regional Command. Answerable to the latter are nineteen Branch Commands, one in each of Syria's fourteen provinces, one for Aleppo city (Damascus City being a province in its own right), and one in each of the country's four universities. Key local officials such as the mayor and police chief are typically members of their Branch Command. Below the branches come party units for provincial districts and city neighbourhoods, and so on down to the level of individual villages.

In theory, members elect delegates to a Regional Congress held every four years. Until 1975 the Congress elected the Regional Command directly. In January 1980, however, at the height of the near-insurrection which the regime faced from the Muslim Brotherhood allied with the secular opposition, a seventy-five-person Central Committee was instituted, with its members elected by the Congress. Its purpose was to improve communication between the Regional Command and the lower party branches, and to elect the Regional Command from its members. The Eighth Regional Congress in January 1985 increased the size of the Central Committee to ninety persons but also empowered Hafiz al-Asad to appoint them. In practice, however, all key party appointments – and none more so than membership of the Regional Command – were decided in advance by Asad. Since 1970 the once important National Command, also headed by Asad, has become an honorary body with only a consultative function. The pretence is nevertheless maintained that it is more important than the Regional Command because (in theory if in nothing else) it oversees pan-Arab affairs and is thus concerned with Arab unity, one of the key strands in Ba'athist ideology. A parallel party system permeates the armed forces down to the battalion level but merges with the civilian party apparatus only at the level of the Regional Command.

As well as being a machine to mobilise loyalty to the President, the Ba'ath Party functions as an important regime watchdog, with agencies shadowing all those in the formal governmental system which must constantly gain party approval for their activities, however mundane. A Military Bureau oversees the armed forces. A Higher Education Office is responsible for the universities. The Ministry of Information's counterpart is a party Indoctrination Office that has an important censorship function. A National Security Bureau – extremely powerful in the late 1960s but now somewhat eclipsed by other security agencies – screens candidates for the People's Assembly, local councils, trade union offices and governing bodies of professional associations. 'By drawing on party members as well as operatives, the bureau's antennae reach into urban neighbourhoods, small towns, and even remote rural areas – places the other *mukhabarat* [secret police] cannot hope to cover effectively,' noted Middle East Watch, a division of Human Rights Watch.[24]

As a patronage system, the Ba'ath Party's main 'resource' is thus its ability to block appointments to jobs. The party's Economic Office has an important voice in the approval of candidates to head public sector enterprises. Academic staff are vetted by the Higher Education Office. Even non-party members must obtain the approval of their local party branch before being employed by some public sector agencies. 'The party, in short, controls personnel more than policies,' commented Volker Perthes. 'Given this function, each member of the party leadership is a powerful patron.'[25]

The Ba'ath's transformation into a political machine to generate loyalty to the President and a watchdog for the regime does not mean that criticism is never voiced. It also functions as a means of channelling complaints to the leadership. Corruption, for example, has been regularly and strongly attacked at party gatherings, but only because the leadership wishes the subject to be vented. Party congresses are carefully stage-managed, and even gentle criticism of the President himself and the main lines of his policy is taboo.

Popular Organisations

As well as witnessing a massive growth in Ba'ath Party membership, the Asad period saw an extension in the number and size of functionally differentiated 'popular organisations' which are directed by the party and which constitute important elements in the Syrian corporatist state. Several were new creations of the Ba'athists while others had long histories as autonomous organisations and had been taken over, gradually or otherwise, since 1963. Like all other state agencies, their function is to demonstrate and enforce loyalty, to assist in the implementation of government directives and to channel complaints upwards in an orderly manner – although certainly not complaints about matters beyond the organisations' immediate spheres of interest. Their status is enshrined in Article 9 of Asad's 1973 Constitution which affirms: 'Popular organisations and co-operative associations are establishments which include the people's forces working for the development of society and for the realisation of the interests of their members.' They may function only in regime-approved ways. Strikes have been outlawed in Syria since April 1959, when the Egyptian labour code was applied to the UAR's northern province. The code also provided for the establishment of a single labour organisation linked to the ruling party. New trade union legislation was enacted in February 1964, following the Ba'athist coup, but the prohibitions on striking and on the formation of an independent national union federation remained in effect. In August 2000 Syria submitted to the UN Human Rights Committee a report on its adherence to the International Covenant on Civil and Political Rights (ICCPR) in which it outlined its trade union structures and asserted, 'The state has avoided the need for workers to resort to strike action' by its reliance on collective employment contracts and through a benign system of conciliation procedures.[26]

Formed in 1964, the General Union of Peasants is the biggest of the popular organisations, with 940,236 members in 2000. Linking farmers' unions and co-operatives, the union is answerable to the party's Peasants' Bureau. Elementary school pupils must enrol in Talai' al-Ba'ath (Ba'ath Vanguards) while for intermediate and secondary pupils there is the Ittihad Shabibat ath-Thawra (Revolutionary Youth Union; see Chapter 5). University students are organised in a national Union of Students. There are the Women's Union, the Writers' Union, the Artisans' Union and so on. Professional organisations for such groups as lawyers and doctors had long traditions of independence and were the last to be brought to heel. Some played an important role in the opposition movement of the late 1970s and early 1980s when their members suffered arrests and torture. The lawyers', doctors' and engineers' associations proved to be the most resilient but in 1980 and 1981 the regime dissolved them and created new, subservient bodies in their place (see Chapter 6).

All trade unions must affiliate to the General Federation of Trade

Unions (GFTU) created in March 1938 but now as much a part of the state as the Ba'ath Party itself. Since 1975 the GFTU has been headed by 'Izzeddin Nasser. From 1980 until the Ninth Regional Congress in June 2000, he also headed the party's (or, to be precise, the Regional Command's) Workers' Bureau. Presently, the GFTU links 194 trade unions with a total membership (in 2000) of 820,050. The unions are divided into eight occupational federations covering textile workers; public service workers; petroleum and chemical workers; construction and woodworkers; transport workers; printing, cultural and information workers; metallurgical and electrical industry workers; and food industry workers.

The great majority of public sector workers belong to unions and they comprise the bulk of union membership. The extent of unionisation in the growing modern private sector (i.e. excluding small workshops and family farms) is uncertain but is unlikely to exceed about 20 per cent. The size of this modern private workforce is equally uncertain but in 2002 it numbered perhaps 400,000. Private employers wishing to avoid the inconvenience of a unionised workforce apparently can and do achieve their ends by bribing party members on their payrolls. Non-unionised private sector workers can toil fourteen or sixteen hours per day and lack job security and proper social security provision.[27]

The unions justify their docility in terms very similar to those used by all the other structures in the system to explain theirs: the President knows perfectly the interests of the country and all its elements, and acts accordingly. Unanimity and harmony therefore prevail, and by definition there can be no place for conflict. It follows that any frictions must be inspired by malice, foreign enemies and the like. The GFTU's 1972 conference affirmed that the role of the unions under Ba'athism was 'political' rather than the 'demanding' unionism which was necessary under capitalism but which was positively counter-productive, indeed a form of sabotage, under socialism. Perthes has well noted: 'Practically, and despite its sound, this "political unionism" meant the abandonment of an independent political role for the unions.'[28]

'Unity' is also invoked to justify Syria's monolithic trade union structures. Addressing academic staff at Damascus University in February 2001 as part of the regime's counter-attack against the civil society movement, Vice President Abdul Halim Khaddam asked: 'Do we have trade unions? Yes, we do. Does the Ba'ath Party control these unions? Yes, it does. Why? Because Ba'athists constitute the majority in these unions. What should they do? Should they vote for their rivals during union elections?' Recalling that the United States had pressed Syria to permit independent trade unions, Khaddam referred to a memorandum demanding 'a multitude of unions in Syria' which Ryan Crocker, US ambassador to Damascus in 1998–2001 (and Deputy Assistant Secretary of State for Near East Affairs as of mid-2002), had presented to GFTU head 'Izzeddin Nasser. 'In other words, he wanted the labour union to become ten,' continued Khaddam, 'which means the fragmentation of the labour movement.'[29]

Bashar and the Party

Despite all the talk of reform and 'modernisation', the party has changed not a jot in the period since Bashar al-Asad took office. True, in late 2000 a decision was taken that party officials should be elected rather than appointed from above. This, however, was hardly the dawning of a new democratic age. It was merely a return to the pre-Corrective Movement practice. Control remains tightly centralised, not least because all candidates for election must first obtain official approval.

A new twenty-one-member Regional Command was elected at the Ninth Regional Congress in June 2000. There were eleven newcomers (other than Bashar himself) including several technocrats, and officials claimed that this was a sign of change and renewal, albeit in the context of continuity. Whatever their merits, however, all were party men – and hence system loyalists – through and through. They included the prime minister, Muhammad Miru; the long-serving foreign minister, Farouk ash-Shara'; and the deputy premier, Muhammad Naji al-'Utari. Key members of the 'old guard' retained their posts, including the two vice presidents, Abdul Halim Khaddam and Muhammad Zuhair Masharqa; the Speaker of parliament, Abdul Qader al-Qaddura; Abdullah al-Ahmar, the assistant secretary-general of the Ba'ath Party, who has held both his party and Regional Command posts continuously since Asad's 1970 coup; and Mustafa Tlass, defence minister since 1972. This hardly looked like a team poised to shake up the ailing system.

The Congress also elected a new Central Committee which included Bashar's younger brother Maher, who is an army major; Manaf Tlass, the son of defence minister Mustafa Tlass; the army chief of staff, Ali Aslan; and the directors or ex-directors of the four main *mukhabarat* networks: Ali al-Houri (retired head of General Intelligence), Hassan al-Khalil (Military Intelligence), Adnan Badr Hassan (Political Security) and Ibrahim Huwaijeh (Air Force Intelligence). The new committee included sixteen women, compared with only three in the outgoing committee. Certainly the changes indicated the rise of a younger generation, often the children of those in the regime, to Syria's elite but few other conclusions could be drawn with any assurance.

Some commentators also saw significance in a reduction to nineteen in the number of party stalwarts in the new government Muhammad Miru formed in December 2001, and a corresponding increase in the numbers of independents and ministers from the Ba'ath's allies in the Progressive National Front (PNF), the Ba'ath-dominated coalition of officially permitted leftist parties (see Chapter 5). The outgoing cabinet, which had been installed under Hafiz al-Asad on 7 March 2000, included twenty-six ministers drawn from the party.[30] Again, however, the signals were mixed and other observers saw the composition of Miru's second government as a sign of regression. 'Dr Miru's new cabinet has arrived without any sign that the new has taken the place of the old,' wrote Subhi Hadidi. 'What is worse than remaining at a standstill, however, is the possibility that the new cabinet may actually be a step backwards.'[31]

Countering the Civil Society Movement: Circular 1075

Nothing has more exposed the Ba'ath's ideological bankruptcy than its response to the civil society movement. From February 2001 senior party officials toured the country denouncing the movement as almost treasonous (see Chapters 2 and 3). The most formal statement of the party's position was Circular 1075, a lengthy tract issued on 17 February 2001 and published in the Ba'ath's in-house journal *Al-Munadil* (*The Struggler*). It is a classic of party rhetoric, asserting that 'the revolution removed its subjective and objective obstacles through the Corrective Movement led by the immortal leader Hafiz al-Asad' and quoting the latter as having said: 'The movement of the party is the movement of history and life.' Hailing the 'national unity' and 'stability' achieved by the regime, the Circular explained that Bashar al-Asad's programme of 'development and modernisation' was a natural sequel to his father's achievements. 'They are as complementary as tree trunk and branches,' affirmed the document.

In the past, 'the comprehensive development process' had suffered shortcomings 'such as poor supervision, lack of competence and institutional weakness'. This had caused 'abnormal phenomena such as corruption, bribery, laxity, irresponsibility [and] bureaucracy' but 'procedures had been instituted to tackle these deformities'. The Circular also pointed to a series of 'objective' hurdles to Syria's development, including rapid population growth, the collapse of traditional markets in the Soviet Bloc and the need for high defence spending. The limited reforms agreed by the regime were presented as an adequate response to Syria's difficulties. The Circular pointed *inter alia* to the reintroduction of internal party elections; the granting of permission for PNF parties to open regional offices and to distribute their own newspapers; and to plans for the introduction of private banks, a stock market and private universities. The Circular insisted that 'development which is not led by an organised and capable, massive and popular force is destined to anarchy and possibly to total collapse'.

The Circular then immoderately attacked the civil society movement as having 'taken advantage of the atmosphere of dialogue'. Some pro-democracy activists were rejects from the political parties to which they had once adhered; some looked to the West; others were 'climber groups whose aim is power'. The Circular warned that it was 'not improbable that some of these individuals are connected with the West'. Some of the civil society activists and groups focused on 'the negative aspects that the party and government have begun to tackle'. Others, however, argued that political reform, involving the termination of the existing system, was the priority. Those demanding radical political change wanted 'to eradicate national unity and stability' and to 'go back to the period of foreign occupation, coups d'état, tension, anarchy and social and economic backwardness', asserted the Circular, which also alleged that the civil society movement had failed to mention 'the Zionist danger' which confronted Syria and the Arab world. 'Whether deliberately or not, these people harm their country because they serve the country's enemies, and they should take responsibility for their acts,' it warned. Party members were urged to step up efforts to counter the arguments of the civil society movement and to 'defend the party's policies, principles and great objectives'.

The problem, of course, is that the party is bereft of policies, principles and even objectives, other than the objectives of power for power's sake and leader-worship. 'Stability', 'national unity' and 'the Zionist threat' are mere excuses for inaction. In reality, Circular 1075, and the moribund party that issued it, offer Syria nothing but stagnation. As for Bashar, in an 8 February 2001 interview with the London-based pan-Arab daily *Ash-Sharq al-Awsat*, all he could say on the subject of the party was that the Ba'ath was 'based on a pan-Arab ideology, the renaissance of the Arab nation ... As I see it, things today are moving in the direction of a pan-Arabist revival, especially after the

Intifada [the uprising in the Israeli-occupied Palestinian territories]. The party is not annulled unless the pan-Arab idea is.'

It is all in the starkest contrast with the idealistic early years of Aflaq, Al-Bitar and Al-Hawrani, when 'self-sacrificing physicians, members of the party, acting on their own and without prompting from their leaders, travelled on foot ... to provide free medical treatment to peasants in out-of-the-way and hitherto neglected villages' and when some Ba'ath activists 'sent promising sons of peasants to secondary schools in the cities at their personal expense or tutored them without charge'.[32]

Headquartered in a heavily guarded block tucked between the Defence Ministry and Air Force Headquarters in the affluent Damascus district of Abu Roumaneh, today's Ba'ath is an utterly cynical instrument of crude power. Failing even to acknowledge that Syria is in crisis, the party admits only to 'mistakes' and 'aberrations' that can be rectified. The membership, not to mention the populace at large, is required to go along with the fiction or stand accused of disloyalty to the regime, even of treason.

In Orwell's *Nineteen Eighty-Four*, the hero, Winston Smith, muses: 'In the end the Party would announce that two and two made five, and you would have to believe it ... The Party told you to reject the evidence of your eyes and ears. It was their final, most essential command.'[33]

Notes

1. Telephone interview with author from Paris, 30 April 2002.

2. Hanna Batatu, *Syria's Peasantry, the Descendants of Its Lesser Rural Notables, and Their Politics* (Princeton, NJ: Princeton University Press, 1990), p. 326.

3. Ibid., p. 135.

4. Patrick Seale, *Asad: The Struggle for the Middle East* (Berkeley and Los Angeles: University of California Press, 1995), p. 42.

5. Ibid., p. 47.

6. Batatu, *Syria's Peasantry*, p. 142.

7. Ibid., p.143.

8. Ibid., p. 144.

9. Ibid., p. 161.

10. Seale, *Asad*, p. 85.

11. Batatu, *Syria's Peasantry*, p. 171.

12. Volker Perthes, *The Political Economy of Syria under Asad* (London: I.B. Tauris, 1995), p. 154.

13. Ibid., p. 154.

14. Baṭatu, *Syria's Peasantry*, p. 176.

15. *An-Nahar*, 6 December 1970.

16. Batatu, *Syria's Peasantry*, p. 177.

17. Ayman 'Abd an-Nur, adviser to President Asad, interview with author, Damascus, 4 December 2001.

18. Nikolaos Van Dam, *The Struggle for Power in Syria: Politics and Society under Asad and the Ba'th Party* (London: I.B.Tauris, 1996), p. 127.

19. Batatu, *Syria's Peasantry*, p. 180.

20. Van Dam, *Struggle for Power*, p. 127.

21. Interview with author, Damascus, 4 December 2001.

22. Batatu, *Syria's Peasantry*, p. 179.

23. Interview with author, Damascus, 4 December 2001.

24. Middle East Watch, *Syria Unmasked: The Suppression of Human Rights by the Asad Regime* (New Haven, CT and London: Yale University Press, 1991), p. 50.

25. Perthes, *Political Economy*, p. 160.

26. UN Human Rights Committee, *Consideration of Reports Submitted by States Parties under Article 40 of the Covenant. Second Periodic Report of States Parties Due in 1984. Syrian Arab Republic*, Geneva, 25 August 2000, p. 69.

27. Interview with a contact who requested anonymity, London, 14 May 2002.

28. Perthes, *Political Economy*, p. 174.

29. *Al-Hayat*, 10 July 2001.

30. Ibrahim Hamidi, 'The A to Z of Syria's Cabinet', *Daily Star* (Beirut), 20 December 2001.

31. Subhi Hadidi, 'Syrian Reform Unlikely', *Al-Quds al-Arabi*, 21 December 2001.

32. Batatu, *Syria's Peasantry*, p. 133.

33. George Orwell, *Nineteen Eighty-Four* (London: Penguin Books, 2000), pp. 83–4.

CHAPTER 5

'The Light of Freedom': Parliament

§ AT 6.00 p.m. precisely a bell is struck to silence the hubbub rising from the nearly 250 members of the Majlis ash-Sha'ab (People's Assembly). Quickly, they come to order. Abdul Qader al-Qaddura, the Speaker, is away meeting European parliamentarians in Athens. One of his assistants reads out the list of absentees. Without eliciting the slightest murmur from the assembled deputies, the names 'Riad Seif' and 'Ma'moun al-Homsi' are included among those unable to attend. Neither Seif nor Al-Homsi is present because both are in prison for demanding the introduction of real democracy in a country whose parliament exists only to support and applaud presidential writ.

The Constitution sounds fine. Syria, it affirms in its preamble, is 'a popular democracy' in which (Article 50) 'the People's Assembly assumes legislative power in the manner defined in this Constitution' and where (also Article 50) 'the members of the People's Assembly are elected by general, secret, direct, and equal ballot in accordance with the election law'. The Constitution goes on to provide a detailed framework for parliament's organisation and role, using terms of which any democrat would approve. It comes almost as a shock when, at Article 107, the underlying reality asserts itself: 'The President of the Republic can dissolve the People's Assembly through a decision giving the reasons.' Article 109 affirms that the President 'may draft project laws and submit them to the Assembly for approval' and Article 111 states that he 'assumes legislative authority when the People's Assembly is not in session'.

A Toothless Watchdog

'From the sanctuary of this Assembly, the light of freedom shines to fill the whole country,' President Hafiz al-Asad declared in an address to parliament. 'And through this Assembly, the practice of freedom, in its right and correct meaning, is insured.'[1] In practice, it is a charade. The People's Assembly – a euphemism for a real parliament – was one of several toothless and subservient institutions created by Hafiz al-Asad to legitimise his rule shortly after he seized power. It was a far cry from Syria's post-independence parliament which had been a vital debating chamber. As Volker Perthes has remarked with telling understatement, under the Ba'athists, 'Parliament has remained very much on the margins of political life.'[2]

That is not to say that it has never taken centre-stage during the recent past. Article 83 of the Constitution states that candidates for the presidency must be over forty years of age. At the time of his father's death, however, Bashar al-Asad, somewhat inconveniently, was only thirty-four. The solution? It was obvious: the Constitution had to be changed to accommodate a president of thirty-four. And it was, on 10 June 2000 – the very same day as his father's demise – and the vote was unanimous. On 27 June 2000 parliament approved – again unanimously – Bashar al-Asad's nomination as President by the Ba'ath Party's Regional Command and set 10 July as the date for a referendum for his candidacy. The state news agency, SANA, recorded that the parliamentary approval of Bashar's nomination had 'crowned a stormy parliamentary session in which speakers pledged full support and loyalty to the persistence of the Late President's march through his son, "the hope", for Syria's immunity, dignity and steadfastness'.[3]

For the members of the People's Assembly, the fate of their jailed colleagues Riad Seif and Ma'moun al-Homsi was not a major issue. It was simply not their job to challenge decisions taken at the top. The People's Assembly is much more a consultative council than a parliament in the European or North American sense. Its opinions are welcomed but it is certainly not expected to rock the political boat. It is all part of the regime's stubborn refusal to concede that there is anything but seamless unity in Syria. Without conflict, after all, what need is there for serious debate and compromise? The one-hour evening session I attended on 16 February 2002 dealt with such mundane matters as double taxation agreements with Italy and Poland; a maritime trade accord with Jordan; and a decree merging the primary and intermediate stages of school into a single basic education stage. A decree to establish a committee of lawyers and judges to review Syria's judicial system was the only potentially controversial subject, in view of the parlous state of the legal system in a country where presidential orders have been the only law that has mattered since the Ba'athist coup in 1963 and where the judicial system is as notorious for corruption and political manipulation as other elements of the state (see Chapter 6).

Legislation is initiated by the government in line with the wishes of the President – whom the government never, ever defies. It is sent to parliament via the President for debate and approval. But with the Ba'ath and its allies enjoying a permanent majority, parliament's basic role is to rubber-stamp presidential decisions. Had there ever been an instance when the President had disagreed with a parliamentary decision? 'No,' confirmed Abdul Qader al-Qaddura, an amiable, fatherly figure who has been Speaker since 1988.[4] He explained, with surprising candour, that everything was fixed from the outset. Noting that the Ba'ath Party was headed by the President, he affirmed: 'When the President would reject something, he will tell his party before. Every party [in the world] does that … The leader of the party will have a meeting [with his party].' If the President's will was all that mattered, what role, if any, was left for parliament? Al-Qaddura, his eyes sparkling slightly as if with humour, preferred to generalise: 'Any president, if he wants something, gets it.'

When it is suggested that Syria's parliamentary democracy is a sham, officials are quick to wrap themselves in the national flag, claiming that their 'democracy' is an authentic product of the country's socio-political conditions and that foreign systems cannot possibly apply. Indeed, they go so far as to suggest that criticism from abroad is tantamount to imperialism. 'It's a different style. You cannot use the same measures,' Ayman 'Abd an-Nur, one of Bashar al-Asad's inner circle of advisers, told me. 'This is very important, and this is one of the most important [difficulties] I encountered with Europeans and Americans. They want to measure everything by their standards. We cannot enforce democracy from outside.'[5]

The oldest part of the magnificent stone-built parliament building in the Salhiyeh district of central Damascus dates from 1932 although it has since been extended. The main meeting hall, topped by an enormous dome, is a monument to local art and handicrafts. Exquisite arabesques abound, perhaps most strikingly in the form of carved, dark wood frames upon white wall panels. The base of the dome boasts panels depicting urban and rural scenes in green and gold, recalling the Byzantine wall decorations of the Omayyad Mosque, little more than a kilometre to the south-east. This must be the most beautiful twentieth-century building in Damascus. Red-upholstered pews for the deputies are arranged in five concentric horseshoes around a central well facing a raised marble platform topped by a dark wooden dais for the Speaker and his assistants. To the left of the dais stands the red, white and black striped national flag with its two green stars; to the right, the black, white, green and red Ba'ath Party flag. Observers (but not the general public) can watch proceedings from balconies surrounding the hall at two levels, perhaps 10 metres and 15 metres above the deputies' heads. Access to the parliamentary compound and to the main meeting hall is controlled by a special khaki-clad police force answerable only to the Speaker, himself the fifth most powerful man in Syria according to the official hierarchy, if not always in reality.

The colours are stunning: the rich, brown woodwork; white walls; red seats; pink, black and white marble; silver tortoiseshell inlay on wall panels; blue, green and red stained glass around the highest part of the dome. Most of the members of parliament wear staid business suits although a significant number sport traditional rural garb: light or dark brown *abayas* or full-length robes with hems decorated with gold braid; and *keffiya* headdresses – white or checked black-and-white or red-and-white. Some wear a mix of traditional and modern: a suit plus a *keffiya*. The women, of whom there are twenty-six in this parliament, are soberly dressed, usually in smart suits, only very few with the headscarves required by Islamic custom. Three sit together, sporting stylish perms.

In seats in front and to the right of the officials on the dais sit Prime Minister Muhammad Miru and his cabinet. In the well of the chamber a cameraman from Syrian TV records the proceedings. Voting is by show of hands and in this session – as in almost all sessions – the majorities are clear and overwhelming.

Ba'athist 'Democracy'

Syria has a long parliamentary tradition. The first assembly was convened in Damascus in 1919 after the Ottoman defeat in the First World War. It comprised representatives from all parts of 'natural' or 'Greater' Syria – the region which is today divided into Syria, Lebanon, Jordan, Palestine and Israel. This 'Syrian Conference' declared the country's independence and promulgated a Constitution. France, having secured a League of Nations Mandate for Syria, occupied the country in 1920 and abolished the Conference. French rule saw a series of national assemblies, although all had limited powers. On 29–30 May 1945, following large demonstrations demanding the withdrawal of French troops from the already nominally independent country, the French bombed the city from the air and shelled the newer quarters of Damascus, killing many people and making thousands homeless. The parliament building was almost totally destroyed and many of its guards killed. A glass-encased model of parliament as it was after the French attack is displayed in a room near the building's main entrance.

Syria became independent in 1946 as a parliamentary democracy, albeit one in which political life was overwhelmingly dominated by a handful of traditional notable families from the main cities. In the early years of independence there were four secular, 'modern' political parties: the Ba'ath, the Communist Party, the Syrian Social Nationalist Party (SSNP, which advocated the unity of Greater Syria), and the Arab Socialist Party (ASP), formed in 1950 by Akram al-Hawrani and drawing support from the Sunni peasantry in the central plains. In 1952 the ASP merged with the Ba'ath to form the Arab Ba'ath Socialist Party. Parliament was dissolved with the military coups of 1949 staged by Husni az-Za'im on 30 March, Sami al-Hinnawi on 14 August and Adib ash-Shishakli on 19 December, but was reinstated in 1954 following Ash-Shishakli's overthrow in another military coup on 27 February that year. In the 1954 elections the Ba'ath won twenty-two seats out of the 142 in parliament. During the 1958–61 union with Egypt, a joint National Assembly functioned, with 200 members from the Syrian 'Northern Province' of the United Arab Republic, although President Nasser monopolised real power and the parliament was correspondingly impotent. After the Syrian secession in 1961, the Assembly was closed down.

The first parliament in the Ba'athist era was a National Council appointed in 1965, two years after the coup, but dissolved after the 1966 counter-coup. That body included key party leaders, representatives of the armed forces and of trade unions, the Peasants' Union, the Women's Union and professional associations. It also included so-called 'progressive citizens', some from Ba'ath splinter groups and from the Syrian Communist Party (SCP) and some acting purely as individuals. Asad appointed his first, 173-member parliament in February 1971, four months after his putsch, or Corrective Movement, as it is officially known. Its composition echoed that of the earlier National Council but it was widened to include representatives from the leftist political parties that were later linked in the Progressive National Front (PNF – Al-Jabha al-Qawmia at-Taqadumiya) and from the main religious establishments and chambers of commerce and industry. Setting the tone for the style and substance of parliamentary life ever since, this parliament quickly nominated Hafiz al-Asad as the sole candidate for the presidency. His nomination was approved by 99.2 per cent of voters in a national referendum on 1 March 1971. The same appointed parliament adopted the country's present Constitution on 31 January 1973. It was overwhelmingly approved by a national referendum on 12 March 1973.

The Progressive National Front

May 1972 saw the formation of the PNF, linking the Ba'ath Party and five leftist and nationalist parties:

- the Syrian Communist Party (SCP)
- the Arab Socialist Union (ASU), a Nasserist group, originally the Syrian branch of Egyptian leader Gamal Abdul Nasser's party of the same name
- the Movement of Socialist Unionists (MSU), a faction which broke away from the Ba'ath Party after Syria seceded from the union with Egypt in 1961
- the Democratic Socialist Unionist Party, a faction which split in 1974 from the MSU
- the Arab Socialist Party, another Ba'athist faction formed in 1964

In addition to co-opting and neutering the Ba'ath's rivals on the left, the PNF's creation also weakened them by causing splits over the issue of collaboration with the regime. Perhaps the most significant defection was the departure from the SCP of a sizeable faction headed by Riad at-Turk and naming itself the SCP–Political Bureau, a group that refused to join the Front. In 1986 the SCP split again, this time over attitudes to Soviet *perestroika*, into factions headed by Khalid Bakdash, the party's traditional, hardline leader, and Yousef Faisal. Both stayed within the PNF, continuing to call themselves the SCP.

The Ba'ath has completely dominated the PNF. 'The parties of the front, as spelled out in the PNF charter and by-laws, have accepted that the Ba'ath party's programme and its conference decisions are the basic guidelines for the front's policies, and that the Ba'ath leads the front and has an absolute majority in all its bodies,' said Perthes. 'Consequently, the other parties cannot even force an issue onto the agenda of a PNF meeting.'[6] The communists have nevertheless sometimes seriously criticised regime policies. In 1974 they strongly opposed a decision to allow foreign oil companies to enter the Syrian market and in 1976 they criticised President Asad's military intervention in Lebanon.

It is hard to gauge to what extent the Ba'ath's partners in the PNF – whose member parties other than the Ba'ath are forbidden from conducting political activity among the armed forces or students – today have independent lives of their own. The two SCP factions have a significant following and a vitality lacking in their tiny fellow PNF member parties. The SCP–Bakdash (now headed by Wisal Farha Bakdash, widow of the party's historic leader, Khalid Bakdash) had 'maybe 12,000 members', said a well-placed contact who requested anonymity.[7] He put the membership of the rival SCP headed by Yousef Faisal at between 8,000 and 10,000. Safwan Qudsi's Arab Socialist Union had between 5,000 and 10,000 members, he said, although he commented: 'I wonder if even they know how many they have.' Fayez Ismail's Movement of Socialist Unionists had the same number of members. The Democratic Socialist Unionist Party (headed until his death in 2001 by Ahmad al-Asad, whose successor had yet to be decided as of May 2002) had 'about 1,000 members'. The Arab Socialist Party, which has subdivided into two factions, headed by Mustafa Hamdoun and Ghassan Othman, had 'a maximum of 1,000–2,000 members', estimated the same source.

As part of its response to the civil society movement which sprang up after Hafiz al-Asad's death, the regime has sought to reform the PNF and thereby give it credibility. Only two measures have been enacted, both in late 2000. The Ba'ath's PNF allies have been allowed to open their own provincial offices; and they have been permitted to sell publicly their own journals (see Chapters 2 and 7). There is no sign that Syria's politically cynical populace regards this as any sort of democratic dawn. No wonder, since 'reactivating' the PNF is nothing new. It is something for which Hafiz al-Asad repeatedly called.

In the months after he became President, Bashar envisaged permitting new political parties (see Chapter 2). By early 2001, however, as the regime's conservatives moved to block any rapid political reforms, he was already back-tracking. In his 9 February 2001 interview with the pan-Arab daily *Ash-Sharq al-Awsat*, he did not rule out new parties, but he stressed that nothing was planned for the short term. 'We as a Party and a Front do not think in terms of there being no development of the work of political parties in Syria,' he said. 'On the contrary. Therefore, all possibilities are open, including the existence of new parties, but without that being linked to a rigid timetable. You cannot embark on a new experiment before evaluating and developing the existing one.' The interviewer, the paper's editor Abderrahman al-Rashed, rightly responded: 'But that could be done in ten days or take twenty years.'

Addressing parliament on 12 March 1992, the late President Hafiz al-Asad declared: 'For more than twenty years we have assured political pluralism ... and the parties which belong to the PNF share responsibility in the state leadership.' Hans Günter Löbmeyer, a keen observer of the Syrian scene, lambasted such fictions thus: 'When considering Syrian political life one cannot avoid the impression that Syria's leadership is talking about any country other than Syria. For reality is quite different and has little or nothing in common with democracy.'[8] He added: 'Still worse than constitutional theory is political practice: with the exception of the Ba'ath Party, the member parties of the PNF have no influence on political decisions and are mere puppets with Asad holding the strings.'

The same point was made with feeling by one of the signatories of the Statement of 1,000, who asked not to be identified: 'Frankly, these parties [of the PNF] do not represent the Syrian people. They are artificial, and fabricated to serve the interest of one person [the President].'[9]

Elections

Several methods are used to ensure that Syrian general elections do not yield unwanted surprises. Most importantly, candidates (of whom there were 7,364 in the 1998 elections) are carefully screened. Voting itself has generally been relatively free and only in 1981, when the regime was facing a virtual civil war, was voting massively rigged. A more perennial problem is that a single person can cast multiple votes, in his own and in any other constituency, because the electoral law, introduced in 1974 and amended in 1984, abolished the use of electoral registers allowing names to be ticked off after votes had been cast. 'The polling station officials are supposed to perforate your identity card to show that you have voted,' explained one politician. 'Usually they don't perforate it. Everyone can go everywhere for the election, and can vote more than once.'[10]

The first general election under Ba'athist rule took place in 1973, when 186 seats were contested, divided between fifteen multi-member constituencies. The Ba'ath and its allies in the PNF were pre-allocated 122 seats (of which the Ba'ath won 120), giving the Front a pre-ordained two-thirds majority in parliament. Independents – deputies approved by the regime but not representing any of the legally recognised parties – were allocated sixty-two seats.

The number of seats was increased to 195 in the 1977 election. In 1990 – reflecting the economic *infitah*, or 'opening', and the need to co-opt the new business class into the system – fifty-five seats were added, all of them reserved for independents. The PNF was allocated two-thirds of the seats in 1973, 81.5 per cent in 1977 (when the number of independents was reduced to thirty-six), 100 per cent in the grossly rigged 1981 elections, and 79 per cent in 1986 (when there were forty-one independents). The Front was allocated 66.8 per cent of the seats in the 1990, 1994 and 1998 elections, in each of which eighty-three seats, or 33.2 per cent of the total, were reserved for independents. The 1973 Constitution stipulates that 51 per cent of parliamentary deputies must be workers and peasants, reflecting the regime's presumed socialist dimension.

Turnout rates are uncertain but definitely low and probably well below 20 per cent. Several times in recent polls, including the 1998 election, an additional day has been allowed for voting – something which is stipulated by law when turnout is less than 50 per cent on the official election day. 'Voter apathy reflects frustration and fear,' recorded Middle East Watch, a division of Human Rights Watch, recounting how a well-known Syrian writer had

> crossed out all the top names on the electoral list in March 1986 as a protest. Shortly after leaving the polling place, an intelligence service summoned him for interrogation. It seems that an agent or informer had observed what he had done. He was told that he would be forgiven if he cooperated. When he refused, he was imprisoned for over two years.[11]

Sa'ad Jawdat Saeed, from the village of Bir Ajman, has more recent experience of official misconduct during elections. He voted 'no' in the July 2000 referendum to confirm Bashar al-Asad as President but he noticed that the polling station clerk had crossed out his reply and ticked the 'yes' box instead. When he protested, Saeed was detained by the local *mukhabarat* and held for several weeks.[12]

Another of Hafiz al-Asad's moves to accord his regime a democratic veneer was the institution of *muhafazat* (provincial) elections every four years, starting in March 1972. Because the provincial councils are mainly concerned with administration and have few political responsibilities, and are anyway subject to the control of powerful provincial governors appointed by the President, these local elections have been surprisingly free. The regime has not even insisted on a guaranteed majority for the Ba'ath and its PNF allies, even though the 1972 poll produced a defeat for the regime.

The Outlawed Opposition

As trains on a ground-level section of London's dilapidated Northern Line underground railway clattered past outside, Ali Sadr ad-Din al-Bayanouni, the grey-bearded *Muraqab 'Am*, or superindendent-general, of Syria's Al-Ikhwan Al-Muslimoun (Muslim Brotherhood), emphasised his movement's commitment to multi-party democracy, human rights and the rule of law. 'The monopoly of power [by the Ba'ath] for some forty years caused all currents to agree on a common position: freedom, plurality, democracy,' he said. 'This regime united the opposition.'[13]

We met in the unlikely setting of a 1920s semi-detached house in a genteel, lower-middle-class district of north-west London which Al-Bayanouni uses when in the United Kingdom. The parquet-floored front room boasts three settees surrounding a brightly patterned carpet. Lace curtains protect the room from prying eyes. Al-Bayanouni wears beige slacks, a light shirt and blue tartan slippers. Passing him on the street, one would never guess his influence. Exiled from Syria in 1980, he lived in Jordan until 2000, but when Bashar al-Asad succeeded his father the Jordanians, wishing to underline their desire for good relations with Damascus, withdrew permission for him to reside there. His wife and three of his seven children still live in the Jordanian capital, Amman. Al-Bayanouni now lives peripatetically: 'I have nowhere to go now.'

Born in Aleppo in 1938 to a devoutly Muslim family, Al-Bayanouni has headed the Ikhwan since 1996 and was re-elected to a new four-year term in July 2002. Like many (perhaps most) leading Syrian politicians, he has suffered for his cause. In 1975–77, at the start of the Ikhwan-led rebellion against the regime, he was imprisoned, spending a year in solitary confinement. In 1979, while he was in Europe, the *mukhabarat* raided his home and seized his son and son-in-law as hostages. 'My son was later released but my son-in-law was killed in prison – although he was not a member of the Ikhwan,' said Al-Bayanouni.

In the late 1970s, at the height of its influence, the Ikhwan's discourse was very different. Much of its success in mobilising armed opposition to the regime was based on its argument that Syria had been hijacked by a sacrilegious and/or atheist, self-aggrandising Alawi minority. The extent of the transformation was strikingly underlined in a *Draft National Code of Honour for Political Action*, issued on 3 May 2001. Presented as 'preliminary ideas' for discussion, the Code affirmed the Brotherhood's belief that 'the modern state is a state of rotation [i.e. where governments change peaceably]' and that 'free and honest ballot boxes are the basis for the rotation of power between all the homeland's sons'. It hailed 'the supremacy of law' and 'the separation of powers', and declared 'the modern state' to be 'a pluralistic one, where there are different views, various policies and different positions'. It made no mention of the Ikhwan's long-standing demand for the application of Shari'a law. The Muslim Brotherhood affirmed: 'The time has gone when one party claims it is the homeland. The utmost that any political group can do is to take its place on the national map according to the size it is given by its actual popularity through the free and honest ballot box.' The past conflict between secular Arab nationalism and Islamism was a 'stage in history that is now past. That confrontation resulted from factors of emotionalism, misunderstandings, and even the ideology that generally prevailed during the post-independence stages.'

'On the principles of this document, there are no differences among Syrians,' said Al-Bayanouni. 'Other documents issued by other factions are very, very similar to ours. The demands of the Muslim Brotherhood, of the communists, of Riad at-Turk's party, of the National Democratic Gathering and of the civil society movement – all have very much in common.'[14]

In August 2002 the Ikhwan – membership of which is still punishable by death under Law 49 of 1980 – convened a meeting in London of some fifty oppositionists aimed at honing the Code into a National Charter encompassing principles for governing a democratic Syria. The conferees included nationalists, leftists and independents as well as Islamists. The most significant, after Ali Sadr ad-Din al-Bayanouni, were Ahmad Abu Saleh, a minister in early Ba'athist governments of the 1960s, and Dr Haytham Manna, a Syrian physician and anthropologist living in Paris who is spokesman for the Cairo-based Arab Human Rights Commission. Issued on 25 August, the National Charter closely echoed the May 2001 Code although it did give greater prominence to the role of Islam, asserting that, with its 'noble objectives, sublime values and perfect legislation', it constituted 'a civilisational authority and distinct identity for the sons and daughters of our nation'. The earlier draft charter had described Islam as 'either a religious term of reference or a cultural affiliation', explaining that it was therefore 'all-encompassing and brings the homeland's sons together, unifies them and protects their existence'.

The Muslim Brotherhood is the most significant of Syria's outlawed political currents. It has always embraced a wide range of opinion. At one end of the spectrum has been a younger, more militant jihadist ('holy struggler') tendency that has co-existed uneasily with an older, traditional, establishment tendency. Dr Samir Altaqi, a member of the politburo of the Yousef Faisal faction of the SCP and a member of parliament for Aleppo, 1994–98, is a shrewd observer of Islamist politics in Syria. Today, the jihadists were gaining ground, he said, because they were being strongly influenced and inspired by the Palestinian Hamas and Islamic Jihad movements and, to a lesser extent, by the Lebanese Shi'a Muslim Hizbollah movement whose guerrilla campaign had forced Israel's withdrawal from southern Lebanon in May 2000.[15]

Whatever its suspicions of the United States and the West, however, the Syrian Muslim Brotherhood is no friend of fanatical groups such as Usama bin Laden's Al-Qa'ida organisation which perpetrated the 11 September 2001 attacks in New York and Washington. 'Our philosophy is moderate,' said Ali Sadr al-Din al-Bayanouni. 'After 11 September, I, with other Muslim leaders, issued a statement denouncing what happened – regardless of who did it and against whom it was done – because it was an horrific act which didn't accord with Islamic realities.'[16] Stressing that the Syrian Ikhwan was 'very, very far from violence', he noted that 'many of the immediate circle around Bin Laden had declared the Muslim Brotherhood to be *kafirs*, meaning non-believers'.

Islamists – who might expect to win perhaps one-third of the vote in a free and fair election – are thought to have infiltrated the Syrian system deeply, despite the strenuous efforts of the *mukhabarat*. This was underlined in late 1999 and early 2000 when hundreds of Islamists associated with the Ikhwan and with the Hizb at-Tahrir al-Islami (Islamic Liberation Party) were arrested. 'Most were military or intellectuals,' according to a well-placed source in Damascus who requested anonymity. 'And 90 per cent were Ba'ath Party members.' Most were released after signing declarations agreeing not to engage in political activities.

As an organisation, Syria's Muslim Brotherhood plainly is now well disposed towards pluralism and democracy, although some analysts have been deeply sceptical of the movement's motives. 'After the failure of its religious strategy in the 1960s and the anti-Alawi strategy in the 1970s and 1980s, [the Muslim Brotherhood] is trying the democratic option in the 1990s,' warned Hans Günter Löbmeyer. 'It is beyond question that democracy is not the Brotherhood's political aim but a means to another end: the assumption of power.'[17] Compromising God's will is inherently difficult, and doubtless the analysis holds for some more extreme Islamists within the movement who seem now a minority voice. The scene has shifted significantly since 1994, when Löbmeyer was writing, and his scepticism today seems excessive.

A substantial part of the secular opposition, grouped in the National Democratic Gathering (At-Tajammu' al-Watani ad-Dimuqrati), has shunned the system and retains a small but significant influence. The Gathering was officially launched in January 1980, at a time when Asad's regime was reeling from the mainly but not exclusively Islamist rebellion. Some of its key elements are splinter groups of parties within the PNF. Although technically illegal, the Gathering is today tolerated and has strongly backed the civil society movement.

The Gathering, which includes every significant secular opposition group except the small Party of Communist Action (PCA – Al-Hizb al-'Amal al-Shuyu'i), links:

- the Arab Socialist Union (ASU), headed by Hassan Ismael Abdul Azim
- the Syrian Communist Party – Political Bureau, headed by Riad at-Turk
- the Workers' Revolutionary Party, headed by Tariq Abu al-Hassan
- the Movement of Arab Socialists, headed by 'Abd al-Ghani 'Ayash
- and the Democratic Socialist Arab Ba'ath Party (formerly the 23rd February Movement), headed by the exiled Ibrahim Makhouss

Hassan Abdul Azim, a lawyer from Damascus, is the Gathering's spokesman. He received me in his modest apartment in the Rukn ad-Din district in north-east Damascus, plugging in an electric fire to take the chill off the winter air and offering the traditional hospitality of thick Turkish coffee. The décor of his guest room is memorably kitsch: richly upholstered Louis XV chairs with ornate legs; fake plastic flowers and greenery around the windows. Discreetly at the side of a glass-fronted bookcase leans a small, framed photograph of the late Egyptian President Gamal Abdul Nasser.

In formal and slightly ponderous style, Abdul Azim tells his story.

The Nasserist ASU, founded in 1964, 'worked with the opposition parties against the Ba'ath Party when it monopolised power'.[18] It stayed in opposition 'until the launch of the Corrective Movement under the leadership of Hafiz al-Asad'. The late Syrian leader 'invited us to take part in government and in the parliament' and promised to create a widely-based Progressive National Front, continued Abdul Azim. 'We entered the Front after being recognised as a party and we took part in parliament, where we had twelve deputies, until April 1973.'

For Abdul Azim's faction of the ASU, the privileged position of the Ba'ath in the 1973 Constitution was the sticking-point: 'Article 8 stated that the Ba'ath was "the leading party in society and the state". We knew then that the Front as a national democratic coalition no longer existed because of the insistence on inserting that text in the Constitution. We therefore called a general conference of the party and decided to quit the Front.' Ruefully, he explained: 'The Front was one of our demands and the Ba'ath accepted it and then went back on its word. The PNF no longer represents a coalition of political parties and political diversity. It's just an external décor, a form without content, colour or activity.' Having left the PNF and split from its mother-party, Abdul Azim's wing of the ASU – then headed by Jamal al-Atassi – went semi-underground. The Gathering, also headed by al-Atassi, 'took part in the events of 1980: strikes, demonstrations and demands for democratic change', said Abdul Azim, adding: 'We tried for a third path, neither that of the government nor that of violent groups which wanted to bring change by force. We wanted a democratic solution.'

How significant were his ASU faction and the Gathering today? Were they not merely marginalised spectators? Abdul Azim, who also helps run a civil society forum for lawyers, conceded that the ASU's membership had fallen but he insisted: 'The Gathering's importance does not lie in the number of its parties but in its opinions, and also in the popularity of its member-parties. Practically speaking, the majority of people are with us. In practical terms, the parties of the Gathering are more popular than the parties of the Front.' Formal membership would increase when a law was issued legalising political parties. Meanwhile 'it's risky to join a non-authorised party'.

Syria's peculiar history since the 1963 Ba'athist coup means that none of its political currents has developed normally. The Ba'ath, a core element of an authoritarian regime, enjoys influence and membership way beyond what might normally have been expected from a party which, while certainly significant, was merely one of several competing socialist nationalist groups. Other parties have become abnormally small after decades of clandestine operation and harassment. For some sections of society – most notably secular, liberal democrats – no representative parties exist. 'None of the parties at this time really reflects the interests of the classes and masses and social layers they are designed to do,' said Samir Altaqi. 'There is a dislocation between actual society and political society.'[19]

Ironically in view of his own emasculation of Syria's political parties, Hafiz al-Asad – routinely dubbed *Qa'iduna ilal-Abad* ('Our Leader for Ever', an appellation inherently negating the requirement for democracy) – severely disapproved of Egyptian President Gamal Abdul Nasser's suppression of parties during the 1958–61 Syrian–Egyptian union:

> We sensed a tremendous hostility towards our [Ba'ath] party, filtering down from Nasser himself, and we started predicting that the union would end in catastrophe. Nasser suffered from a persistent paranoia about political parties, a seemingly incurable condition which no doubt stemmed from his experience of the corrupt parties of pre-revolutionary Egypt. He used to say – and his remarks would get back to us – 'I'm an honest and decent man, so what need have we of parties?'[20]

The Speaker's Role

Abdul Qader al-Qaddura has a clear view of his role as Speaker of the People's Assembly: 'The Speaker chairs parliament's meetings, without intervening unless required to do so for clarification. Decision-making is the responsibility of the Assembly.' In addition, he 'speaks on behalf of the People's Assembly and represents it in international and regional parliamentary meetings'.[21] Outside analysts see it differently. Volker Perthes described Al-Qaddura as 'a core member of the Ba'ath Party Regional Command who has functioned as the regime's supervisor of parliamentary affairs rather than as parliament's representative in the leadership'.[22] An example was the Speaker's determined response to an attempt by parliament to vote down a proposed change in the tax law in 1991. Both leftist trade unionist deputies and independent members from the business community agreed in committee to amend the law so as to exempt from taxation the first 18,000 Syrian Pounds of both business profits and wage income. In the plenary debate the minister of finance declared the amendment unacceptable as it would cost too much in lost revenues. Despite his protestations, the amended text was approved by a majority. The then prime minister, Mahmoud Zu'bi, protested. Al-Qaddura promptly adjourned the meeting, insisting there had been no quorum. That afternoon, parliament reconvened for another vote. Again the amended text was passed. The Speaker asserted that there had been a majority against. In the face of protests by many deputies, Al-Qaddura agreed another vote, by call rather than by show of hands, in which each member would individually declare for or against the amendment. In an effort to bring wavering Ba'athists into line, the Speaker reminded them that the tax law had been drafted by the Party's Regional Command and that President Asad himself had been directly involved. In effect, he turned the vote into a test of loyalty to the regime. About sixty members left the meeting in protest at these tactics. 'Qaddura then put the entire bill in its original form to a vote and finally, against the votes of a couple of trade unionists, got the majority wanted, demonstrating … the limitations of parliamentary participation – even in one of the less critical policy fields,' wrote Perthes.[23]

Not-so-independent Independents

The expansion of the number of seats reserved for independents in the 1990 elections (although this was achieved not by reducing the number earmarked for the Ba'ath and PNF but by expanding the total number of parliamentary seats) was hailed as a landmark in a process of ever-widening democratisation. Most of the independents in the earlier parliaments were educated middle-class professionals and businessmen and tribal and religious leaders. Many of those in the parliaments since 1990 have been from the new bourgeoisie, underlining the regime's desire to create at least the appearance of representation for a community that has played an increasing role in the national economy since the 1980s. At the same time, parliamentary debate on economic policy has widened, in tandem with the parallel encouragement of such discussion in the media and wider society. Economic policy has become an area – albeit the only one – where parliament can have a real influence on the government. Addressing parliament in December 1991, Prime Minister Mahmoud Zu'bi opined that the Assembly was a crucial element in Syria's 'democratic system' and the means by which 'the people participate in the making of all decisions which relate to their economy and their daily affairs'.[24] Matters such as defence, foreign affairs and internal security plainly remained off-limits.

Some independents were loud advocates (with official approval) of major economic reforms that have since been embraced as regime objectives. A notable example was Ihsan Sanqar, a businessman with wide interests including food-processing plants and vehicle importing. Sanqar entered parliament in 1990 where, from a position of solid loyalty to the regime, he pressed strongly for measures including the establishment of a stock market, the introduction of private banks, the lifting of price controls, the cancellation of laws which discouraged investment and the establishment of new industrial cities.[25] Many of the new industrialists owe their success to close ties to the regime and are generally keen supporters of the status quo. They are only 'independent' in the sense that they are not affiliated to any political party. Like other parliamentary candidates, the independents are carefully scrutinised by the authorities before being allowed to stand for election. As Löbmeyer noted: 'They are allowed to articulate their special interests only for as long as their demands do not contradict the regime's general policy.'[26]

Riad Seif and Ma'moun al-Homsi, both independents from Damascus, were two who went too far, in the regime's opinion, and they paid the price (see Chapter 3). Seif, a key figure in the civil society movement, was arrested in September 2001 after holding a meeting of his National Dialogue Forum at his home without permission from the Interior Ministry. Al-Homsi was detained in August after declaring a hunger strike in support of demands including a lifting of the draconian and oppressive Emergency Law. The arrests came as part of a wider crackdown on the 'Damascus Spring'. Syria's Constitution guarantees immunity to members of parliament but this is not absolute. When parliament is in session, it is up to a parliamentary committee to decide. Otherwise, as in the cases of Seif and Al-Homsi, it is a matter for the Speaker. Insisting that he had acted properly and in accordance with the law, Al-Qaddura asserted that freedom of speech had not been violated: 'Neither was arrested for what he said but for what he did.'[27]

The two jailed deputies took a different view. In a written statement issued from 'Adra prison on 14 November 2001, Seif maintained that he had been arrested because he had been pressing in parliament for full disclosure of payments surrounding a mobile telephone contract, and because the high attendance at his Forum had worried 'the security apparatus ... who feared the disappearance of the fear barrier they had planted in the people for long decades'.[28] Al-Homsi, who was vilified in the official media after his arrest, issued a similar statement from prison denying any wrongdoing and asserting that he and Seif had been 'arrested and imprisoned with no reason and in violation of the Constitution'.[29]

At least one stint in prison is almost a *sine qua non* for those engaged in politics in Syria, a badge of authenticity. Even Hafiz al-Asad spent a few days in spring 1962 being interrogated in the notorious Mezzeh political prison in western Damascus, near the highway to Beirut, which his son Bashar finally closed in 2000.[30] Al-Qaddura told me proudly that in a political career stretching back to the 1950s he too had been imprisoned three times for his political activism on behalf of the Ba'ath Party.[31] The first occasion was during the rule of General Adib ash-Shishakli, who seized power on 19 December 1949 and who was overthrown in a coup on 27 February 1954. At that time, said Al-Qaddura, he was merely 'a member of the Ba'ath Party, a small member'. His second spell in prison was in 1961 'in the revolution to separate Syria from the United Arab Republic [the union with Egypt]'. His third, and longest, incarceration started on 23 February 1966, when Salah Jadid's extremist civilian wing of the Ba'ath seized power. At the time, Al-Qaddura was a science student at Damascus University and a high-profile student activist. First he was held in Tadmor, the infamous desert prison near the enchanting ruined classical city of Palmyra, and then he spent one month in Mezzeh. This was followed by six months in the Qal'a (the old citadel of Damascus, used for years as a jail but now converted into a museum) 'and the rest in Damascus'. Al-Qaddura was freed after fifteen months, on 10 June 1967. He joked: 'Anyone who wants to engage in politics may become a minister or he may become a prisoner.'

Notes

1. People's Assembly, *The People's Assembly: One of the Great Achievements of the Glorious Correctionist Movement*, 2nd edn (Damascus, 1999).
2. Volker Perthes, *The Political Economy of Syria under Asad* (London: I.B. Tauris, 1995), p. 167.
3. 'Syrian Parliament Okays Lt. Gen. Bashar Assad's Nomination', *SANA*, Damascus, 26 June 2000.
4. Interview with author, Damascus, 3 December 2001.
5. Interview with author, Damascus, 4 December 2001.
6. Perthes, *Political Economy*, p. 164.
7. Interview with author, Damascus, February 2002.
8. Hans Günter Löbmeyer, 'Al-dimuqratiyya hiyya al-hall? The Syrian Op-

position at the End of the Asad Era', in Eberhard Kienle (ed.), *Contemporary Syria: Liberalization between Cold War and Cold Peace* (London: British Academic Press, 1994), p. 82.

9. Interview with author, Damascus, 1 May 2001.

10. Interview with author, Damascus, February 2002.

11. Middle East Watch, *Syria Unmasked: The Suppression of Human Rights by the Asad Regime* (New Haven, CT and London: Yale University Press, 1991), p. 37.

12. Haytham Manna, 'Syria: A General Amnesty as the Springboard for Reform', *Al-Quds al-Arabi*, 3 August 2000.

13. Interview with author, London, 19 July 2002.

14. Ibid.

15. Interview with author, Damascus, 1 December 2001.

16. Interview with author, London, 19 July 2002.

17. Löbmeyer, 'The Syrian Opposition', p. 90.

18. Interview with author, Damascus, 4 December 2001.

19. Interview with author, Damascus, 1 December 2001.

20. Patrick Seale, *Asad: The Struggle for Power in the Middle East* (Berkeley and Los Angeles: University of California Press, 1995), p. 61.

21. Interview with author, Damascus, 3 December 2001.

22. Perthes, *Political Economy*, p. 221.

23. Ibid., p. 223.

24. *Ath-Thawra,* 1 January 1992.

25. Interview with author, Damascus, June 1995.

26. Löbmeyer, 'The Syrian Opposition', p. 83.

27. Interview with author, Damascus, 3 December 2001.

28. Riad Seif, *It is Impossible to Hide the Sun with a Sieve*, Declaration from Prison, 14 November 2001.

29. *Statement of Muhammad Ma'moun al-Homsi, Independent Member of Parliament and Member of the French–Syrian Friendship Committee inside Parliament*, undated (approximately December 2001).

30. Seale, *Asad*, p. 70.

31. Interview with author, Damascus, 3 December 2001.

CHAPTER 6

'Subject to no Authority but the Law': The Legal System

§ ENTERING the central hall of the Qasr al-'Adl (Palace of Justice) – popularly dubbed the Palace of Injustice – one is confronted by a large and crudely painted mural depicting the late President Hafiz al-Asad in the black robes of a judge. He stands at the head of a group of twelve other judges, one of them a woman in a headscarf, and gazes upwards towards an open book hovering above and ahead of him in an electric blue sky. The book carries a verse from the Qur'an: 'God instructs you to restore property to its rightful owner; and if you judge between people, do so righteously.' Flitting awkwardly through the mural's sky are several doves – of peace, no doubt.

Noon on a rainy December day and the Palace of Justice, on Nasser Street, almost opposite the entrance to the famed Hamidiya *suq*, is thronged. The central hall is an atrium overlooked by three balconies marking each floor of the building, which was constructed during the French occupation. A hubbub rises from the 200-strong crowd who present a microcosm of Syrian society: lawyers in sharply tailored Italian suits; their clerks and clients, also besuited but far less grandly; tanned villagers wearing suit jackets over robe-like *abayas*. Perhaps 10 per cent of the throng are women.

A corridor to the right of the main entrance leads to a series of small courtrooms, high-ceilinged and perhaps 6 metres by 10 metres, reserved for the lowliest cases. To left and right in one of these, neon lights are mounted on bare, grey walls. Ahead is a window and on one side a portrait of the late President. In front of the window, from wall to wall, extends a raised wooden bench piled high with files. Immediately before the bench stands a wooden table topped with a sheet of glass, cracked diagonally. Rows of spartan wooden benches for the litigants and their legal teams face the judges' bench. Judge

Feiha al-Asad, a handsome woman in her thirties from the port city of Lattakia, presides over a case involving a man accused of working without the correct permits. She is assisted by male clerks, one on each side of her. None of the actual parties is present but two lawyers representing them stand below the bench, both in suits. Judge Al-Asad says that she can hear as many as thirty of these cases per day.

In a bigger courtroom with two-tone grey walls, on the second floor of the Palace of Justice, another female judge presides over the case of a man who opened a shop without the necessary official permits. Above and behind her is a portrait of Hafiz al-Asad and another, smaller, one of his heir, Bashar. Around twenty people sit on the wooden pews while the lawyers stand immediately before the judge's bench. Although my visit has been approved by the Information Ministry, the judge says that I can stay only with permission from the Ministry of Justice.

On one wing of the third floor is the Economic Security Court which deals with those who fall foul of the Emergency Law's provisions on economic crimes (see below). Entry to the wing is via a locked steel-barred gate, guarded by uniformed police. Beyond this barrier, at the end of a corridor is a large courtroom. Steel cages to house the accused extend the length of two sides of the room. On this occasion they are empty. A third wall has windows and the fourth accommodates a raised wooden bench. A judge in a black gown trimmed with gold lace speaks into a microphone. Before him, a witness, flanked by his lawyer, claims that he knows nothing. The case concerns a man who borrowed money with a monthly interest of 3 per cent and who was unable to repay the loan. A dozen people sit attentively on the wooden pews facing the judge's bench. Only the witness and his lawyer are standing. The atmosphere is formal and deeply respectful of the judge.

It is not long before my visit encounters the customary bureaucratic obstacles. In the corridor a lawyer suggests that I should go to the press office of the Palace of Justice. In turn, they say that I should go first to the *Muhami al-'Am* (solicitor-general). He says that he requires an introductory letter from the Minister of Justice. It is a classic example of the upwards buck-passing which afflicts all Syria's official institutions.

The casual visitor to the Palace of Justice might gain the impression that the rule of law prevails in Syria. Officially, it does. The Constitution affirms: 'The supremacy of law is a fundamental principle in society and state'; and that 'Citizens are equal before the law in their rights and duties'. It states that all Syrians have 'the right to participate in the political, economic, social and cultural life' and that 'the law regulates this participation'. It further affirms that 'every defendant is presumed innocent until proven guilty'; that 'no one may be kept under surveillance or be detained except in accordance with the law'; that 'the right of litigation, contest and defence before the judiciary is safeguarded by the law'. It affirms that 'the judicial authority is independent. The President of the Republic guarantees this independence'; that 'judges are independent. They are subject to no authority except that of the law'; and that 'the honour, conscience and impartiality of judges are guarantees of public rights and freedoms'.

Crushing the Lawyers

Haitham al-Maleh, lawyer and president of the Syrian Human Rights Association, is profoundly unimpressed. 'The problem here – the main problem – is that the country is controlled by orders, not by the law,' he said. 'The law is in books, not in everyday life.'[1]

Until 1980 the Bar Association and several other professional associations, for example those for engineers and doctors, had retained their independence from the regime and played important roles in the non-violent opposition movement of the late 1970s. The lawyers were at the fore. On 22 June 1978 the Damascus Bar Association passed resolutions demanding an immediate lifting of the Emergency Law which had been in effect since December 1962 (see below), condemning the use of torture and warning lawyers that they would be disciplined by the Bar if they took part in unlawful activities in concert with the authorities. On 29 June a plenary session of the Syrian Bar Association adopted similar resolutions and on 17 August 1978 the president of the Syrian Bar, Sabah ar-Rikabi, presented the authorities with a memorandum demanding respect for the rule of law and the release of people imprisoned without trial. On 11 November the general congress of the Aleppo Bar voted to support the Damascus Bar's June decisions.

On 1 December the Syrian Bar Association met in emergency congress and demanded independence for the judiciary, an end to the State of Emergency and the disbanding of the special courts (see below). Shortly after, a lawyer and his wife were assaulted on a Damascus street by members of the Defence Companies, a praetorian guard headed by Hafiz al-Asad's brother, Rif'at. A one-day protest strike called by the Damascus Bar was supported by the bars in Homs, Hama, Aleppo and Deir ez-Zor.

Despite harsh repression by the authorities, the tide of dissent, including an intensifying campaign of bloody armed attacks by Muslim Brotherhood militants, continued to rise. On 31 August 1979 the Damascus Bar passed a further resolution demanding democratic rights and an end to the State of Emergency. On 28 February 1980 the national congress of the Engineers' Association passed a resolution demanding the lifting of the State of Emergency, the release of all political prisoners and freedom of expression and association. On 2 March the Aleppo Bar Association staged a two-hour strike to underline its demand for reform. On 8 March – the anniversary of the Ba'athist coup of 1963 – Syria was convulsed by anti-regime strikes and demonstrations. The following day the professional associations in Homs issued a joint demand for reform and this was echoed two days later by a declaration from the professional associations in Hama.

As the crisis deepened, the regime increasingly resorted to brute force. In March 1980 army Special Forces soldiers killed between 150 and 200 protesters in Jisr ash-Shughour, a small town on the Orontes river between Aleppo and Lattakia. The same month security forces killed about fifty demonstrators in Idlib and Ma'arra, to the north-east of Jisr ash-Shughour. The Syrian Bar Association called a national strike for 31 March and was backed by the Medical Association, the Engineers' Association and other professional groups. The government's response, on 9 April, was a decree dissolving all the professional associations on the grounds that they had been 'infiltrated by reactionary elements' and were a danger to society. The following day compliant replacement bodies with executive committees loyal to the regime were created. The *mukhabarat* arrested and imprisoned almost all the authentic leaders of Syria's professions including over 100 doctors and health professionals, 100 engineers and fifty lawyers. Many of the detainees were tortured and some were killed.

Having dissolved the independent associations and replaced them with officially appointed bodies, the regime moved to ensure that they could never regain their independence. Law No. 39 of 21 August 1981 required the bar to act 'in conformity with the principles and resolutions of the Arab Ba'ath Socialist Party' and to 'work in co-ordination with the competent office of the [party's] Regional Command'. The law stipulated that Bar congresses could convene only if called and attended by a party representative, and it empowered the government to dissolve the executive committees of the national or regional Bar associations at any time. Further, it placed the Bar under the supervision of the Ministry of Justice. The new law forbade lawyers from joining any Arab or international organisation without the written permission of the Bar Association (itself now an agency of the regime). *Mukhabarat* agents were empowered to arrest lawyers and search their offices if they acted for clients deemed to be 'security threats' and the law threatened lawyers with disbarment for equally vague offences. Henceforth, lawyers could act for foreign clients only with the permission of the minister of justice. Similar laws were issued to regulate the other previously autonomous professional associations.

Haitham al-Maleh, who was part of the legal team that defended the ten civil society activists arrested in August and September 2001, including MPs Riad Seif and Ma'moun al-Homsi, is clear: 'The Syrian Bar Association is under the control of the government, like the engineers and the doctors. They fixed them all to the wheel of the regime.'[2]

Lawyers who remained recalcitrant faced severe harassment. *Mukhabarat* agents might be posted outside a lawyer's office to deter clients, or judges might be pressured consistently to rule against the clients of a particular lawyer.[3]

Haitham al-Maleh's Ordeal

Al-Maleh, then a member of the Bar's Freedom and Human Rights Committee, was one of the victims of the regime's assault on the lawyers, and his ordeal lasted seven years. His office is a charming stone building, about seventy years old, in the Baramkeh district of central Damascus. During the Mandate, it was the home of the head of French Intelligence. Al-Maleh, whose painful history and advancing years – he is slightly older than his office – have failed to dim his great courage and dignity, received me in his guest chamber, a small rectangular hall with a tiled floor and lined with chairs. Hanging on the walls are three remarkable framed bead-works, products of his years in jail. The biggest, in green and beige, is the Muslim invocation *Bismallah ar-Rahman ar-Rahim* ('In the name of God, the Beneficent, the Merciful'). It comprises an astonishing 96,000 beads and took Al-Maleh three months to make. A second bead-picture carries a saying of Moses from the Qur'an: 'He said: "My God, you were so generous to me that I will not support criminals."' It is half the size of the biggest and took six weeks to complete. The third and smallest depicts the sword and scales of justice and carries the legend: *Al-Haqq wa al-'Uruba* ('Justice and Arabism'). It also shows Al-Maleh's name, and the words: *Dhikra Difa'a 'an al-Hurriya wa Siyadat al-Qanun* ('Commemorating the Defence of Freedom and the Rule of Law').

Having arranged for me the customary glass of sweet tea, Al-Maleh told his story. Initially, he and his colleagues had been held in a General Intelligence prison in a discreet, tree-lined square surrounded by bland apartment blocks in the Tijara district in north-east Damascus. They were then moved to a Military Intelligence facility in an elegant stone-built mansion fringed with palm trees in the Halbouni district, near the Hejaz railway station, the northern terminus of a narrow-gauge line built by the Ottomans to carry pilgrims and troops to Medina in what is today Saudi Arabia. The mansion was once the home of Shaikh Taj ad-Din al-Hasani, a prime minister and later President of Syria during the French Mandate. Here, the lawyers were kept for only a few days, sharing a small cell in the basement. Subsequently, the prison was closed and the building was repaired and renovated by Muhammad Bashir an-Najjar, a senior *mukhabarat* chief, for use as his home and office. He, too, later fell foul of the regime and is now in jail.

Al-Maleh and the other lawyers were then moved to the headquarters of General Intelligence, an unsightly complex with a tall communications tower on the Kafr Sousa roundabout in south-west Damascus. Surrounded by a high wall, the complex includes a central office block and a series of squat, bunker-like structures. Plain-clothed agents carrying Kalashnikov automatic rifles and wearing ammunition belts stand guard outside – as they do outside all *mukhabarat* installations and the homes of senior secret police chiefs. 'We stayed at Kafr Sousa a long time, about two years,' recalled Al-Maleh, adding that some of the detained engineers were being held there at the same time. 'About twenty people were held together in a cell 4 metres by 4 metres,' he continued. 'We were lucky. The guards told us that sometimes forty people were jammed into that room.'[4] Some of the guards there were vicious, especially when high on drugs, Al-Maleh recalled, although others were pleasant. 'One refused to beat some female prisoners on the soles of their feet,' he said. 'As a result, he was himself imprisoned.'

After Kafr Sousa, the lawyers were moved to a prison in an old, Ottoman-era building adjacent to a cemetery in the Shaikh Hassan district of the Old City. Six months later they were transferred to the Qal'a military prison in the old Damascus citadel, a stone's throw from the Palace of Justice. The prison was closed in 1984 and the citadel has since been renovated as a tourist attraction. They stayed in the Qal'a for two years before being taken back to Sheikh Hassan (also now closed), where they remained 'for two or three months'.

They were then transferred to the civil prison at 'Adra, some 25 kilometres north-east of Damascus on the road to Homs, where they were kept for two years. In late 1986 they were moved to a Military Intelligence centre in the Jamarik (Customs) district in west-central Damascus, just behind the Carlton Hotel. The Jamarik, Kafr Sousa, Halbouni and 'Adra facilities all feature in a list of prisons in Damascus holding political prisoners included in a 1991 report by Middle East Watch, a division of Human Rights Watch. The report notes that the list is 'partial'. It also identifies eight prisons and detention centres in Aleppo.[5]

In the ugly, utilitarian Jamarik complex with its different building blocks painted brown or yellow, Al-Maleh was held for thirty-six days as part of a group of ten lawyers. 'They were preparing us for release,' he recalled. 'They put us in a cell 3 metres by 3 metres, with a toilet and sink. The guards told us: "You're in the Sheraton here," because usually they put about thirty people in that cell. One cannot imagine how prisoners could sleep like that.' At length, they were released, said Al-Maleh, 'after seven years in prison without having done anything illegal. Everything we did was in accordance with the law.'[6]

Endless 'Emergency'

The judicial system dealing with non-political matters draws loosely on Islamic Shari'a law (the Constitution stipulating: 'Islamic jurisprudence is a major source of legislation'), based on pre-independence Ottoman legislation and, especially, on the French legal tradition. Its structures and procedures are largely unexceptional. Civil and criminal courts – such as those operating within the Palace of Justice – are overseen by the Ministry of Justice. Defendants are presumed innocent, they may appoint their legal representatives and can confront their accusers in open court. Judgments may be appealed first to provincial appeal courts and ultimately to the Damascus-based Court of Cassation, or supreme court. A separate Administrative Court, located in the Mezzeh district of western Damascus, sits to adjudicate disputes over decisions of the country's bureaucracy. Personal and family status, including marriage and divorce, are adjudicated by religious courts serving each of Syria's religious faiths. Certain matters – marriage and inheritance, for example – are the subject of national law but are regulated through these religious courts. Generally, each religious community's customs are respected.

These conventional legal structures, however, are shadowed by a parallel and infinitely more powerful system dealing with political and security offences. At its heart is a State of Emergency which has been in effect without interruption since late 1962 and which effectively gives the regime and its security agencies *carte blanche* to behave without even a pretence of due process. The State of Emergency was originally declared by the previous regime in Legislative Decree No. 51(5) of 22 December 1962. In Military Command No. 2 of 8 March 1963 it was reissued by the Ba'thist regime the day it seized power and it was formalised the following day as Legislative Decree No. 1. This gives extraordinary powers to a presidentially appointed martial law governor (the prime minister) and his deputy (the interior minister). They may restrict freedom of movement and assembly, including the preventive arrest of anyone 'suspected of endangering public security and order'; censor letters and other communications, publications and broadcasts; seize property; and close media organs. The law lists five categories of offence: contravention of orders from the martial law governor; offences 'against the security of the state and public order'; offences 'against public authority'; offences 'which disturb public confidence'; and offences that 'constitute a general danger'.

The legality of the State of Emergency Law is questionable. It is based on Decree 51 of 22 December 1962 but this stipulated that a 'State of Emergency shall be declared by a decree from the Cabinet, presided over by the President of the Republic. It must be carried out by a majority of two-thirds and be made known to the chamber of deputies at its next meeting.' The March 1963 law, however, was promulgated as a military order. It has never been approved by the government or submitted to parliament. No less important, the State of Emergency Law plainly violates the International Covenant on Civil and Political Rights (ICCPR; see above) and it is a well-established principle that domestic legislation cannot frustrate the application of a country's international legal obligations.

Officially, the State of Emergency Law is justified in terms of the military threat from Israel. In August 2000 Syria submitted to the UN Human Rights Committee a report on its adherence to the ICCPR in which it asserted that the Emergency Law was

> an exceptional constitutional regime, based on the concept of imminent threat to the country's integrity, under which the competent authorities are empowered to take all the measures provided by law to protect the territory, territorial waters and air space of the state, in

whole or in part, from the dangers arising from external armed aggression by transferring some of the powers of the civil authorities to the military authorities.[7]

The report explained that Syria had been under 'a real threat of war by Israel' since that state's establishment in 1948 and that this 'gave rise to an exceptional situation that necessitated the rapid and extraordinary mobilisation of forces in the Syrian Arab Republic and, consequently, the promulgation of legislation to ensure the Administration's ability to act rapidly in the face of these imminent threats'. Syria ratified the ICCPR in 1969 and has been legally bound by its terms since it entered into force in 1976. The report submitted in 2000 should have been presented in 1984.

In reality, Syria's State of Emergency has little to do with the Israeli threat; rather, it is, in the words of Middle East Watch, 'the central legal mechanism and justification for the Syrian repressive system'.[8] Middle East Watch further commented: 'After twenty-eight uninterrupted years [now 40 years] of a state of emergency ... there is now an overwhelming presumption that the "emergency" is simply an excuse for the regime to suppress legitimate domestic opposition.'[9]

Special Courts

The State of Emergency Law provides for violators to be tried by military courts, and subsequent legislation has built on this. Decree No. 6 of 1 July 1965 established exceptional military courts which had even fewer safeguards for defendants and which were used mainly as arenas for political cases. The decree also created vaguely worded categories of crime including 'actions considered incompatible with the implementation of the socialist order, whether they are deeds, utterances or writing'; 'offences against the security of the state'; and 'opposing the unification of the Arab states or any of the aims of the revolution or hindering their achievement'. In March 1968 came Decree 47, replacing the exceptional military courts with a Supreme State Security Court (SSSC), to try political and security cases, and an Economic Security Court to deal with cases involving financial crimes. The decree explicitly states that the procedural rules of the new courts would not be 'confined to the usual measures' that apply to civil courts. Middle East Watch noted that 'evidence could be introduced that had no ordinary standing in law, such as hearsay or even the opinion of the prosecutor'. It added that as there were no rules of procedure 'there could never be an appeal on procedural grounds'.[10] The Economic Security Court is in the Palace of Justice. The SSSC is located a kilometre to the north, near the Basil al-Asad School on Abu Zer al-Ghifari Street, itself leading from 29th May Street, one of the city's main thoroughfares.

A further type of special court, the military field tribunal, was created by Decree No. 109 of 1968 which stated that such tribunals could be established anywhere during 'armed confrontation with an enemy'. In practice, they have been used almost exclusively to dispose of domestic enemies of the regime, notably during the repression of the armed uprising of 1976–82.

In these new types of special court, commented Middle East Watch,

> proceedings are closed and decisions unappealable. At best, legal counsel appointed by the court only goes through the motions of representing the accused. After a verdict is reached, the President is required to confirm the decision, but this step can usually be taken for granted. The President – or the minister of defence in the case of the field tribunals – appoints the judges, who are not required to have any legal training and in practice usually do not. Most are drawn from the ranks of military officers, Ba'ath party officials, and the like. The courts are therefore completely outside the ordinary judicial system. Decisions usually appear to be reached in advance by the security agencies that made the arrest. With these courts in place, summary judgment has become the order of the day.[11]

Almost incredibly, Syria's above-mentioned report to the UN Human Rights Committee in August 2000 asserted: 'In principle, the composition of the Higher State Security Court [which embraces both the Supreme State Security Court and the Economic Security Court] and the procedures that it applies do not differ from the composition and procedures of the ordinary courts empowered to hand down final judgments.'[12] The report went on to assert, equally brazenly, that 'defendants appearing before this Court enjoy the same guaranteed right of defence that they would have before the ordinary courts'.[13]

These are far from being the only occasions on which it is hard to believe that the report is actually about Syria. In a section dealing with the death penalty, for example, the report informed the UN Human Rights Committee that 'the last death sentence imposed in Syria was handed down on 2 August 1987 against Samih Fahd Awwad, who was found guilty of felonious complicity in the murder of his father. The last judgment confirming a death sentence was handed down on 6 June 1993 against the same person.'[14] The report also recorded that 'no death sentence has ever been carried out on an offender against whom a final judgment has not been handed down or before completion of the legal procedures needed to confirm its enforceability after it has become final'.[15] This from a regime which, according to Middle East Watch in 1991, has 'killed at least ten thousand of its citizens in the past twenty years'; which 'continues to kill through summary executions and violent treatment in prison'; and which 'routinely tortures prisoners and arrests and holds thousands without charge or trial'.[16] Without doubt the regime's conduct has improved significantly since early 2000, and especially since Bashar al-Asad became President in July 2000. Abuses nevertheless continue, and the structure of repression remains intact.

It might be imagined that the authorities, ever anxious to stress their commitment to the rule of law, would take care to respect the elaborate and sweeping legal pretexts they created to intimidate and silence dissenters. Not so. *Mukhabarat* officers have often made arrests without valid warrants signed by the martial law governor, as required by the State of Emergency Law. Sometimes blank warrants are used that have been signed in advance; all that needs inserting is the name of the person to be seized. Middle East Watch – reporting just over a decade ago in 1991, it must be stressed – commented then that the *mukhabarat* 'now ignore the courts altogether and do not bother even with the most perfunctory official charge and trial'.[17]

Middle East Watch (in 1991, again) graphically summed up the progress of Syria's legal system during the Ba'athist period thus: 'Through a series of steps begun under the initial State of Emergency Law and continued through decrees and administrative action, the regime moved from a modicum of legality to a total disregard for legality; from courts, to summary courts, to no courts.'[18] It was uncomfortably close to the situation in the fictitious state of Oceania in Orwell's *Nineteen Eighty-Four*, where keeping a personal diary 'was not illegal (nothing was illegal, since there were no longer any laws), but if detected it was reasonably certain that it would be punished by death, or at least by twenty-five years in a forced-labour camp';[19] and where 'the arrests invariably happened at night … In the vast majority of cases there was no trial, no report of the arrest. People simply disappeared, always during the night.'[20]

While heavily reliant on the State of Emergency Law to crush dissent in the late 1970s and early 1980s, the regime has tried to portray itself as an upholder of the rule of law, to the extent of criticising the structures it had itself created. On 27 September 1979 the Progessive National Front (PNF), which is entirely captive to the Ba'ath Party (see Chapter 5), issued a ringing declaration calling on the regime 'to apply firmly the principle of the sovereignty of law; strengthen the [independent] authority of the judiciary; respect and implement legal verdicts; and to restrict the jurisdiction of the Supreme State Security Court to crimes against the security of the state'.[21]

In his address to the Ba'ath Party's Seventh Regional Congress in January 1980 Hafiz al-Asad himself (and surely no one else could be held more responsible for the abuses) demanded 'the establishment of ordinary courts' dominance over the special courts as soon as possible'. He revealed that 'instructions have been issued to the [Supreme] State Security Court to avoid looking into any case that does not deal with security'.[22] A decade later he was making similar calls. As his personal power was absolute, one may conclude that his appeals were, to put it mildly, disingenuous. In 1990 certain categories of economic crime were transferred from the Economic Security Court to the ordinary courts but that did not mean an end to the Economic Security Court or that the Supreme State Security Court dealt only with what might reasonably be defined as cases involving national security, as opposed to regime security.

The wholesale destruction of the rule of law in Syria under the Ba'athists might have been less easy to effect had the crowning element in the court system, the Supreme Constitutional Court, had any teeth. The Constitution stipulates that this court, which rules solely on electoral disputes and the constitutionality of laws and decrees, should have five members 'of whom one will be the President, and all of whom are appointed by the President of the Republic by decree'. It sets a four-year renewable term for the court's members. Like every other entity in the country's political and administrative system, the Supreme Constitutional Court is a creature of the regime and in particular of the President.

The President's grip on the judiciary is also assured through his chairmanship of a High Judicial Council that appoints, transfers and dismisses judges. Comprising senior civil judges, the Council is charged under the Constitution with 'assisting' the President in guaranteeing the independence of the judiciary. Like so much else in Syria, it is a cross between Kafka and *Catch-22*, with doses of Márquez and Dali.

'Hafez al-Assad's personal governance has sapped the rule of law and made Assad's despotism possible,' commented Middle East Watch in its 1991 report, which remains largely valid today. 'Loyalty has become more important than legality.'[23] In a biography of Hafiz al-Asad which is not unsympathetic to the late President's foreign policy at least, the British historian of Syria Patrick Seale said much the same:

> There was no truly independent judiciary, no freedom of information, association or expression, and no autonomous university ... People longed for laws which everyone would respect, and in their absence it seemed as if, at the end of the day, the only protection lay in the Arab tradition of *wasata*, that is, having connections in high places to intervene on one's behalf.[24]

A Self-defying System

Close to the Palace of Justice is the now closed Al-Ahli Laboratory, a small medical establishment owned by two doctors. One of them, a woman, lives in Damascus. The other fled to Germany after being targeted by the *mukhabarat* because of his Islamist political beliefs. Apparently motivated by a desire to punish him, the Interior Ministry ordered the laboratory's closure and sent police to implement the instruction. The owners complained to the Administrative Court, which decisively ruled in their favour. 'In their decision, the Administrative Court nullified the Interior Ministry's closure order,' said Haitham al-Maleh, who acted for the laboratory's owners. 'This was four years ago and they continue to refuse to implement the decision of the Court, even though it has the same weight as a law.'[25]

Another of his cases involves a plot of privately owned land which the Ministry of Labour and Social Affairs has been using as a car park for decades. Some thirty years ago the land-owner informed the ministry that he wanted to build on the plot but the ministry refused to relinquish it. Although the owner obtained a court judgment in his favour, the ministry persists in holding the land. Officials at the ministry have either bought time by agreeing to consider the case and then doing nothing, or have demanded payment for complying with the court's decision. Such flagrant defiance of the law was 'normal', said Al-Maleh. 'Many lawyers have had this experience in cases against government bodies.'

The same point was made in an open letter to President Bashar al-Asad in late 2000, signed by seventy lawyers. They complained that 'court judgments are not applied by most state administrations, organisations and ministries, especially the Ministry of Defence and the Interior Ministry'. The letter – itself a remarkable display of independence in view of lawyers' past treatment by the regime (see above) – noted that decrees issued in 2000, allowing defendants charged with economic crimes to be freed on bail and granting an amnesty for a range of smuggling and currency control offences, were being flouted, even by the courts. While the Economic Security Court was allowing defendants to be freed on bail, it was demanding sums way beyond the defendants' means. The minister of justice had instructed judges at the Economic Security Court 'not to release any prisoner until he has spent several months in prison, regardless of his crime or whether his guilt had been proved', said the lawyers.

Although the penalty for changing sums of up to 100,000 Syrian Pounds on the black market had been reduced to confiscation and a fine, the Economic Security Court had 'continued to imprison those accused of such crimes', said the lawyers. They also noted that the *mukhabarat* continued to hold people for smuggling and foreign currency offences covered by the amnesty decree. It 'has not applied this law to those it detains, nor does it transfer them to the courts for trial', the letter said. 'Instead, their detention continues and is extended.' The lawyers also complained about the refusal of police and security agencies to allow detainees access to lawyers. Affirming their support for Bashar's programme to 'modernise all aspects of society, including the most important: the laws which organise and steer the movement of society', the lawyers insisted that judges and other legal personnel had a central role to play in the debate about modernising the legal system. They noted that the Ministry of Information had excluded judges from the debate by issuing a directive 'forbidding [them] from discussing any law through the media without the ministry's approval'.

Selective Prosecution

The regime also undermines respect for the law by using legislation highly selectively to destroy those it perceives as its enemies. In Syria corruption is a routine and usually tacitly accepted facet of the system. It is widely understood that modest financial irregularities often mean the difference between survival above the poverty line and real hardship. Although anti-corruption campaigns are periodically launched, these are mainly intended to appease a public that, while accepting small-scale financial improprieties, has no sympathy for the large-scale commission-taking which has grossly enriched senior regime figures. Those at the top remain untouchable, and the anti-corruption campaigns inevitably have limited results.

When the regime has decided to undermine politically significant figures, however, allegations of financial irregularity offer a convenient weapon. Laws that are normally ignored are suddenly invoked with vigour against regime targets. The classic case was that of the former prime minister, Mahmoud Zu'bi, who was arrested for alleged bribe-taking and subsequently committed suicide (see Chapter 1). It was no surprise at all that the MPs Riad Seif and Ma'moun al-Homsi, who have been jailed for their civil society movement activism, should have been accused by the authorities of tax evasion, although this was not included in the formal charges filed against them.

Another striking example of the way in which the authorities can suddenly discover a zeal for applying the law came in late 1999 when the long-running feud between Hafiz al-Asad and his younger brother Rif'at (see Chapter 1) exploded into violence with the enforced closure of an 'illegal' jetty run by Rif'at near the northern port of Lattakia. The official version was that Rif'at had ignored a series of decrees from the Transport Ministry going back to 1995 ordering the demolition of his jetty and an accompanying complex of buildings that had been established on 11,410 square metres of publicly owned land. Eventually, in October 1999, the police were sent to enforce the closure of the premises. They encountered small-arms fire and retreated. The security forces then attacked and occupied the port in an operation in which two people were killed. Later, the then information minister, Muhammad Salman, warned that Rif'at could face criminal charges if he returned to Syria. 'It was a matter of the rule of law,' an Information Ministry official told me at the time, invoking a theme that the authorities had recently started propagating in apparent deference to the rhetoric of economic liberalisation. It was never explained why, in view of this respect for the law, the illegal port had been tolerated for four years.

The truth was that Rif'at, who had returned from exile in Europe in 1992, had been raising his public profile in a way deemed by his brother to be an affront and had not taken the hint in February 1998 when he had been stripped of his (albeit empty) title of vice president for security affairs. During 1999 Rif'at had attended the funeral of Morocco's King Hassan. He had performed the *Hajj*, or pilgrimage, to Mecca and had been shown with his son Somer on television being received by Saudi notables; and Somer had paid a visit to Yasser Arafat, the head of the Palestinian Authority. A month before the Lattakia incident, Rif'at's office in central Damascus had been raided and documents listing recipients of funds had been taken away. At about the same time, Rif'at left Syria for renewed exile.

'With the presidential succession under way, Asad is working to remove all obstacles to the transfer of power to his son Bashar, and this raising of Rif'at's profile was judged to have exceeded acceptable limits,' one well-placed local observer told me in late 1999.

Corruption

Conceptual and procedural shortcomings are by no means the only problems facing Syria's judicial system. Demoralised by decades of abuse by a regime which cares nothing for the law except as a tool of repression; riddled with officials owing their positions to family contacts or political favouritism; and with a workforce suffering from low salaries, it is as prone to corruption as other parts of the system. Although 'the regular court system generally displays considerable independence in civil cases, political connections and bribery at times influence verdicts', said the US State Department in a May 2002 human rights report on Syria.[26] This was putting it mildly.

'Until the United Arab Republic [the 1958–61 union with Egypt], the Syrian judiciary was one of the cleanest, strictest, most objective judiciaries in the Middle East,' said Professor Muhammad Aziz Shukri, chairman of Damascus University's Department of International Law and one of Syria's most highly regarded legal experts. 'Now it is one of the dirtiest, most unskilled and definitely corrupted. Now you can get to the judges either through "public relations" or money.'[27] Explaining that by 'public relations' he meant 'women, drinking, friendship', he continued: 'I know of some lawyers who know nothing about law but who win all the cases. And I know that these lawyers – I'll refrain from mentioning names – receive one million Syrian Pounds [$19,230] as a down-payment. These lawyers deal with drug-trafficking, murders, conspiracies against the state … the really big, heavy cases.' Corruption existed in 'all the courts, even in the so-called military [Supreme State Security and Economic Security] courts', he said. 'The overwhelming majority of the good judges are either in retirement or they have been released from their work.'

A confidential source within the legal system told me that in the criminal and economic courts bribery affects 'between 80 and 100 per cent of cases' although bribes cannot swing verdicts in murder cases 'unless you are one of those above the law'. He added: 'Regardless of the case, the richer and more influential a person, the higher the likelihood of a bribe.' Prices are relatively well defined. 'There's a set scale of charges,' he explained. 'Prostitution: $500; smuggling: 20 per cent of the value of the smuggled goods; manslaughter: between $1,000 and $2,000; fraud: 20 per cent of the value of the theft.' Rather than take payment directly, judges use intermediaries. 'Every judge has his middleman,' said the source. Bribes are not used only to secure a favourable verdict. 'Someone has a car accident and kills an innocent bystander,' said the confidential source. 'You bribe the judge to grant bail until you reach a settlement with the victim's family.' In such a case, months might otherwise be spent in prison.

Corruption was 'relatively rare in civil cases, mainly because of the difficulty in falsifying the evidence', he continued. 'The best you can hope for [via bribery] there is to delay the issuing of a verdict against you or to extend the case's duration in court as a stalling action.'

No Change under Bashar

In his inaugural address to parliament on 17 July 2000 President Bashar al-Asad reaffirmed his commitment to 'development and modernisation' and he stressed 'the importance of the judiciary and the need to provide it with efficient and clean cadres so that it can play its full role in ensuring justice, safeguarding citizens' freedom and overseeing the implementation of laws'. Addressing the government of Muhammad Miru, which had been installed that day, Bashar on 22 December 2001 declared that 'nobody should be above the law'.[28]

Fine words, but by autumn 2002 there had been no sign of any serious moves to reform the country's legal system and in particular to annul the notorious State of Emergency Law. Instead, officials have merely reiterated the tired old pretexts for what amounts to a complete absence of legal process. At a press conference on 29 January 2001 Information Minister Adnan Omran claimed that the State of Emergency legislation was 'effectively frozen' and went on to cite the Israeli threat as the reason for its continued existence.[29] Exactly the same line had been taken earlier in Syria's report to the UN Human Rights Committee on its adherence to the International Covenant on Civil and Political Rights. 'Although the Emergency Act remains in force, in actual fact it is virtually in abeyance since it is applied only in a limited number of cases solely involving offences against the security of the State.'[30]

The essential falsity of the claim was underlined by the arrests of civil society activists in August and September 2001. While MPs Riad Seif and Ma'moun al-Homsi were charged and tried under the criminal justice system, the other eight detainees were arrested under the State of Emergency legislation and tried in the Supreme State Security Court. Commentators noted that the treatment of Seif and Al-Homsi was a break with the past, when such cases would have been handled under the State of Emergency legislation. In reality, the change was more of style than substance. 'The difference now is that they are being referred to ordinary courts instead of state security courts,' said Haitham al-Maleh. But he added that these were 'ordinary courts that they [the authorities] control and that pose no danger' to the regime.[31] Does Al-Maleh see any prospect of the Emergency Law being lifted in the near term? 'No. No. There's no possibility,' he told me. 'They [the authorities] need it. They feel that it protects them.'[32]

He was speaking in December 2001. Late the following August Al-Maleh was tipped off that the *mukhabarat* planned to 'invite' him to report to them. At once, he fled to Jordan, just before a military court issued a warrant for his arrest, and for the arrest of three other SHRA activists: Muhammad Farouk al-Homsi, Muhammad Khair Bek and Ghasoub Ali al-Mulla. The trigger was SHRA's publication without official authorisation of *Tayyarat* (*Currents*), a magazine dealing with legal aspects of human rights. The four were charged with circulating illegal publications, spreading false rumours, forming an unauthorised political association and publishing material likely to destabilise the country. Already in May 2002 Al-Maleh and Anwar al-Bunni, another lawyer helping to defend the detained civil society activists, had had their membership of the Lawyers' Association suspended for three months in retaliation for comments they had made about the trials of MPs Riad Seif and Ma'moun al-Homsi.

Quite apart from the human rights dimension, the failings of Syria's legal system have profound economic implications. Countering the civil society movement, President Bashar al-Asad asserts that the economy is his top priority and that democracy and human rights will have to wait their turn. The pro-democracy activists, however, insist that the two are inextricably linked. In particular, they warn that desperately needed foreign investors will steer clear of the country until they can trust its legal system (see Chapter 2). Strong support for this stance came in the UNDP-sponsored *Arab Human Development Report 2002*, which presented a devastating analysis of the reasons for the region's backwardness relative to other parts of the world. This affirmed that economic and human progress required 'a transparent rule of law, a visibly fair and appropriately swift legal system, and an efficient and professional judiciary'.[33]

Further endorsement of the civil society activists' position came in an editorial in April 2002 in the internet magazine *The Syria Report*. This concerned a dispute between the Egyptian firm Orascom, the operator of Syriatel, one of the country's two mobile phone licensees, and its local partner, with Orascom claiming that the local judiciary was biased towards the local partner, Rami Makhluf, son of Muhammad Makhluf, President Bashar al-Asad's maternal uncle.[34] 'The largely perceived lack of independence of the Syrian judiciary will be attracting much attention from foreign would-be investors,' said *The Syria Report*. 'Will the interests of this major company [Orascom] be preserved? Will its long-term involvement and investment be simply discarded?' Noting that eleven years after the promulgation of Law No. 10, which set out incentives for foreign investors, the share of foreign direct investment in private capital investment stood at a mere 13 per cent, the journal explained: 'The reason for that is simple, and has not much to do with investment laws and their different incentives. What foreign investors are looking for is a reformed and independent judicial system.'

Notes

1. Interview with author, Damascus, 4 December 2001.
2. Ibid.
3. Middle East Watch, *Syria Unmasked: The Suppression of Human Rights by the Asad Regime* (New Haven, CT and London: Yale University Press, 1991), p. 87.
4. Interview with author, Damascus, 4 December 2001.
5. Middle East Watch, *Syria Unmasked*, p. 161.
6. Interview with author, Damascus, 4 December 2001.
7. UN Human Rights Committee, *Consideration of Reports Submitted by States Parties under Article 40 of the Covenant. Second Periodic Report of States Parties Due in 1984. Syrian Arab Republic*, Geneva, 25 August 2000.
8. Middle East Watch, *Syria Unmasked*, p. 23.
9. Ibid., p. 24.
10. Ibid., p. 26.
11. Ibid.
12. UN Human Rights Committee, *Consideration of Reports*, paragraph 52.
13. Ibid., paragraph 54.
14. Ibid., paragraph 80.
15. Ibid., paragraph 74.
16. Middle East Watch, *Syria Unmasked*, p. 146.
17. Ibid., p. 24.

18. Ibid., p. 27.

19. George Orwell, *Nineteen Eighty-Four* (London: Penguin Books, 2000), p. 8.

20. Ibid., p. 21.

21. *Foreign Broadcast Information Service*, 29 September 1979.

22. Ibid., 7 January 1980.

23. Middle East Watch, *Syria Unmasked*, p. 29.

24. Patrick Seale, *Asad: The Struggle for Power in the Middle East* (Berkeley and Los Angeles: University of California Press, 1995), p. 458.

25. Interview with author, Damascus, 4 December 2001.

26. US Department of State, Bureau of Democracy, Human Rights, and Labor, *Country Reports on Human Rights Practices – 2001, Syria*, 4 March 2002, p. 5.

27. Interview with author, Damascus, 1 December 2001.

28. *BBC Monitoring Service*, 23 December 2001, quoting Syrian TV report of 22 December 2001.

29. *Al-Hayat*, 30 January 2001.

30. UN Human Rights Committee, *Consideration of Reports*, paragraph 55.

31. 'Reforms Continue in Syria', *Las Vegas Sun*, 23 January 2002.

32. Interview with author, Damascus, 4 December 2001.

33. UNDP, *The Arab Human Development Report 2002* (UNDP: New York, July 2002).

34. 'The Independence of the Judiciary, a Prerequisite for Foreign Investments', *The Syria Report*, 17 April 2002.

CHAPTER 7

'Balanced, Objective and Ethical': The Media

§ 'THE new media law legalises martial law – and that's all it does,' declared journalist and human rights activist Nizar Nayyouf shortly after his release from prison.[1] 'While the authorities may now allow articles which are slightly more free than before, journalists will be repressed if they cross the red lines.' The law was so loosely worded, he added, that it 'allows the authorities to do anything they want'.

Nayyouf was referring to Decree No. 50, promulgated by President Bashar al-Asad on 22 September 2001, just when the *mukhabarat* were rounding up leading civil society activists. The new press law, hailed by the authorities as a sign of liberalisation, permits privately owned newspapers but subjects all publications to such draconian regulation as to allow the authorities total control. Threatening punishments ranging from fines to three years' imprisonment, the law bans the publication of articles and reports about 'national security, national unity, details of the security and safety of the army, its movements, weapons, supplies, equipment and camps'; 'details of secret trials'; 'books, correspondence, articles, reports, pictures and news affecting the right to privacy'; and 'details of cases of libel, defamation, slander or calumny'.

Covering publishers, printers, distributors and retailers, the law forbids the publication of 'falsehoods' and 'fabricated reports', and it stipulates that the heaviest penalties should apply where 'such acts have been committed by reason of ill-will, or caused public unrest, or harm to international relations, offence to state dignity, national unity, the morale of the army and the armed forces, or caused some damage to the national economy and the currency'. The decree prohibits the publication of 'propaganda' financed 'directly or indirectly' by foreign countries, companies or foundations. All periodicals – including those of 'legally established political parties' – must obtain licences to publish from the prime minister, who may refuse an application 'for reasons he deems to be related to the public interest'. Publications 'calling for a change in the Constitution by unconstitutional means' will be closed down.

Nayyouf knows very well how the regime acts when it feels that 'falsehoods' have been published. A journalist from the coastal city of Lattakia who contributed to Jordanian, Lebanese and Palestinian publications, he was released on 6 May 2001 after nine years in prison for 'disseminating false information', 'membership of an illegal organisation' and 'receiving money from abroad'. His real 'crimes' had been to help found the Committees for the Defence of Democratic Freedoms and Human Rights (CDF) and to edit their monthly newsletter *Sawt ad-Dimuqratiyya* (*Voice of Democracy*). The authorities had been particularly incensed by a CDF leaflet distributed in December 1991 which had criticised irregularities in President Hafiz al-Asad's 're-election' for a fourth seven-year term earlier that month. As usual, the President had won 99 per cent approval on a 99 per cent turnout of eligible voters. Nayyouf was arrested in January 1992 as part of a country-wide crackdown on the CDF. He and seventeen other CDF activists were tried by the Supreme State Security Court in February and March 1992. Nayyouf was sentenced to ten years' imprisonment with hard labour.

Nizar Nayyouf's Ordeal

During his incarceration Nayyouf was tortured horribly – and then denied medical treatment for his injuries. A speciality was the 'German chair' torture, involving a metal chair with moving parts that is used to hyper-extend the victim's spine and places severe pressure on the neck and limbs. On his release he could walk only with crutches. A few weeks later, the UN Committee on Economic, Social and Cultural Rights was being told by a Syrian delegation that 'clinics, hospitals and dispensaries existed in prisons and any prisoner was provided with health care free of charge' and that 'a prisoner could visit a specialist if needed and could also be operated on free of charge'.[2]

While in prison, Nayyouf won UNESCO's World Press Freedom prize and other prestigious awards. His release followed repeated protests from human rights and media organisations world-wide, culminating in an intervention by Pope John Paul II. During his highly publicised visit to Damascus in early May 2001, he passed to President Bashar al-Asad a plea for Nayyouf's release from the French campaigning organisation Reporters sans Frontières (RSF). According to Nayyouf, on 20 June – the day before a press conference at which he planned to highlight *mukhabarat* atrocities – he was seized by plain-clothed security agents in Damascus while on his way for medical treatment. 'They tried using enticement and threats against me,' he told the Qatar-based *Al-Jazeera* satellite television station. 'At first they tried to tempt me with incredible financial offers in return for keeping silent on all that I knew. When they failed, they resorted to threats.' He was warned: 'We will cut off your tongue and feed it to the dogs.'[3]

The official Syrian Arab News Agency (SANA) insisted that Nayyouf had faked his detention in order 'to remain in the centre of attention and under the spotlight'.[4] At the invitation of RSF, Nayyouf arrived in Paris on 15 July for treatment at the Pitié-Salpêtrière Hospital. Undaunted, he held a press conference the following day and gave a series of interviews detailing his experiences. In retaliation, the Syrian authorities in early September issued a warrant for his arrest on charges of 'seeking to change the Constitution by illegal means', 'issuing false reports from a foreign country' and 'incitement to inter-religious strife'. 'I wanted to return to Syria,' Nayyouf told me, 'but my friends stopped me. They even hid my passport to stop me travelling back.'[5]

Like many of Syria's laws, the new press law is buttressed by other legislation. The 1963 Emergency Law (see Chapter 6) lists a comprehensive array of offences 'against the security of the state and public order', 'against public authority', 'which disturb public confidence' and 'which constitute a general danger', all of which can be invoked to justify the repression of writers and publications. Legislative Decree No. 6 of 1965 outlaws 'acts which are considered contrary to the implementation of the socialist system in the state, whether they take place by action, speaking or writing or by any other means of expression or publication'. The same decree outlaws 'opposition to or obstruction of any of the aims of the revolution … by publication of false information with the intention of creating a state of chaos and shaking the confidence of the masses in the aims of the revolution'.

All this is apparently unknown to Syria's delegates to the Geneva-based UN Human Rights Committee, which in early 2001 was considering Syria's compliance (or lack of it) with the International Covenant on Civil and Political Rights that was ratified by Syria in 1969 and has been in legal effect since 1976. Damascus had been required to submit a progress report in 1984 but did so only in 2000 – a seventeen-year delay. Answering questions about the report, Abboud Sarraj, Dean of the Faculty of Law at Damascus University, asserted that 'conscience was the only restriction' on freedom of expression in Syria. 'No restrictions were imposed on journalists, even during the state of emergency' (which has lasted without interruption since 1963), he told the Human Rights Committee. For good measure, he added that 'radio and television had full freedom of expression'.[6]

The Preamble of the 1973 Constitution declares that 'freedom is a sacred right', while the Ba'ath Party's own Constitution, dating from 1947, affirms that 'freedom of speech, of association, of belief and of science are sacred and may not be limited by any government whatsoever'. Somewhat more honestly, if menacingly, another clause of the Ba'ath's Constitution asserts: 'The state will be responsible for protecting the freedoms of speech, publishing, association, protest and of the press *within the limits of the higher interest of the Arab nation*' (my italics). From the regime's viewpoint, this all makes a certain sense. If the Ba'ath Party is in power and represents all the people and is the embodiment of Arabism and the nation's 'higher interests', then plainly it must stand above any criticism; which could, by definition, only come from traitors not worthy of the normal freedoms.

The Media in the Ba'athist Era

Between independence in 1946 and the Ba'athist coup in March 1963 Syria enjoyed a lively media, albeit one that was censored after military coups and during the 1958–61 union with Egypt. The only title that survives today is *Al-Ba'ath* (*Renaissance*), the official organ of the Ba'ath Party, which was founded in 1946. On seizing power in 1963 the Ba'athists closed all independent journals. Apart from *Al-Ba'ath*, the only national daily in the early years of Ba'athist rule was *Ath-Thawra* (*The Revolution*), which was published by the state-owned Al-Wahda (Unity) Press, Printing and Publishing Establishment. *Ath-Thawra* originally had been launched as *Al-Wahda* (*Unity*) in 1958 by Al-Wahda Press. In mid-1963 this organisation was transferred to the Information Ministry and the daily was relaunched under its new name with the mission of publishing material that would 'promote national socialist awareness among the masses in all Arab countries'.

Today, the Wahda Establishment, headquartered in a gaunt office block on a busy roundabout in the Kafr Sousa district of Damascus, near the headquarters of the much-feared General Intelligence

Directorate, also publishes local papers for Aleppo (*Al-Jamahir al-'Arabiya – The Arab Masses*); Lattakia (*Al-Wahda – Unity*); Homs (*Al-'Uruba – Arabism*); and Hama (*Al-Fida' – Sacrifice*). In addition, it publishes a weekly cultural supplement to *Ath-Thawra* and a weekly sports journal, *Al-Mawqif ar-Riyadi* (*The Sporting Situation*). The Wahda Establishment employs 1,300 people. Of these, 400 are journalists, of whom 250–300 work for *Ath-Thawra*. *Al-Ba'ath* and *Ath-Thawra* were joined in 1975 by *Tishreen* (*October*, after the October 1973 Arab–Israeli war), published by the state-owned Tishreen Organisation for Press and Publishing which was created by presidential decree in 1975 because of the urgent need to 'struggle against imperialism and Zionism'. In mid-2000 *Tishreen*'s daily circulation was about 60,000.[7] Also published by the Tishreen Organisation is Syria's only foreign-language daily, the *Syria Times*, which has a daily circulation of 5,000.[8]

These publications tend to cover much the same stories, centred on the utterances and activities of the President and other leading regime figures. The main foreign story for years has been the Arab–Israeli struggle. This uniformity reflects the heavy reliance of all the state newspapers on the Syrian Arab News Agency (SANA). Created in June 1965, SANA now has a staff of 370, including 200 journalists, and maintains bureaux in sixteen cities abroad. The SANA internet site asserts that the agency 'precisely covers local, Arab as well as international news from their different sources in a balanced, objective and ethical way'. It is an outrageous claim from what is in reality a propaganda organisation charged with singing the regime's praises. Syria's state-controlled broadcasting services, overseen by the Directorate-General of Radio and Television, are no less propagandist and are treated with disdain by ordinary Syrians. They rely instead on foreign satellite broadcasts (see below).

Despite the web of mutually reinforcing prohibitions and the best efforts of the *mukhabarat*, Syria has a long tradition of underground publishing. 'Seditious' journals continue to circulate clandestinely from hand-to-hand, echoing the old Soviet Bloc's *samizdat* publications. A good example is *Ar-Rai'* (*Opinion*), the journal of the illegal Syrian Communist Party – Political Bureau (SCP – Political Bureau) faction, headed by Riad at-Turk, which split from the SCP in 1972 over the latter's decision to join Hafiz al-Asad's Progressive National Front (PNF). Although Kurds form about 9 per cent of the population, Kurdish-language publications and broadcasts are outlawed; this has not prevented the circulation of Kurdish publications.

Syria's entire media system is closely overseen by the Ministry of

Information. The minister is, for example, chairman of both the Tishreen Organisation and SANA. In the realms of theatre productions, films and books, the Ministry of Culture and National Guidance has the same combined role as publisher and censor as that of the Information Ministry in the media field. Both ministries, but especially the Information Ministry, are closely supervised by the presidency 'since information policies are part of the President's main concerns'.[9]

Self-censorship by Journalists

In Syria, journalists like Nizar Nayyouf are very much the exception. The great majority take care not to cross the 'red lines'. The country's media are almost all state-owned, and their journalists are thus state employees. Loath to risk their jobs or otherwise jeopardise their careers, they prefer self-censorship. As the prestigious anti-censorship organisation Article 19 noted: 'Even state-employed journalists weigh every word carefully before submitting their pieces and, even then, take the further precaution of consulting close friends or family members as well.'[10] Middle East Watch, a division of Human Rights Watch, has noted that 'a Syrian journalist is simply not expected to have a personal opinion'.[11]

Fuad Mardood, editor of the *Syria Times*, made the point succinctly, if unintentionally, when I asked him if any of his writers had ever attacked the regime. 'I cannot imagine that there's anyone in Syria who wants to attack our policy,' he replied, adding: 'You can find people who have personal motives who may attack the system, but it's only to achieve personal goals.'[12] Muhammad Khair al-Wadei, then editor of *Tishreen*, confirmed that his paper, too, firmly supported the regime. 'We are not calling for a change of the system,' he agreed.[13] Al-Wadei said that *Tishreen*'s aims included 'explaining Syrian policy', 'creating unity within Syria and the Arab states' and 'deterring Israel's aggressive policy and encouraging the peace process'. He insisted, however, that it was also his paper's job 'to keep an eye on government organisations in Syria' and 'to criticise anything that's wrong'.

In January 2000 businessman and independent member of parliament Riad Seif, who would later be imprisoned for his activism in the civil society movement, was able to publish a letter in *Tishreen* describing the private sector as 'afraid, confused, shackled and unable to perform its proper role in the development process' because of inadequacies in the legal system and the absence of a proper investment framework. The state-owned banking system, he wrote, was unable to support trade and had been reduced to 'a channel for providing loans to those who don't deserve them'.[14] Such criticism in the economic and financial fields has been permitted only since the late 1980s, with the launch of Syria's latest economic *infitah*, or 'opening'. Before then, as Volker Perthes noted, the term businessman (*rajul a'mal*) was not used in the Syrian media and 'it was not uncommon to speak of the parasitic bourgeoisie. Rarely were parts of the bourgeoisie referred to in a positive fashion. By 1988, however, Syria's newspapers had started to mention businessmen by name, in a positive context, by 1990 to interview them and occasionally publish their photographs.'[15]

By early 2000, as the political atmosphere lightened (see Chapter 2), the frontiers of criticism had extended into the political realm, albeit only a short way. Even abuses by the *mukhabarat* could be exposed, said Al-Wadei, referring to a full-page exposé he ran in spring 2000 about an incident in Aleppo in which a man had been detained by security officers and beaten to death. 'We criticised this and the government responded,' said Al-Wadei. 'All those responsible were arrested.' On 1 July 2000 – less than a month after Hafiz al-Asad's death and before Bashar had officially taken office – *Tishreen* carried a careful, coded call for greater democracy. In a top corner of the back page of that day's issue appeared a small opinion piece on democracy, by Walid Ma'amari. The author cited the hypothetical example of a headmaster who took complete control of his school 'while it would have been better for him to have shared it with an administrative board which took decisions by majority'. Earlier, the writer noted that democracy could be applied from 'the lowest unit of society's hierarchy – the family – to the highest'; and that the example of the headmaster 'can be applied to any company or organisation'.

Syrian editors understand the limits. If they have criticised specific cases of mismanagement or corruption it is because those running the system have permitted it. Criticism of the presidency or fundamentals of the system have been taboo. The populace understands well that corruption and inefficiency are endemic to the system and they cannot take too seriously media exposés of low-level misconduct. As Article 19 has observed: 'Government appointees berated in newspaper columns for waste or neglect can only be scapegoats, as they have no scope for personal initiative and simply follow orders issued by heads of the security forces and the Ba'ath Party.'[16] The same point has been well made by Hans Günter Löbmeyer:

> Anybody who dares to allot responsibility for major corruption to the Asad regime or to hint at the involvement of high-ranking officials can expect an invitation to see the *mukhabarat*. The same applies to criticism of foreign and internal policies, the security apparatus, the predominance of Alawis in the power centres, or permanent violation of human rights, to say nothing of Asad being in power. All the subjects are strictly banned from public debate.[17]

As might be expected in such a context, what does get printed is almost always extraordinarily bland. 'People's Support for President's Nomination Unlimited', was one of the front-page stories in the *Syria Times* on 10 February 1999. It revealed that the then Local Administration Minister Yehya Abou Asali had 'stressed that nominating President Asad for a new constitutional term confirms the Syrian people's support for the wise and brave leadership of President Asad and their continuous readiness to scarify [*sic* – i.e. 'sacrifice'] to consolidate Syria's steadfastness'. On 26 November 2001 the same paper's lead story was headed 'Gratitude, Appreciation Cable to President'. This disclosed that Bashar al-Asad had 'received a cable of greeting and appreciation sent by the Secretary General of the Syrian Communist Party on the occasion of the Party's 9th conference'. It further revealed that 'the cable extended to the President most sincere greetings of appreciation for the great role he plays in enhancing the country's position in the Arab and international arenas, expressing determination of Syrian communists to continue making efforts to meet the requirements of the people's interests and those of the Arab nation and world peace'. *Tishreen* on 1 July 2000 informed its readers in a headline on page 3 that 'General Dr Bashar al-Asad is the Shining Future and his Election is a Continuation of the Path of the Late Leader'. On the same day – nine days before the plebiscite in which Bashar al-Asad was confirmed as President – *Ath-Thawra*'s page 3 carried a story headed: 'Yes to the Lion Cub [i.e. Bashar, whose family name means *lion* in Arabic], Progeny of the Family of Struggle, Dignity and Arabism'.

Sometimes, despite their best efforts to comply with the system's demands, editors make mistakes, which can be tragi-comic. One editor was questioned after printing a photo of Hafiz al-Asad in which he appeared short and pot-bellied, even though the photo had been issued by the presidential press office.[18] More absurd still, another editor was targeted because of a typographical error. He had intended to describe Hafiz al-Asad as a *batal,* or 'hero', but two letters were transposed and the Syrian leader was instead dubbed a *tabal*, meaning 'dolt' or 'windbag' in colloquial usage. Air Force Intelligence interrogated the unfortunate editor for a week.[19]

Bashar and the Press

In the months before Hafiz al-Asad's death in June 2000 the limits of economic policy debate in the media widened noticeably and even some guarded discussion of political issues was countenanced. With Bashar's succession to the presidency in July 2000 the debate expanded further to include the civil society movement and related issues of democracy and human rights. In his inaugural address to parliament on 17 July 2000 he affirmed that Syria's 'educational, cultural and media institutions must be reformed and modernised' although he added the telling proviso that this should be done 'in a manner that serves our national and pan-Arab issues, strengthens our genuine heritage, renounces the mentality of introversion and negativity and treats the social problems that negatively affect the unity and security of society'.

Shortly after taking office Bashar underlined his desire for change by replacing the heads of Syrian radio and television and of the three main dailies, *Ath-Thawra*, *Al-Ba'ath* and *Tishreen*. The ex-editor of *Tishreen*, Muhammad Khair al-Wadei, was appointed ambassador to China. *Al-Ba'ath*'s ex-editor, Turki Saqr, became ambassador to Iran. *Tishreen*'s ex-editor, Amid Khouri, retired. At the same time, tentative steps were taken to expand the range of media outlets. Syria's first privately owned newspapers, *Ad-Dommari* (*The Lamplighter*) and *Al-Iqtisadiya* (*Economy*), both weeklies, were launched respectively in February and June 2001. By early December that year fourteen applications for licences to publish privately owned journals were pending. They included two political publications, *Al-Qabbas* and *Ash-Sham*. An application had also been submitted for a private satellite television channel.[20] In January 2002 the government approved in principle the establishment of privately owned radio stations, although stipulating that they would not be permitted to broadcast news or political items.

In November 2000 the Ba'ath Party had resolved that the six other legally authorised member parties of the Progressive National Front (PNF) should be allowed to print their own newspapers. Previously, they had been allowed to distribute their journals only privately, and not through news-stands. The first to appear, in January 2001, was *Sawt ash-Sha'ab* (*Voice of the People*), the twice-monthly organ of the Syrian Communist Party headed by Wisal Farha Bakdash (SCP–

Bakdash). February saw the launch of the weekly *Al-Wahdawi* (*The Unionist*) by Safwan Qudsi's Arab Socialist Union (ASU). In May the other Syrian Communist Party in the PNF, headed by Yousef Faisal (SCP–Faisal), started publishing *An-Nour* (*The Light*). That was followed by *Al-'Arabi al-Ishtiraki* (*Socialist Arab*), the monthly organ of Mustafa Hamdoun's Arab Socialists.

An-Nour's first issue was typical of the new journals. As well as reports on the Palestinian uprising, or *intifada*, there was an exposé of poverty in some districts of Damascus while another article highlighted the parlous state of the national economy, declaring: 'We must recognise that the state's economic policy is responsible for the situation.' By Syria's past standards, such material was bold indeed.

Ad-Dommari

The 28 February 2001 launch of *Ad-Dommari* – the first privately owned newspaper since the 1963 Ba'athist coup – was a landmark. Owned by Ali Farzat, one of the Arab world's leading cartoonists, the weekly satirical journal was initially highly successful, despite selling at 25 Syrian Pounds – five times the price of the four official dailies. 'There were two editions of the first issue, each of 75,000 copies,' said Farzat in April 2001.[21] 'But we distributed only 75,000 copies because of printing and other errors. Since then, we've fixed our weekly print-run at 75,000.'

The broadsheet paper of twenty-plus pages, heavily illustrated with cartoons by Farzat, is based in a modest apartment behind a doctor's surgery on Pakistan Street in the Sabi' Bahrat ('Seven Ponds') district near the north-east wall of the Old City. Until he left to resume his work in the Gulf, the editor-in-chief was Ali's brother, Adnan, who presided over a twenty-strong team of journalists plus ten administrative and support staff. 'I had the idea for this newspaper ten years ago, and the recent changes helped to realise it,' said Ali Farzat, a genial, bearded figure from the central city of Hama who exudes enthusiasm. He explained: 'By "changes" I mean there is a greater possibility for expression.'

Ad-Dommari targets mismanagement, inefficiency and waste. Typical was a story on 30 April 2001 about conditions in the 'Adra civil prison, in the Damascus satellite town of Duma. 'They Transformed it into a Five-star Prison because they Knew about our Visit,' the headline blared. 'We found that inside there's one prison for the poor and another for the rich,' Ali told me. 'The more you pay, the more comfortable is your stay.' The same issue carried a story about paedophilia in Syria – a taboo subject for the mainstream press. 'Children in the Mouth of Human Wolves,' the report was headlined. It argued that paedophiles needed treatment and asserted that academic institutions were obstructing studies of the problem.

The paper certainly has had an impact. Ministers and members of parliament regularly telephone or visit to complain. 'This makes me happy but unfortunately my office isn't big enough for all of them,' Farzat smiled. *Ad-Dommari* is nevertheless careful not to cross the 'red lines' of Syrian journalism. Civil society activists criticise the paper for focusing on symptoms while ignoring the underlying disease and claim that this lies behind a steady drop in its sales. For his part, Farzat shows no enthusiasm for the civil society activists and uses depressingly familiar arguments against them. They were 'trying to pull the people towards imported ideologies far from the spirit of our country and the soul of our people', he said. They were going too far, too fast. They 'want to put the horse behind the carriage and not before it', he asserted. 'We believe in developing the [existing] institutions to develop civil society, and not the opposite.' The activists wanted rapid change 'because their aim is not civil society' but 'political positions'. Farzat insisted: 'I don't work in politics. I work with national feeling – the feeling of belonging to your homeland, outside the ideological realm.'

If *Ad-Dommari* wanted to leave the Syrian system alone, its wish was not reciprocated. Initially the paper was sold through private channels. After the tenth issue, however, the authorities insisted that it should be distributed through the state's General Establishment for Printing and Publishing, which charged 40 per cent of the cover price for its services, and that advertisements should be arranged via the state advertising company, which charged 27.5 per cent of gross advertising revenues. 'They mess our distribution up,' complained Ali Farzat in late 2001. 'We hear about copies not arriving at many outlets. They are slack.'[22]

Despite Farzat's caution, *Ad-Dommari* also felt the censor's knife. On 17 June 2001 the paper appeared with two pages blank but for cartoons. They should have carried an article critical of the government's performance and another on an imminent cabinet reshuffle. Prime Minister Muhammad Miru took offence, claiming that the articles amounted to a personal attack on him, and ordered the cut, with the support of Information Minister Adnan Omran. The instruction to cut the two articles came after printing had started. Thousands of copies could not be distributed and the affair cost the newspaper about $4,000. Ironically, the articles, which did not carry by-lines, had been penned by Ayman 'Abd an-Nur, one of President Asad's close advisers.

In the second half of 2001 the paper was also hit by resignations of key staff members, including the editor-in-chief, Adnan Farzat. There was grumbling that *Ad-Dommari* had lost its early cutting edge and was instead offering satire for satire's sake. Certainly it lost its novelty value as the months passed. By the year's end, circulation had fallen to only about 15,000. On 22 January 2002, less than a year after its launch, Ali Farzat announced the suspension of publication, claiming that continued enforced use of the costly and inefficient state distribution system and of the state advertising company would lead to unsustainable losses. The suspension lasted only three weeks but it underlined the extent to which the initial dreams had faded.

Ath-Thawra

Despite its credentials as a pillar of the regime in a state where there has been no distinction between the media and the system, *Ath-Thawra* was a key platform for the civil society movement. At first sight the late Mahmoud Salameh, appointed as editor-in-chief by the President just weeks after Bashar took office, was an unlikely choice for such a sensitive job. Although he had written three novels, Salameh, a former member of parliament, had spent most of his career working his way up Syria's trade union hierarchy, ending as economic affairs secretary to the General Federation of Trade Unions. He then moved to become permanent secretary of a committee formed to advise Hafiz al-Asad on economic and administrative reform. Not only had he not been a journalist, he had not even been a member of the Ba'ath Party. 'I was a member of the [Nasserist] Arab Nationalist Movement,' he told me. 'But now I'm independent.'[23]

On assuming the editorship, Salameh contacted the leading figures of the civil society movement, which was then gaining momentum, and offered to carry articles from them. Michel Kilo, for example, wrote a double-page feature for *Ath-Thawra*; Arif Dalila published a series of articles in the paper. 'Ours was the only newspaper that opened a dialogue about civil society,' said Salameh, with evident pride. 'Syrian, Lebanese and some Moroccan intellectuals participated – hot discussions about civil society and the prospects for its development.'

Like other Syrian dailies, meanwhile, *Ath-Thawra* also highlights specific instances of malpractice or maladministration. 'We have a daily page entitled "public surveillance",' Salameh explained. 'We receive complaints and publish them. And opposite them we publish the official responses. We are neither judges nor inspectors.' Like all other Syrian editors, however, Salameh understood that there were limits: 'We don't accept everything. There are three areas that must not be touched: the fundamentals of the political system; national unity; and national security. Apart from these, everything is allowed.'

How closely did the information minister monitor his editorial decisions? 'It's a relationship of co-ordination and political supervision. We discuss strategic matters with the minister but our day-to-day activities are independent.' Sometimes opinions differed sharply. 'Discussions may occur, and even heated ones,' said Salameh. With one eye on the anti-civil society current which by then was strengthening, he opined that 'the civil society forums exceeded what is related to the concept of civil society and started presenting issues that are more akin to the issues of a political party'. He noted that Riad Seif (whom he described warmly as 'my friend') had himself announced plans for a political party. Seif 'knows that there is a big difference between the activity of political parties and that of clubs talking about civil society'.

He was speaking in May 2001, when the regime 'old guard' had already started its campaign to check the civil society movement (see Chapter 3). Just three days after I met him in his busy editorial office, Salameh was ousted from his post and appointed head of research in the cabinet office. In a glowing tribute in the Beirut daily *An-Nahar*, Michel Kilo noted that Salameh 'believed that intellectuals constituted a force that could help Syria emerge from its dilemma – a force for dialogue and compromise that could mobilise significant sectors of the middle class behind a programme for change'. He had 'met from the beginning with a grumbling resistance' especially 'in the (Ba'ath) Party and the Ministry of Information'. Despite all the obstacles, Kilo continued, Salameh's 'original vision, to develop *Ath-Thawra* into a tool for dialogue between the state and society, distinct from Syria's other official papers *Al-Ba'ath* and *Tishreen*, crystallised more with each passing day'. As a result, sales had increased and the paper's editorials had attracted wide interest 'especially the one following the [early 2001] government campaign against intellectuals in which he said that Syria had chosen reform as its destiny and that there was no turning back'. Salameh's dismissal suggested that 'the anticipated process of change still has not started – or that, if it has, it had started so weak that it could not protect its few supporters in the Party and in the government'.[24]

Mahmoud Salameh died of natural causes shortly after his ouster from *Ath-Thawra*. Under its new editor, Khalaf al-Jarad, the paper has reverted to its old stock-in-trade, memorably described by Joel Campagna, senior programme co-ordinator for the Middle East and North Africa at the US-based Committee to Protect Journalists (CPJ), as 'fawning coverage of the President, numbing stories about the activities of government ministers and vociferous criticism of Israel'.[25]

The Technology Revolution

For authoritarian regimes like Syria's, the advent of satellite television and the internet has been a nightmare. Bans on TV receiver dishes and the control of internet access are notoriously difficult to enforce. But the real issue is *control* itself, rather than preventing 'negative' information reaching the public. Syria is a small country with large families and nothing of significance evades notice and comment. Despite the censors and the secret police, Syrians are well-informed about internal affairs and can rely on foreign radio broadcasts for information about world affairs. In the mid-1990s two-thirds of the weekly radio audience listened to foreign stations – far more than those who listened to local state-run services.[26]

The regime's dogged insistence on censorship of domestic news outlets is in essence much the same as its requirement for 99.9 per cent approval rates in presidential plebiscites and its stage-managed pro-regime street demonstrations by 'the popular masses'. No one in Syria or anywhere else is fooled, but that's not the point. What *really* matters about such absurdities is that they are an expression of regime power. That said, over the years only sporadic and half-hearted attempts have been made to jam foreign broadcasts, none of them since Bashar took office. Arabic-language satellite television services – and notably the Qatar-based *Al-Jazeera* station, which is renowned for its objective current affairs coverage – have become a major source of news for Syrians. While the state-controlled media largely ignored the civil society movement in 2000–2001, *Al-Jazeera* carried extensive reports that undoubtedly hastened the movement's rapid spread from Damascus to the rest of the country. Initially, as satellite TV stations proliferated world-wide, the authorities sought to dissuade people from installing dishes. In November 1994, for example, the then prime minister, Mahmoud Zu'bi, warned that there would be 'no future' for those doing so.[27] This was no surprise in a state whose near obsession with controlling information had included a ban on the import of fax machines that was lifted only in 1993. Despite official misgivings, at least one-third of Syrian homes can now receive satellite TV although regulations governing the import of receiver dishes were not officially approved until July 2000. In his 8 February 2001 interview with the London-based pan-Arab daily *Ash-Sharq al-Awsat*, Bashar al-Asad insisted that 'the presence of open media [such as satellite TV] does not mean that things are out of the Information Ministry's control'. Rather, it was 'clear evidence that the state wants citizens to be informed'. He explained that, had the state not been so benevolent, 'it would have banned all satellite dishes, which would not be difficult for the state to do'. The true explanation may be somewhat less prosaic, albeit unsurprising in a system so riddled with corruption. The anti-censorship group Article 19 has noted that the authorities tolerated the spread of dishes 'for reasons widely assumed to relate to the profits earned by well-connected individuals from the sale of satellite equipment'.[28]

The obsession with control has also slowed the development of internet and e-communications services. A pilot internet project was implemented by the state-run Syrian Telecommunications Establishment (STE) in early 1997 but was limited to 150 subscribers from ministries and other state organisations. This was followed by an interim project that allowed connections only by public and private sector businesses and by professionals such as doctors and engineers. Work started in 1998 and the project was completed a year later. As of mid-2000 full public internet access was available only at a series of STE 'internet cafés'. The first to be established were in the Muhajirin district on the slopes of Jabal Qasioun, the mountain which dominates the Syrian capital; on Nasser Street, near the shabby terminal of the Hejaz railway, the line which never recovered from T. E. Lawrence's First World War exploits; in the Asad National Library, a bunker-like Ministry of Culture edifice overlooking Ommayad Square, the latter named after Islam's first dynasty which ruled from Damascus; at STE's Damascus headquarters; and in the transit and arrivals halls of Damascus International airport.

'Already we have 5,000 internet and e-mail subscribers,' said Ghatfan Kandel, system administrator for the pilot internet project, in mid-2000. He added: 'Demand is very, very strong.'[29] The use of passwords meant that users outnumbered subscribers by far. One estimate put the number at 20,000 in 2000.[30] The STE has since opened internet cafés in Aleppo and other cities but the spread of unofficial cafés has been far more rapid. In January 2002 Telecommunications Minister Muhammad Bashir al-Munajid disclosed plans to license these unofficial establishments.[31] After taking office Bashar al-Asad (a former head of the Syrian Computer Society) declared that there would be 200,000 new internet connections by 2001. The STE charges subscribers an initial one-off fee of 5,000 Syrian pounds ($100) plus a monthly fee of 1,000 Syrian Pounds ($20) and a connection fee of one Syrian Pound ($0.02) per minute: way beyond the means of most Syrians. In mid-2002 a project had been launched to provide internet access in rural areas by means of a specially equipped fleet of buses, one for each of Syria's fourteen governorates. The scheme was being implemented by the Fund for the Integrated Rural Development of Syria (FIRDOS), which is headed by Bashar's wife, Asma al-Akhras. Technical advice was being provided by the Children of the Web, a French non-governmental organisation devoted to extending internet use.[32]

Internet access is carefully monitored and websites deemed undesirable for moral or political reasons are censored. Surfers can gain unfettered access only by dialling to service providers in neighbouring Lebanon or Jordan. If discovered, however, they are fined and have their phones disconnected. Foreign diplomats are not spared. In 1999–2000 the telephone lines of several European embassies and the residence of a US diplomat were cut, apparently because they had been used for internet access outside the sole approved channel. The fate of those who transgress the rules was highlighted in December 2000 when the wife of a prominent and well-connected Aleppo businessman received by e-mail a cartoon showing a donkey, with the Syrian President's head, buggering another donkey with the head of the Lebanese President, Emile Lahoud. The recipient (who shall remain nameless to spare her unnecessary embarrassment, but who will be known to all who followed the story) was sufficiently amused by this astute comment on Syria's relationship with its western neighbour to forward the message to friends in Damascus. Regrettably, one of them informed on her to the authorities. She was promptly arrested by the *mukhabarat* and remained in jail for nine months in deplorable and deliberately humiliating conditions. The episode, coming just as regime hardliners were counter-attacking the civil society movement, is thought to have been used by the conservatives to denigrate Bashar al-Asad's relative liberalism. 'The security people went to the President and said: "Look what you have done, by allowing e-mail,"' said a Brussels-based European Commission official familiar with Syrian affairs. 'I think Bashar was embarrassed but (a) it happened and (b) I think the old guard is using it.'[33]

The offending cartoon was certainly more entertaining, perhaps even more enlightening in its way, than most official websites. Take, for example, that of the Ministry of Economy and Foreign Trade in 2001. An introductory page by the then minister, Muhammad Imady, declared that the ministry 'will remain loyal to the special and distinguished strategy planned by our immortal leader President Hafez al-Assad. As such, the Ministry will keep on upholding the principles, basics and the socio-economic achievements brought about under his leadership.' Or one may visit www.assad.org, which is dedicated to 'the immortal leader'. There he is, smiling benevolently from the computer screen. 'Good bye', says a caption. 'Thank you for leaving Syria in good hands … Your Spirit will remain in all of us forever.' Somewhat superfluously, it is explained: 'This Site is designed as a tribute to the legacy of the Late President Hafez Assad.' Pride of place should perhaps go to the Ministry of Information which, like all state institutions in Ba'athist Syria, is heavily overstaffed by underskilled staff, a defect which shows in sometimes bizarre ways. A visit to the ministry's website on 3 November 2001 offered, *inter alia,* the weather forecast for 5 October. Subsequent checks in January 2002 proved fruitless as the ministry website did not work at all.

The Information Ministry is housed in what must be one of the ugliest buildings in Damascus. It occupies the upper floors of the *Dar al-Ba'ath,* (Ba'ath Publishing House), a squat, bland office block a few kilometres from the city centre along the Mezzeh *Autostrade* that also houses the party daily *Al-Ba'ath*. The building's cheap tiled façades were recently refurbished after years in which no effort had been made to hide the results of a 1980s bomb attack. A concrete-block barrier in the road now offers protection from car-bombers. The poor quality of construction and the lack of maintenance are evident throughout the building. One or more of the three central lifts is always dysfunctional. Windows are caked with sandy dust. Lethargic officials sit behind desks piled high with paperwork and old newspapers. Much time is spent chatting and drinking tea as there's no incentive to do more than the absolute minimum of work. Computer screens are a rare sight. All the talk of 'progress' and 'modernisation' means nothing here.

In George Orwell's *Nineteen Eighty-Four* the hero, Winston Smith, works in the Ministry of Truth, 'an enormous pyramidal structure of glittering white concrete, soaring up, terrace after terrace, three hundred metres into the air'. High up were inscribed 'the three slogans of the Party:

WAR IS PEACE
FREEDOM IS SLAVERY
IGNORANCE IS STRENGTH'[34]

Syria's grubby Information Ministry is not so grand. In the weeks following Hafiz al-Asad's death in June 2000 it was bedecked with banners bewailing the national loss. As one ascended the broad, tiled steps leading to the main entrance one could look up and see the Ba'ath Party's logo in the shape of a circular plaque about a metre in diameter. In the centre was a map of the Middle East and North Africa, with the Arab states shaded in green against a yellow background. The red, white, black and green Ba'athist flag was portrayed, its pole planted firmly in Syria. The lower part of the plaque's rim was decorated with green laurels. The upper part carried the party's slogan:

UNITY
FREEDOM
SOCIALISM

Notes

1. Telephone interview with author, 14 January 2002.
2. UN Committee on Economic, Social and Cultural Rights, Press Release, 15 August 2001.
3. *Al-Jazeera* Television, Doha, 22 June 2001.
4. Gary C. Gambill, 'Continuing Detentions and Disappearances in Syria', *Middle East Intelligence Bulletin*, 3 (6), June 2001.
5. Telephone interview with author, 14 January 2002.
6. UN Human Rights Committee, Press Release, 30 March 2001.
7. Muhammad Khair al-Wadei, then editor of *Tishreen*, interview with author, Damascus, summer 2000.
8. Fuad Mardood, editor of *Syria Times*, interview with author, Damascus, summer 2000.
9. Volker Perthes, *The Political Economy of Syria under Asad* (London: I.B. Tauris, 1995), p. 237.
10. Article 19, *Walls of Silence: Media and Censorship in Syria* (London, June 1998), p. 49.
11. Middle East Watch, *Syria Unmasked: The Suppression of Human Rights by the Asad Regime* (New Haven, CT and London: Yale University Press, 1991), p. 113.

12. Interview with author, Damascus, summer 2000.

13. Interview with author, Damascus, summer 2000.

14. *Tishreen*, 30 January 2000.

15. Perthes, *Political Economy*, p. 236.

16. Article 19, *Walls of Silence*, p. 48.

17. Hans Günter Löbmeyer, 'Al-dimuqratiyya hiyya al-hall? The Syrian Opposition at the End of the Asad Era', in Eberhard Kienle (ed.), *Contemporary Syria: Liberalization between Cold War and Cold Peace* (London: British Academic Press, 1994), p. 84.

18. Middle East Watch, *Syria Unmasked*, p. 114.

19. Ibid.

20. Ayman 'Abd an-Nur, adviser to the President, interview with author, Damascus, 4 December 2001.

21. Interview with author, Damascus, 30 April 2001.

22. Andrew Hammond, 'Slow but Steady Progress in Syria', *The Middle East*, December 2001, p. 38.

23. Interview with author, Damascus, 5 May 2001.

24. *An-Nahar*, 28 May 2001.

25. Joel Campagna, *Syria Briefing* (New York: CPJ, September 2001).

26. BBC survey, May 1994; cited in Article 19, *Walls of Silence*, p. 29.

27. *Summary of World Broadcasts*, BBC, 21 November 1994; cited in Article 19, *Walls of Silence*, p. 31.

28. Ibid.

29. Interview with author, Damascus, spring 2000.

30. Central Intelligence Agency, *The World Factbook: Syria* (Washington, DC: CIA, 2001).

31. 'Telecommunications Minister Confirms Internet Investment', *The Syria Report*, 30 January 2002.

32. 'IT Reaches Syria's Rural Population', *The Syria Report*, 19 August 2002.

33. Interview with author, Brussels, 16 February 2001.

34. George Orwell, *Nineteen Eighty-Four* (London: Penguin Books, 2000), p. 6.

CHAPTER 8

'Creating a Socialist, Nationalist Generation': Education

§ HIDING behind the University of Damascus's College of Arts and Social Sciences is a delightful garden, although its central pond is dry. Red and green wood-slatted benches stand along walkways lined by date palms and conifers. It is a glorious sunny morning in mid-February and the birds are singing. A ginger cat steps carefully through the fresh, bright green grass. Students, casual and relaxed, stroll through this oasis of calm. The sole discord is the roar of traffic on the Mezzeh *Autostrade*, one of the city's main thoroughfares, some 50 metres away behind a college building.

The atmosphere is equally relaxed in the unusual pedestrian subway beneath the highway a few hundred metres away. Perhaps 30 metres long and 5 metres wide, the passage has stairways at each end whose walls are plastered with posters advertising social and other events. On one side is a snack stall and then a row of hole-in-the-wall shops selling books and stationery. Most of the shop spaces on the other side are unoccupied and shuttered. The only functioning establishment is the Ghassan Medical Bookshop. Facing the snack stall, tiny plastic stools are set around twelve larger, violet stools that serve as tables. It is a convenient place to take a thick, black Turkish coffee or a glass of tea – almost too hot to touch – before attending classes.

Most of the passers-by are students, displaying the fashions typical of modern Damascus. A girl, aged perhaps twenty, with long dark hair, gold earrings and high heels, wears corduroy jeans and a grey roll-neck sweater. A couple in their early twenties walk together, he in khaki anorak and blue jeans, she in jeans and wearing a headscarf. Two modest Muslim girls, both headscarved, walk arm-in-arm. One wears a long, beige jacket and loose trousers, the other a long dark raincoat over blue jeans. None of the women is wearing a face veil, and while a fair proportion of the young men sport light beards this should not automatically be taken as a sign that they are 'fundamentalists'. The beards may be a statement of Muslim identity but they are also a matter of fashion. Even Hafiz al-Asad's late son Basil wore a beard, and the last thing the Asad family could be accused of is religious fundamentalism.

More traditional modes are also present. A grandmother, almost as round as she is tall, wearing black from head to calf, grey stockings and loose sandals, walks stolidly through the subway, only her face visible. A villager in a black *abaya* and red-and-white checked *keffiya* strides by, followed a few metres behind by his wife, in full-length, wine-coloured dress.

The atmosphere in the Mezzeh highway subway and in the garden of the College of Arts and Social Sciences is beguiling. Behind the tranquillity, however, lies another story. Syria's universities, like all its institutions, must function as integral parts of a system that values loyalty to the regime above all else – and certainly more than academic standards – and which punishes disloyalty without pity. As Middle East Watch noted: 'The battle over ideas in Syria has been most organised and intense in the universities.'[1]

Reminders of this underlying reality are not hard to find. At one end of the tranquil garden are two freestanding metal noticeboards each perhaps one metre square, one extolling the virtues of President Bashar Al-Asad, the other praising those of his father. As students emerge from the subway and pass through the main entrance to the College of Arts and Social Sciences, they are confronted by a 4-metre-high statue of the 'Immortal Leader', perched on a small roundabout. Spray-painted on the side wall of the college building lying between the garden and the Mezzeh highway, in metre-high letters, is the slogan *Nahnu ♥ Hafiz al-Asad* ('We love Hafiz al-Asad'). It is plainly a few years old and the black paint has faded; but the requirement for loyalty has not.

Ba'athist Education

The Ministry of Education website offers excerpts from an undated speech by the late Hafiz al-Asad in which he declared that the purposes of education included the 'enhancement of homeland adoration' and the 'inculcation of national values in the minds of citizens and students'. At least he made no bones about it. Nor did the 1973 Constitution, which at Article 21 affirms: 'The educational and cultural system aims at creating a socialist nationalist Arab generation which is scientifically minded and attached to its history and land, proud of its heritage and filled with the spirit of struggle to achieve its nation's objectives of unity, freedom and socialism, and to serve humanity and its progress.' Article 23 affirms, *inter alia*, that 'the state undertakes to encourage and protect this education'.

The Ba'athist regimes that have ruled Syria since 1963 have been strongly committed to expanding educational opportunities. They have been equally determined to exploit the education system's rich potential for political control and indoctrination, and never more than in the Asad era. The expansion of education has been enormously complicated by the country's rapid population growth: over 3 per cent per year during the 1980s and still about 2.5 per cent. School attendance is compulsory and free for children aged six to eleven. Six years of primary education lead to three years of intermediate school providing general or vocational training. This is followed by three years of academic or vocational training at secondary school. In 1970–76 enrolment at the primary, intermediate and secondary levels increased by 43 per cent, 52 per cent and 65 per cent, respectively. By 1984 one million boys and 818,000 girls were attending primary schools. Intermediate and secondary schools were attended by over 700,000 pupils.

The 1976–80 Fourth Five-Year Development Plan set a target of full enrolment of boys of primary school age by 1980 and of girls by 1990. The target for boys was reached by the early 1980s although only about 85 per cent of girls were attending primary school at that time. In 1996 the primary school enrolment rate was 91.2 per cent although the figure for girls was only 87.3 per cent.[2] Primary school attendance by girls varies significantly from one part of the country to another. In remote rural areas it is often well below the national average. In 2000 girls accounted for 46.25 per cent of rural primary school enrolment nationally but for only 42.3 per cent in the Euphrates Valley province of Raqqa and 44.1 per cent in the far north-eastern province of Hassaka. Most Syrian children do not go on to intermediate and secondary level. In 1996 only 38.1 per cent of children were enrolled at such schools, and the proportion of suitably aged girls was only 36.1 per cent.[3] By 2000 the school population had risen to 3,730,212 of whom 2,774,922 were in primary schools, 783,565 in intermediate schools and 171,725 in secondary schools.[4] While private schools (mainly run by religious communities) and schools for Palestinians operated by the UN Relief and Works Agency (UNRWA) for Palestine refugees play significant roles, state schools dominate, accounting for 98 per cent of elementary schools and 96 per cent of intermediate and secondary schools in 2000. In addition, 139,344 students were enrolled at post-secondary school technical colleges specialising in areas such as agriculture, commerce and manufacturing industry. There were 92,592 students in training institutes operating under the auspices of government ministries.

The eradication of illiteracy has been a persistent aim. In the early 1970s about 60 per cent of the population was illiterate.[5] For 2000 the World Bank put the illiteracy rate for males aged fifteen and over at 11.7 per cent and the equivalent figure for girls at 39.5 per cent.[6]

The regime has always understood that education is a double-edged sword. While skilled workers are essential to develop the economy, educated people are also the most likely to question and challenge the system. After all, many of the key figures in the regime – and most notably Hafiz al-Asad himself – had started their political careers as high school activists. Political control and indoctrination have therefore been central features of the education system. Batatu has noted: 'The significance that the regime attaches to the political assimilation of the students may be gathered from the fact that they constitute one of the two elements of the population – the other being the armed forces – among whom political activity is forbidden to the non-Ba'athist organisations incorporated in the Asad-sponsored National Progressive Front' (see Chapter 5).[7]

For elementary pupils, enrolment in the Talai' al-Ba'ath (Ba'ath Vanguards) is compulsory. Their slogan, chanted in unison, is: *'Bir-Ruh, bid-Damm, Nafdeek, ya Hafiz!'* ('We sacrifice for you our souls and our blood, O Hafiz!'). At about age nine, the Vanguards attend summer camps where they undergo basic military training. For intermediate and secondary pupils there is the Ittihad Shabibat ath-Thawra (Revolutionary Youth Union – RYU), membership of which is not officially compulsory but which confers considerable privileges including bonus marks in the final school-leaving exam. 'It's very Nazi-like,' recalled Subhi Hadidi, the exiled Syrian writer and critic who himself went through the system, graduating from Damascus University with a degree in English literature in 1974. 'It's all about loyalty to the leader and the party, to the extent that it becomes your duty to inform the authorities of any political misconduct by your colleagues.'[8]

The Universities

University education has also expanded dramatically. By far the biggest establishment is the University of Damascus, which in 2000 had 75,678 students, 56 per cent of them male. It was officially founded in 1923 although the oldest faculty, of medicine, was founded in 1903 as the Institution Médicale Turque. Aleppo University, founded in 1958, had 37,410 students in 2000. Tishreen ('October', after the October 1973 Arab–Israeli war) University in Lattakia was formed in 1974 and had 25,660 students in 2000. The smallest and newest is Al-Ba'ath University in Homs which opened in 1979 and which in 2000 had 16,389 students.[9]

Entry to university depends on the results of a final school examination, or baccalaureate, but political factors can play a big part. In particular, one quarter of university places are reserved for members of the RYU. In the past, the political dimension loomed even larger. In 1975 the Ba'ath Party's Sixth Regional Congress appointed the President's brother, Rif'at al-Asad, then the second most powerful man in the country, as head of the Regional Command's Bureau of Higher Education, which oversees all higher education. He held the post until 1980. His projects included a scheme to train young men and women as parachutists to prepare them for future battles in defence of their homeland. As compensation for the time they spent on training, the students were awarded bonus points in their school-leaving exams. As entry to the most sought-after university faculties such as those of medicine and dentistry depends on the exam results, such bonus marks proved critical.

At university level, membership of the state-sponsored Students' Union and of the party is not obligatory but it certainly helps. Both offer a range of benefits including cheap lodgings, travel and scholarships. Like the Vanguards and the RYU, the Students' Union plays an important coercive role. It has been praised for detecting among students 'forces inimical to the party and the revolution'. It has been expected to 'evaluate politically' Syrian students abroad and to monitor 'inimical elements' amongst them.[10] 'The education system is just another tool of the regime,' said Subhi Hadidi. 'This is especially so at university level, since schools are free whereas the range of benefits available at university offer a further means of manipulation.'[11]

A much rosier picture is painted by Professor Hani Mourtada, a former dean of Damascus University's Medical School who in April 2000 was appointed president of the university. 'This country's higher education policy since the Ba'ath Party took over has been that it is free for everyone,' he told me. 'And it's not only free education. It's also heavily subsidised books and even accommodation. We have living accommodation for 17,000 students at Damascus University where [Syrian students] pay 25 Syrian Pounds ($0.50) per month.'[12]

Underlining the potential of universities as sources of trouble for the regime, each of the four institutions has its own full branch of the party. Even though their membership is just a few thousand, they have organisational equivalence to party branches in *muhafazat*, or provinces, where party membership runs into many tens of thousands. Albeit less so now than in the past, the university party branches have as much if not more power than the formal university authorities. Their responsibilities are open-ended, and include the approval of teaching staff appointments.

Even more than other institutions, the universities are saturated with agents and informers of the *mukhabarat* or secret police. The student branch of Al-Amn as-Siyassi (Political Intelligence) has a particular responsibility for the surveillance of higher education establishments. 'Faculty are under heavy pressure to conform,' said Middle East Watch, in a report which although published in 1991 remains largely valid in today's less oppressive conditions. 'Failure to do so can easily cost them their jobs. Students are reminded constantly that independent thought is dangerous and co-operation the best route to jobs and economic success.'[13]

Damascus University students were the first to demonstrate against Hafiz al-Asad's November 1970 Corrective Movement, chanting: 'Down with dictatorships! Down with military regimes!' Fifty of them were reportedly arrested.[14] The universities were key centres of dissent – and hence repression – in the late 1970s and early 1980s when the regime faced a tide of opposition which included an armed uprising by the Muslim Brotherhood. In autumn 1979, when Aleppo University students marched on the *mukhabarat* headquarters in the as-Sabil district, security agents opened fire, killing three and wounding many. Hundreds of demonstrators were arrested. The protests continued, prompting ever harsher measures from the authorities. Aleppo University was occupied by the army. There and in Damascus and Lattakia hundreds of students were detained and tortured. Some died in captivity.

Teaching staff were equally under pressure. From late 1979 until mid-1980 over one hundred lecturers openly critical of the regime or suspected of disloyalty were dismissed or transferred to bureaucratic jobs. Others were detained by the *mukhabarat*. 'The teaching program at the Faculty of Medicine [at Damascus University] was disrupted for over two years,' noted Middle East Watch, adding: 'No anatomy professors remained, though there was certainly no shortage of cadavers.'[15] The official mood in that dark period can be gauged from a decision of the Ba'ath Party's Seventh Regional Congress, staged from 22 December 1979 to 7 January 1980. It was agreed 'to charge the comrade Minister of Education to eliminate all trace of adverse thought in his sector and modify the educational programmes to coincide with the interests of the party and the revolution'.[16] The universities, like the rest of Syria, were cowed. As recently as 1989, however, the regime's nervousness was still apparent. 'At the Mezzeh arts campus of Damascus University', reported Middle East Watch, 'armed security agents guarded the campus entrance and four armoured cars stood under tarpaulin covers outside a lecture hall.'[17]

The Mood Softens

Damascus University President Dr Hani Mourtada stressed that Syria's current more liberal political atmosphere started before Hafiz al-Asad's death in June 2000. 'The Ba'ath Party policy during the last two or three years of President Asad's regime was relaxed,' he said. 'Everyone was asked to express his opinion.'[18] The Damascus University branch of the Ba'ath Party is headed by Adel Safa, a former dean of the Agriculture School. He chairs a seven-member committee that meets monthly to review developments. Before each meeting, Mourtada is consulted closely. 'If they have to take a decision, they will know exactly the position of the university administration,' explained Mourtada – who is not a party member.

He also stressed that the party was much more inclined than in the past to accept staff appointments suggested by university administrators. 'The administration is no more decided by the party,' he said. 'Ninety-five per cent of what we suggest is being done. With the other five per cent the party consults me and says: "We have so-and-so on this person. Do you still want him?" If there were some real deficiencies, I say "no".' He conceded, however, that the final decisions rested with the party: 'If it wants to change something, it can.'

The civil society activists – who include university teachers such as Arif Dalila who in August 2002 was sentenced to ten years' imprisonment – had 'taken advantage' of the liberalisation. Those attending civil society forums were 'either interested in politics or they want to create problems,' opined Professor Mourtada. 'The people who really want to develop higher education in this country express their opinion in our board meetings, in meetings at different levels of the university,' he continued. 'I hear things as president of the university in my board meetings that never used to be said before.'

In mid-2000 Dalila had been dismissed as head of the Economics Faculty but Mourtada denied that this had had anything to do with his political views. 'He did lose his job but it had nothing to do with what happened,' said Mourtada. 'We're in the process of changing heads of department and I'm responsible for that. Just recently I changed four or five heads of department. It came from me, not even from the Ba'ath Party.'

I asked Professor Mourtada if I might be permitted to attend a typical lecture. He said that I should put my request in writing. 'You could write it here', he offered, 'and I'll refer it to the head of the University Branch of the Ba'ath Party.'

Professor Shukri Remembers

If the system has become more flexible it is not immediately obvious to other senior university figures. For them, the salient feature remains the absence of autonomy. Professor Muhammad Aziz Shukri, chairman of the university's Department of International Law and one of Syria's most highly regarded legal experts, recalls that when he was a student at the university all academic administrative posts were decided by internal elections. Professors at the Law School, for example, would elect the dean, and the government would confirm that person in the post. In turn, the deans would elect three candidates to head the university, one of whom would be selected by the government.[19]

'The universities have [since] been greatly, greatly politicised. Now, every academic administrative position is decided by the government upon the recommendation of the party,' said Professor Shukri, stressing that an academic's ties to the party could be critical for his career. The Students' Union's role had expanded dramatically since his time as a student. 'They intervene in everything. They intervene in the curriculum, in the examination timetable, and at times they side with lazy students against strict teachers.'

Even if the political atmosphere has lightened and the margins of expression widened since the start of the decade, however, the educational system remains in the grip of a bitter legacy. Rapid expansion with limited resources has taken its toll on the quality of facilities and teaching. Despite constant clean-up campaigns, corruption and political favouritism are as endemic here as elsewhere in the system. The problems are compounded by fear of upsetting the authorities and a related fear of taking initiatives, and by a tradition of rote-learning which discourages independent and creative thinking.

'Damascus University was one of the best in the Middle East,' insisted Professor Shukri. 'It was a tough, sober university which allowed the cream of Arab intellectuals to graduate – students not only from Syria but also from Lebanon, Jordan, Iraq, Palestine.' Standards at all Syria's universities fell as a direct result of a policy, instigated by Hafiz al-Asad, of assuring a university place for all high school graduates. Shukri conceded that it was 'a noble idea in principle' but facilities and teaching staff could not cope with the vast increase in student numbers. The Law School, established in 1919, 'still maintains its old, falling-apart building, its falling-apart classrooms. There are fifty professors for 17,000 students.'

Sub-standard Staff and Students

Dr Amr al-Azm, an energetic British-educated lecturer in the university's Archaeology Department and son of the Syrian philosopher Sadiq Jalal al-Azm (see Chapter 2), was scathing about the quality of students produced by the school system. Although there was now an attempt to raise standards by raising the school-leaving exam pass-mark for university entrance, he said this was being nullified by the absence of any improvement in the criteria used to mark the exams. 'All they're doing is asking for stricter and stricter adherence to the original text that the students are being set at school,' said Al-Azm. 'The better you are at memorising by rote, the higher your average. So you're getting these parrots. We're getting more and more parroty students. Any form of independent thinking, any form of intelligence is immediately snuffed and punished by being given a lower mark.'[20]

In addition, many students manage to qualify for university entrance only because of bonus marks in their school-leaving exams granted as rewards for political loyalty. 'We have a variety of extra marks than can be acquired by a student,' explained Dr Al-Azm. 'Doing a paratrooper's course entitles him to 15 extra marks on the baccalaureate. If you're a party member you get extra marks – depending on your rank you get five, ten extra marks. If you're in the *Shabiba* (the RYU) you get extra marks. And they all add up. Our students can gain up to 30 extra marks on their baccalaureate – which is the difference between going into an institute for a two-year course or entering the university.'

Rote learning is also standard at university level, and examinations are mainly tests of memory. 'They memorise headings and chapter headings, and then they expect questions on a chapter heading which they are then able to regurgitate,' continued Al-Azm. 'Ask them any intelligent or sensible question, ask them any question requiring any form of analysis, any general question that requires them to link ideas from different sources, and they're totally incapable of doing that.'

The quality of many, perhaps most, lecturers is also questionable. Many are the product of a highly controversial programme which started in 1985 under which around 3,500 assistant lecturers were sent for training to Eastern Bloc countries, especially East Germany. The results were disastrous. The lecturers, many of whom had been selected for foreign training not because of their intellectual abilities but because of their political loyalty, returned with woefully inadequate academic standards. 'The plan at the time was to raise the quality of higher education,' said Hani Mourtada. 'The training of some people in the Eastern Bloc was not up to the standard we expected. We didn't know that the results would be like that. When we did know, we started sending people to the West, to the UK, Germany, France. Some have already returned and are doing extremely well.'[21]

Another problem is that for nationalistic reasons Arabic has been stressed as the key teaching medium at the expense of English and French, the leading languages of modern academic discourse. As a result, Syria's students have been marginalised from the international academic mainstream. Dr Samir Altaqi, a surgeon who is also a member of the politburo of the Yousef Faisal faction of the Syrian Communist Party, noted that many countries have educational problems 'but an Egyptian doctor, for example, because he was taught medicine in English, can at any time pick up a book in English and become updated with what's going on in the world'.[22] He urged improvements to Syria's system which would enable Syrian students to do the same.

An experienced medical academic, who requested anonymity, told me that the shortcomings of overseas training programmes, which had favoured the politically loyal above the academically excellent, had created 'a salad of doctors, one coming from the Soviet Union, one from China, one from Cuba. And many of them gained their diplomas through their political background.'[23] He complained: 'I would approve if they said: "Yes. We don't know much and we want to learn more."

That would be acceptable. Now, they just defend their ignorance.' As a result of the incoherent training programmes for doctors, there was no consensus within Syria about the treatment of particular illnesses. 'I can't now say what is the protocol for treating this or that illness in Syria,' said the academic. 'There is nothing. There's no reference, no hierarchy and no tradition. It's personal.'

Outdated and inadequate Arabic textbooks pervade Syria's education system. Dr Amr al-Azm, who as well as teaching at Damascus University is director of the national Department of Antiquity's scientific and conservation laboratories, noted that university rules insist that 80 per cent of each course must derive from a core Arabic textbook.[24] 'If the textbook was written twenty-five years ago, I'm still bound by that,' he said. 'If the core textbook is full of mistakes – as most of my core textbooks are – then I'm bound by those as well. If I correct a mistake and a student quotes the original words in the textbook then, technically, I'm bound to give him that mark, even though it's wrong.'

Dr Al-Azm, who confessed, 'I'm reaching the end of my tether', cited one of the core textbooks which asserts, bizarrely and contrary to all the scientific evidence, that *homo sapiens sapiens* evolved from Neanderthals and did so in the Middle East, making him Arab. All this, said Al-Azm, was 'patently untrue and has been proven to be untrue. It's crap.' Worse is that the textbook adds a proviso to the effect that those disputing this version of the origin of modern man were 'imperialists'. Al-Azm recounted how he had confronted the book's author, asking him: 'How am I going to convince these poor students that I'm right when it says in your book that you're an imperialist lackey if you don't agree with me?'

Regardless of their academic merits, textbooks must be ideologically correct, although this was more of a problem during the repression of the 1980s than now. Their authors know that antagonists among their colleagues or students will be keen to highlight political 'errors' in the books, thereby subjecting the writers to investigation by the party and even the *mukhabarat*.

Corruption

Despite the best efforts of the university authorities, corruption is widespread. One senior insider who requested anonymity estimated that 'between 20 per cent and 30 per cent' of all degrees granted by Damascus University are obtained through bribery. Dr Al-Azm thought that 'perhaps 10 per cent' of exam passes in his department were the result of bribes. Some colleges are far more susceptible to corruption than others, said the senior insider: 'In some, like the Medical School and the Engineering School, it's impossible. It's common in the School of Economics, in the Law School, in the School of Letters. I hate to say it, but it's now common.' Paradoxically, the corruption has a moral dimension. 'I think there's a view here that we don't play with people's lives,' explained the confidential source. 'I mean, if you lose a case in court it's a problem, but if you lose a life it's a catastrophe. Thus far, we've not had a single case of corruption in the Medical School or the Pharmacy School, nor in the three Schools of Engineering; nor, of course, in the School of Shari'a [Islamic Jurisprudence].'

The corruption takes several forms. Students may assure their success in exams by paying a lecturer, either directly or through a middleman, or *miftah* ('key'). The price for a full degree is about 100,000 Syrian Pounds ($2,000) for each year of a degree course. For most subjects, the course takes four years although it is five years for engineering, pharmacy and dentistry and six years for medicine. 'It ranges from subject to subject,' explained Dr Al-Azm. 'It depends on which faculty you're in, which department you're in, on whether you want a high grade or a low grade.'[25] The bribery may involve the provision of goods rather than cash. In a recent case, a Law School lecturer was found to have accepted a new suite of bedroom furniture. Sometimes it is a matter of favours. 'It can be *quid pro quo*,' said Dr Al-Azm. 'Your father is an important man in something, and he will then do you a favour. And you get a reputation for whether you are willing to do this or not.' If a senior party or security official 'requests' a favour, however, it can be difficult not to comply. There have also been high-profile cases where lecturers have demanded sexual favours from their students who, if they refused to acquiesce, were failed.

Cheating in examinations is another major headache for the university authorities. Professor Shukri described a particularly elaborate system used by well-connected students, often the sons and daughters of regime big-wigs. As soon as an examination paper is distributed, someone inside the examination room passes a copy to a group of lawyers and even judges outside who rapidly write correct answers, each taking responsibility for one part of the paper. Their answers are then passed back to the student, who copies them out.[26]

Crude threats and intimidation can also feature. Patrick Seale, one of the best-informed observers of Syria, recounts how 'The daughter of one security chief turned up for her examination with a posse of bodyguards and insisted that the professor write her papers.'[27] In one bizarre case in the early 1990s a law student who was caught cheating responded by producing a hand-grenade and pulling the pin. He then ran out of the examination hall and was pursued across the campus by university guards, who dared not shoot at him for fear of the deaths that might result if the primed grenade exploded. His car number plates showed that it had been issued by the presidential palace, which claimed, somewhat unbelievably given draconian presidential security, that the vehicle had been stolen.

Beyond doubt, many of the privileged offspring of Syria's ruling elite have obtained university degrees fraudulently, in some cases 'without ever having opened a book', according to one confidential and well-placed source with direct knowledge of the phenomenon. In his biography of Hafiz al-Asad, Patrick Seale records that 'resentment at the unfairness of life, a nascent class consciousness, was probably Asad's first political emotion'. Ironically, it was the outrageous cheating at school of the offspring of the then bourgeois elite that was apparently among the key factors which turned Hafiz al-Asad to Ba'athism. The late President is quoted as saying: 'Rich boys didn't bother to work [at school], but simply gave themselves what marks they wanted at the end of the year, and very few were the teachers who dared stand up to them.'[28] In many ways, only the names and backgrounds of Syria's elite have changed, while the unfairness remains, despite the 'socialist' rhetoric of the Ba'ath revolution.

Graduate Unemployment

Although highly prized, a university degree is by no means a passport to employment. Wages in the bloated public sector are unattractive. The monthly pay of a heart surgeon is a mere 8,000 Syrian Pounds ($160). The private sector requires skills – especially proficiency in English – that not all graduates possess. As a result, many graduates do not work in their area of academic specialisation. An official survey of the 1998 labour market put the proportion who did not at 35 per cent.[29] Reviewing the problems facing Syrian graduates, the pan-Arab daily newspaper *Al-Hayat* commented: 'The graduates' stories are similar: they are unqualified for work because the educational curricula are outdated.'[30] The same point was made forcefully by an intellectual who preferred anonymity: 'There's very high unemployment among engineers. But if a big Western or Japanese company came to Syria to build something it wouldn't be able to use these engineers because their information is so old-fashioned, so theoretical, so distant from any practical experience. It wouldn't be able to use them even as skilled workers, never mind as engineers. The big problem in Syria is not only of the educational system, but also the rehabilitation of the workforce, which is completely out of date.'[31]

Many of the better graduates are therefore forced to emigrate, in a brain-drain that deprives the country of its most talented young people. Thousands of Syrian doctors, engineers and teachers work abroad, particularly in the Gulf countries and the United States.

Professor Hani Mourtada, president of Damascus University, did not feel that the education system was in a crisis although he readily agreed that mistakes had been made that required correction. 'Reasonable people … who do not work in politics will say that a lot of good things were done during the Ba'ath Party regime,' he said. 'There are some mistakes which we can look at and correct. This is for the benefit of the country. But to change the subject from reform or repairing some few things to change completely [as civil society activists were demanding], this I think is a wrong move for everybody in this country.'[32]

His view mirrors that of the regime. In his inaugural address to parliament on 17 July 2000, Bashar al-Asad acknowledged the importance of 'reforming and modernising' educational establishments although he stressed that this should be done in a way which served Syria's 'national and pan-Arab issues' and which 'treats the social problems that negatively affect the unity and security of society'. By autumn 2002 only a handful of educational reforms had been enacted, none of them addressing core issues. A decision was made to end the distinction between the primary and intermediate stages of schools. In mid-2001 Arabic language ceased being taught as a subject in all university departments. Military training for students was confined to one month in summer. Previously they had been obliged to attend training camps weekly throughout the year. It was decreed that university students who failed their final examinations would be given the chance to re-sit. A legal change permitted the establishment of private universities although no moves were yet under way in response to the change. A more notable development was the launch in September 2002 of an internet-based Virtual University, the first in the region – although it remains to be seen how successful it will prove.

Plainly, in education as in other spheres, the regime seeks gradual change, hoping that painful root-and-branch reform can be avoided. Many leading Syrians feel that the problems are far greater than the government is prepared to acknowledge, and that urgent and sweeping changes are needed if the educational system is to become part of the solution to Syria's problems rather than one of its biggest headaches. The anonymous intellectual was unequivocal: 'There's a very, very big gap between what is being taught within the universities and the actual life of society. And another gap between what is being taught in the universities and what is really needed for the country and its future.'[33]

Notes

1. Middle East Watch, *Syria Unmasked: The Suppression of Human Rights by the Asad Regime* (New Haven, CT and London: Yale University Press, 1991), p. 131.
2. World Bank, *World Development Indicators Database* (Washington, DC: World Bank, July 2001).
3. Ibid.
4. Office of the Prime Minister, *Statistical Abstract 2001*, Central Bureau of Statistics, Syrian Arab Republic.
5. Moshe Ma'oz, *Asad: The Sphinx of Damascus* (New York: Weidenfeld and Nicolson, 1988), p. 80.
6. World Bank, *World Development Indicators Database.*
7. Hanna Batatu, *Syria's Peasantry, the Descendants of Its Lesser Rural Notables, and Their Politics* (Princeton, NJ: Princeton University Press, 1990), p. 187.
8. Interview with author, Paris, 20 March 2002.
9. Office of the Prime Minister, *Statistical Abstract 2001.*
10. Volker Perthes, *The Political Economy of Syria under Asad* (London: I.B. Tauris, 1995), p. 172.
11. Interview with author, Paris, 20 March 2002.
12. Interview with author, Damascus, 2 May 2001.
13. Middle East Watch, *Syria Unmasked*, p. 131.
14. Ibid., p. 131.
15. Ibid., p. 132.
16. Ibid., p. 11.
17. Ibid., p. 133.
18. Interview with author, Damascus, 2 May 2001.
19. Interview with author, Damascus, 1 December 2001.
20. Interview with author, Damascus, 18 February 2002.
21. Interview with author, Damascus, 2 May 2001.
22. Interview with author, Damascus, 1 December 2001.

23. Interview with author, Damascus, December 2001.

24. Interview with author, Damascus, 18 February 2002.

25. Interview with author, Damascus, 18 February 2002.

26. Interview with author, Damascus, 1 December 2001.

27. Patrick Seale, *Asad: The Struggle for Power in the Middle East* (Berkeley and Los Angeles: University of California Press, 1995), p. 344.

28. Ibid., pp. 24–5.

29. Ahmad Qodjai and Wa'il Yousef, 'Syrian Graduates Between Two Fires', *Al-Hayat*, 22 January 2002.

30. Ibid.

31. Interview with author, Damascus, December 2001.

32. Interview with author, Damascus, 2 May 2001.

33. Interview with author, Damascus, December 2001.

CHAPTER 9

'Our Leader ... for Ever'?: Whither Syria?

§ THE Havana *maqha* (coffee shop), on the corner of Al-Mutanabi Street and Port Said Street in central Damascus, is a traditional haunt of intellectuals and politicians, and of young lovers, the latter frequenting the establishment's gallery, sitting upright in the upholstered chairs gazing into each other's eyes across low coffee tables. The Havana has style, albeit faded and dated. The floor is of light grey marble, the slabs divided by embedded brass strips. The walls are marble-faced and the tables marble-topped. The dark wooden ceiling, sporting arabesques in the traditional local style, complements the wood latticework balustrade defining the gallery. Around the walls, dark green plants are set in large brass pots. The only discordant note in this 1940s elegance is the inevitable poster of President Bashar al-Asad, on the wall between the till and the dispenser of the locally produced sweet drink 'mandarin'. The scenes through the darkened plate-glass windows recall the age when the Havana was new. Al-Mutanabi Street still boasts the uneven black cobbles laid during the French Mandate. Between them, remnants of tram lines lead into a forgotten terminus.

The Havana's origins are disputed. According to one account, it was built in the 1940s by a Syrian émigré who had returned after making his fortune in Cuba.[1] Another version is that it was built in 1947–48 by Edward Sabbagh, a Lebanese Christian. It was apparently so named as there was then another coffee shop across the street, named Brazil.[2] In 1978, during a campaign to Arabise the names of businesses, it was renamed Sulwan. The name did not stick. The clientele persisted in calling it the Havana, and in the late 1980s the Arabic name was abandoned.

It was in the Havana that I met Dr Samir Altaqi, a member of the politburo of the Yousef Faisal faction of the Syrian Communist Party.

'Syria is entering a critical period, a long period of transition,' he said. 'Bashar's strength is that the old, bureaucratic, sclerotic system is dying. His weakness is that the new is not yet born. This is the dilemma. Will Bashar be able to be the bridge towards the next system? This is the question.'[3]

'Qa'iduna ilal-Abad', declares the slogan writ large above the wide entrance of the Officers' Club on Shukry al-Quwatly Street in central Damascus, near the five-star Meridien Hotel. 'Our Leader for Ever'. It was the slogan which epitomised Asad's regime, especially during his final years. After his death, therefore, it was at least logical that he should become 'Our Immortal Leader', and that Bashar, as his son, should be his natural, almost inevitable successor on Earth. At this rhetorical level, Syria's future has already been settled. A land at peace with itself but vigilant against its enemies, pursuing principled Arab nationalist policies abroad and socialism at home, will move steadily forwards under the benevolent shadow of its Immortal Leader. As always in this long-suffering country, reality and rhetoric differ vastly. By the time of Asad's death in June 2000 Syria was in deep trouble. 'The power structure feels and knows that it is in crisis,' said philosopher Sadiq al-Azm. The regime knew that 'returning to the old ways is not possible; that freezing the situation is not possible; that there are unintended consequences to whatever they do'.[4] At the dawn of the new millennium, there was only one strategic question on Syria's political agenda: what would replace a system that had manifestly failed on all fronts? The key measure of Bashar al-Asad's performance would be the extent to which he succeeded as midwife to a new order.

Asad's Crisis of Legitimacy

The crisis facing Bashar is essentially the same nagging, tenacious crisis of legitimacy which has dogged the regime since the late 1970s when both the Islamist and secular opposition rose in rebellion against the regime, the one with bombs and Kalashnikovs, the other with words and ideas. Then, the regime was vilified as a rapacious Alawi clique which ran the country as its personal fiefdom, whose looting of the nation's wealth was impoverishing the masses; and whose power was based on a network of secret police agencies responsible for barbaric violations of human rights. The Ba'athist slogan 'Unity, Freedom, Socialism' had been exposed as so much hot air.

The regime survived the uprising, albeit by dint of such atrocities as the Hama massacre of early spring 1982, but it never regained the genuine popularity it had enjoyed in its early years, when it was seen as an improvement on the previous Ba'ath ruling clique. There would be no repeat of the spontaneous shows of public affection for Asad which took place in 1970–71 (even in solidly Sunni cities like Hama and Aleppo whose residents had traditionally viewed Alawis with disdain, and which would later be major centres of the Islamist uprising) when 'crowds ... carried him and his car exultantly on their shoulders'.[5] The regime weathered the 1983–84 succession crisis when the President's brother, Rif'at, tried to advance his position while his brother was ill. It survived the stark austerity of the 1980s when the economy was crippled by foreign exchange shortages (see Chapter 1). Having defeated its internal enemies and with newly discovered oilfields in the Euphrates Valley providing desperately needed income, the regime felt able to relax its iron grip slightly in the 1990s and the private sector was allowed a bigger role, but with croneyism always at the forefront of business dealings.

Never, however, were the fundamentals of the system touched. Asad and his colleagues were genuinely non-sectarian in outlook but in Syria, as in the wider Middle East, family and clan loyalties count for much. At base, the regime was centred on Asad's minority Alawi community and it depended for its existence on a military-security system in which key positions were held by Alawis. Beyond the Alawi community, the regime's main support groups were the poorer peasantry, workers in state-owned enterprises and the vast state bureaucracy. These key characteristics tied the regime into a Gordian knot.

Asad wanted to widen his support base in order to boost his legitimacy. That meant winning the endorsement in particular of the Sunni Muslims who constitute three-quarters of the population, who have traditionally dominated the petit bourgeois business community and who have historically regarded the Alawis with some contempt as backward mountain peasants. Concessions to the Sunnis, however, could not be so generous as to threaten the interests – especially the financial interests – of the regime's Alawi core. It would of course be a gross over-simplification to describe Asad's regime as exclusively or simply Alawi; but the dictates of power politics meant that it often behaved as if it was a confessional enterprise – providing rich fields for the propagandist ploughs of the Sunni Muslim Brotherhood.

Nikolaos Van Dam notes:

> However idealistic some Ba'thist leaders may originally have been, they

> could not evade the socio-political reality that without making use of primordial ties they could not monopolise power in Syria, let alone maintain themselves.
>
> Without their well-organised sectarian, regional and tribally based networks within the Syrian armed forces, the security services and other power institutions, the Ba'thists who have ruled Syria since 1963 would not have been able to survive for so long.[6]

A second Gordian knot arose from the patent need to reform the ramshackle economy. In practice, reform meant a bigger role for the private sector. This, however, implied a relative marginalisation of the poorer sections of society which had the highest stakes in Ba'athist rule. The beneficiaries of such limited liberalisation as Asad permitted, often with regime connections if not regime figures, displayed their wealth conspicuously, causing much resentment in a country where hundreds of thousands lived well under the poverty line. Economic reform was therefore sometimes constrained by the need to appear to appease – or at least not provoke – the very classes upon whose support the regime could traditionally count.

It was the same in the area of corruption. Although the target of successive clean-up campaigns, corruption persisted and the higher levels of the regime were always untouched by the campaigns because, in the final analysis, Asad valued political loyalty above all else. Van Dam again:

> Various campaigns to eradicate corruption were successful only to a very limited extent, as the corrupt elements of the high-placed Alawi (and for that matter also non-Alawi) military elite belonging to the direct entourage of the President, as well as their clientele, were to a great extent left untouched. Disciplinary action against the most important supporters of the President could have directly undermined the whole regime, and therefore was not undertaken ... After having enriched themselves and having obtained all kinds of privileges to defend, the same elite turned into a major obstacle to the reform of abuses enveloping the state.[7]

Caught between these dilemmas, Hafiz al-Asad's reforms were unconvincing and *ad hoc* and never amounted to more than what Volker Perthes has termed 'regime maintenance'.[8] Israeli writer Eyal Zisser has described them as 'more than cosmetic and yet not enough to offer any substantial changes to the political reality and the structure of the governing system'.[9] During the 1990s the *mukhabarat* were far less obtrusive than before, but their powers were not reduced. In particular, the Emergency Law stayed in place. The media were permitted to air certain issues – particularly economic matters – that had been taboo, but the debate had clearly defined limits. The President and the system itself were beyond criticism. The number of independent members of parliament increased, but all were loyal to the system that, again, could not be questioned beyond limits drawn by the President.

Economic changes were equally half-hearted. Private sector economic opportunities were distributed selectively to entrepreneurs close to the regime. Measures to stimulate investment such as the much-vaunted Law No. 10 of May 1991 had far less impact than had been hoped because it was political patronage above all that determined the success or failure of an enterprise. Incentives such as tax holidays hardly mattered if an investor was unable to secure the support (by means of the usual hefty commission payment) of a key regime figure. By the end of 1998 1,494 projects valued at about $8.5 billion had been approved under Law 10. Over 75 per cent of them, however, never went beyond the planning stage.[10]

Although generally reluctant to criticise his father's political legacy, Bashar al-Asad has not flinched from criticising his handling of the economy. In his inaugural speech to parliament in July 2000 he affirmed that 'performance in the economic field fluctuated sharply' and that the response had been to issue 'laws, decrees and decisions that were sometimes characterised by experimentation and at other times by improvisation. Yet others were a reaction to a certain situation.' This approach had only rarely 'been effective in taking the initiative and pre-empting events'. The reason was that 'there were no clear strategies on which the laws were based. The economic strategy was the outcome of all the laws that were issued. Thus, it was weak and had many loopholes. It was also responsible to a certain extent for the hardships we are facing today.' He went on to call for 'steady, yet gradual, steps towards introducing economic changes through modernising laws, removing bureaucratic obstacles to the flow of domestic and foreign investments, mobilising public and private capital and activating the private sector and giving it better business opportunities'. Another objective would be to 'achieve a competitive strength for the public sector in foreign markets'.

Bashar's Dilemmas

In essence, the regime under Bashar al-Asad must grapple with exactly the same dilemmas as it faced under his father: how to win legitimacy by widening the support base and boosting economic performance without fatally undermining the Alawi core and traditional support groups. At one end of the spectrum of debate are the hardliners of the 'old guard', men from Hafiz al-Asad's inner circle such as Vice President Abdul Halim Khaddam and Defence Minister Mustafa Tlass; and also a younger group with the same outlook, including Bashar's brother-in-law Asef Shawkat, the deputy head of Military Intelligence, and Prime Minister Muhammad Miru. Broadly, their views are echoed by the staff of the inefficient state-run industrial and commercial establishments and by the bureaucracy – many of whom form part of Syria's legions of incompetent under-employed, who have good reason to fear that reform might affect their livelihoods. In their view, nothing beyond the correction of 'mistakes' is required. In all its essentials, the system can and should persist.

A second group, essentially technocratic and headed by Bashar himself, believes that the system – and especially the economy – is capable of reform and 'modernisation'. At the same time, it insists that changes must be careful and gradual and it foresees no fundamental revision of the system such as the introduction of genuine liberal democracy or unfettered media. At the other end of the spectrum is the loose alliance of groups and trends committed to democracy, including the civil society movement, the National Democratic Gathering and the recently reformed Muslim Brotherhood. They demand nothing less than the replacement of Syria's authoritarian system with a multi-party liberal democracy replete with an independent judiciary, a free press and respect for human rights. Within this alliance there are marked differences as to the pace of the desired reform, and the extent to which the regime should be involved in the process.

A majority is realistic enough to accept that, barring any unforeseeable eruption of internecine rivalries within its inner core, the regime is as firmly in control as at any point since the early 1980s; and that change therefore can be effected only with support from within the regime, whatever their doubts may be about the ability of the system as a whole to transform itself. Bashar and his technocratic modernisers are seen as potential allies – not without reason, as until early 2001 the President appeared to be encouraging the civil society movement (see Chapter 2). 'Reform in Syria is not easy after forty years of political and economic corruption,' agreed the Muslim Brotherhood's superintendent-general, Ali Sadr ad-Din al-Bayanouni. 'We believe if he [Bashar] co-operates with other political groups and opens to the people, he will be able to overcome these problems.'[11]

It would be mistaken, however, to draw too big a distinction between the different currents within the regime or to imagine that conservatism will simply fade away with the deaths of the older regime figures. The conservatives and modernisers may differ but they are at least capable of a mutual compromise, while neither can reach any real accommodation with the civil society movement. Ibrahim Hamidi, Damascus correspondent for the pan-Arab daily *Al-Hayat*, warned: 'We should be very careful when we talk about the "old guard" and "reformists". I know some of the "new guard", and they are not very different from the old.' Some of the 'new guard' were 'worse than the "old guard"', he continued. The latter had come to power with an ideology. 'They were clever and charismatic. They had experience. Some of the "new guard" appear as if they are open, or would like to be open, but they lack clear vision. The maximum they want is just to change some names, to get rid of some people. Their goal is continuity, not to make substantial changes beneficial for the whole people.'[12]

The Economic Challenge

However much one may admire the ideals and courage of the civil society movement, it would be foolish to pretend that it commands wide support. The regime denigrates the activists as a tiny minority of middle-class intellectuals, and plainly they are – although this does not mean that their ideas will not eventually triumph. For most Syrians, the priority is the daily struggle to make ends meet. It is on its economic performance rather than its record on democracy or human rights that the regime is most vulnerable, and it is economic pressures above all that are driving the reformers within the regime.

The scale of the challenge was underlined by the May 2002 *Euromoney* semi-annual survey of 185 countries which ranked Syria 102nd – down from ninety-seventh in the previous survey – and fifteenth among eighteen Middle East and North African states. Syria was ahead of Guatemala, New Caledonia and Samoa and came immediately behind Bangladesh, Ukraine and Honduras. The surveys assess economies on the basis of economic growth, monetary stability, current account, budget deficit or surplus, unemployment and structural imbalances. The world's projected best-performing economy for 2002 and 2003 would score 100. Syria received a score of 34.10 points.[13]

Although Syria's population growth rate has slowed from well over 3 per cent per year to 2.8 per cent per year in 1996 and 2.5 per cent per year in 2000, economic progress is still a race against population growth.[14] In 2001, 53.8 per cent of the population were aged nineteen or below[15] and at least 200,000–250,000 job-seekers enter the labour market each year. Unemployment is officially put at 11.2 per cent[16] but the real rate is estimated at 25–30 per cent[17] while under-employment is a major problem, especially in the public sector. Mass protests, sometimes involving rioting, at falling standards of living have rocked other Arab countries – Algeria, Morocco, Egypt, Jordan and Lebanon – in the past and the regime is well aware of the potential for unrest posed by mass unemployment. Yet the public sector, including the government bureaucracy, has created no more than 20,000 jobs per year since the mid-1990s. Perhaps 40,000–60,000 jobs per year were created by the private sector in the same period.[18] Each year, therefore, at least 120,000 of the new entrants to the labour market fail to find work.

Combating unemployment is a governmental preoccupation, but planned measures appear confused and even contradictory. The then Planning Minister Issam az-Za'im told a *Euromoney* conference in London in July 2001 that ministries and other public establishments had been working on a five-year reform programme which would be approved by parliament 'soon'. The overriding aim would be job creation, with the first three years being devoted to administrative reforms and the final two years to an acceleration of economic growth. Total investment would rise from 18.2 per cent of Syria's gross domestic product (GDP) in 2000 to 26 per cent in 2003 and 27 per cent in 2005. The public sector would account for 69 per cent of the total investment. He affirmed: 'We do not intend to privatise, at least at the moment. But we will make sure that the public sector is market-oriented and profit-making, through changing its organisational structure and altering its relationship with the Finance Ministry.' Az-Zaim insisted: 'We want to move to having an independent, accountable public sector, governed by market prices and with management separated from ownership.'[19]

Interviewed by the local daily *Tishreen* in January 2002, Az-Zaim – who had been appointed industry minister in a December 2001 cabinet reshuffle – said that the accumulated losses of Syria's state-owned industries had reached $1.6 billion in 2001 and that they were 'threatened with extinction if they remain in deficit'. Again, privatisation was ruled out and, again, it was not explained how loss-making industries could be rendered profitable without major job losses.[20]

In October 2001 Prime Minister Muhammad Miru announced a $1 billion programme to create 440,000 public and private sector jobs in 2002–2007 through the establishment of small enterprises, mainly in rural areas. In May 2002 it was reported that the Kuwait Fund for Arab Economic Development had approved a $100 million loan for the scheme. However laudable, the job-creation programme will plainly fail to provide employment for all the projected new entrants to the labour market. In December 2001 Bashar signed a law establishing a government job-creation agency. The following month the retirement age, previously sixty for men and women, was lowered to fifty-five for men and fifty for women, provided they had over twenty years' service. The new rules also permitted employees who had worked for twenty-five years to retire at any age. In early March it was reported that Bashar had issued an instruction that all public sector employees aged over sixty should be retired compulsorily. Over 80,000 people were affected, most of them managers. If those taking voluntary or compulsory retirement are replaced, the measures could help ease unemployment. Replacing the retirees, however, does not square with the other government objective of streamlining the bureaucracy and making public sector companies profitable.

Unemployment is only part of the economic threat to regime stability. Falling living standards are another. GDP at constant prices stagnated in the second half of the 1990s while the population continued to expand fast. The result was a decline in real per capita GDP from 43,682 Syrian Pounds in 1998 to 40,844 Syrian Pounds in 2000. Real per capita GDP had reached 42,853 Syrian Pounds in 1980 and had fallen as low as 32,145 Syrian Pounds in 1990.[21] Boosting economic expansion to a rate significantly greater than the population growth rate is plainly essential to avert an escalation of discontent that could destabilise the regime. According to the World Bank, real GDP growth of over 5 per cent per annum will be required.[22] In a communiqué issued on 8 March 2002 marking the thirty-ninth anniversary of the 1963 Ba'athist coup, the government said that GDP at current prices had grown by an impressive 5.9 per cent in 2001. The figure is unlikely to have been much different when allowance is made for inflation because retail prices have been virtually static since the mid-1990s after spiralling by around 20 per cent per annum in the 1980s. One swallow does not make a summer, however. The communiqué did not explain the sudden GDP spurt in 2001 but it is likely to have resulted from a happy coincidence of factors essentially external to the 'real' economy. The illicit import at discretionary prices of 150,000–200,000 barrels per day of Iraqi crude oil in violation of UN sanctions against Baghdad may well have played a big part. This trade enabled Syria to export more of its own oil at full market prices. Whatever the reasons for the sharp GDP growth in 2001, however, they certainly did not include any overnight infusion of efficiency into the main body of the economy.

Since the mid-1980s Syria has been highly dependent on its oil industry. Crude oil and petroleum products have accounted in recent years for 60–70 per cent of export earnings and 40–50 per cent of the state budget. Already half of Syria's output of about 530,000 barrels per day is destined for domestic consumption (if oil smuggled in from Iraq is excluded) and the country could become a net oil importer as it was before the rapid development of its new Euphrates Valley oilfields in the 1980s. Assuming no new discoveries and no change in production levels, Syria's oil reserves will be exhausted by about 2012. That the creaking edifice of the non-oil economy, on which most Syrians depend, has managed to avoid collapse for so long is more than anything the result of oil income. If this declines, the consequences for the rest of the economy could be severe.

Arab and other (mainly European Union) aid will continue to help keep Syria afloat but the regime understands well that the private sector and foreign investment must be a major – and probably the biggest – part of the answer to the economic crisis. In January 2002 Economy and Foreign Trade Minister Ghassan ar-Rifai (who had worked with the World Bank before becoming a minister in the December 2001 cabinet reshuffle) affirmed:

> The fundamental challenges, as I see them, are accelerating growth on a sustainable basis by modernising and diversifying the economy and, in doing that, creating sufficient employment to absorb the rapidly growing and young labour force. To achieve these goals I see a great need to invigorate the role of the private sector, domestic and foreign, and to give it the opportunity *to lead the growth process* [my italics].[23]

Reflecting the regime's long-standing dilemma about the widening of social gulfs associated with private sector activity, Ar-Rifai stressed that he had in mind 'a private sector that is responsible and caring, a private sector that should be a partner in this process, with rights but also with commensurate obligations towards the economy and the country as a whole'. He also stressed that the government 'is not considering at this point in time the privatisation of the state companies'.

Any significant growth in private investment will require a major overhaul of Syria's financial sector and a start was made in 2000–2002. In December 2000 the Ba'ath Party announced its approval of plans to allow the country's first private banks, establish a stock market and float the local currency. In March 2001 parliament passed a law permitting private banks provided that they were at least 51 per cent Syrian-owned. As of September 2002, none had yet been established although several foreign banks, including France's giant Societé Générale and Germany's Hypovereinsbank, were showing interest. Earlier, in April 2000 (shortly before Hafiz al-Asad's death), a presidential decree had been issued permitting foreign banks to operate in free zones within Syria. Six Lebanese banks took advantage of the measure, although they could offer services only to companies based in the free zones, but in September 2002 it emerged that all had ceased operations because of excessive restrictions. In March 2002 Bashar signed a law establishing a Monetary and Credit Council to regulate the financial market. To be chaired by the Central Bank governor, the new council's responsibilities will include approving applications from private banks wishing to operate in Syria. Plans were meanwhile in hand for the reform of the tax system and trade regulations and for the establishment of a special committee to promote private investment.

External Threats Bolster the Hardliners

By mid-2002 it appeared that Bashar's reform programme might be losing momentum. Partly, this was because of passive opposition from a bureaucracy and Ba'ath Party loath to assist in changes from which they would very likely be losers. In April Ghassan ar-Rifai said that reforms were facing unabated resistance at all levels.[24] At the same time, and while trials of civil society activists were being staged as part of the wider crackdown on the pro-democracy movement that had been under way since February 2001 (see Chapter 3), the hardliners were reasserting themselves. Israeli and Western threats to the region, they argued, made it the wrong time for reformist measures which might upset domestic unity and stability. For Syria and the wider Middle East, the outside world has been historically anything but benign. Syria's experience as the hapless victim of successive invasions and dismemberment means that external threats cause an even greater patriotic closing of ranks than they might do in some other parts of the world. At the same time, however, foreign threats present hardliners with highly convenient pretexts to maintain the status quo and silence their domestic critics. Not for nothing had the conservatives been seeking to demonise the civil society activists shamelessly as '*foreign* agents' and '*foreign*-financed' (see Chapter 3).

The greater the external threats, the better the hardliners' arguments played. In February 2001 the militarist Ariel Sharon had become Israel's prime minister. In April and again in May 2001 Israeli warplanes had attacked Syrian radar stations in Lebanon. Following a spate of suicide bombings in Israel by Palestinian militants, the Israelis in April 2002 had bloodily reoccupied almost all of the West Bank. The invasion was undertaken with the approval of a United States preoccupied with its global 'war on terrorism' sparked by the 11 September 2001 attacks in New York and Washington by Usama bin Laden's Afghanistan-based Al-Qa'ida organisation. Incredibly, President George W. Bush had described Sharon as a 'man of peace', prompting outrage in the Arab world. Bush was meanwhile planning a major military assault on Iraq with a view to replacing Saddam Hussain's government with a regime more friendly to US interests. Arab public opinion, already angered by the devastating impact on ordinary Iraqis of UN sanctions against Baghdad, imposed after the 1991 Iraqi withdrawal from Kuwait, was incensed at the prospect of a US attack that was not even being justified as part of the war on terrorism, which itself had been discredited after being used by despotic governments world-wide as an excuse to crack down on local political dissent.

Angered by Syria's breach of UN sanctions against Iraq and spurred by the powerful pro-Israeli lobby in Washington, the USA in early 2002 started leaning on Syria itself, thereby helping to tip the internal regime balance even further against Bashar. This US pressure came even though Syria had been providing the Americans with information about terrorist groups. On 27 January the US Sixth Fleet stopped and searched two Syrian cargo ships, the *Capitane Mohammed* and the *Hajji Rahma*, north of Cyprus. The vessels, loaded with citrus fruit, had been sailing to Syria from the Turkish port of Mersin. Nothing suspicious was found and the vessels were allowed to complete their voyages. The freighters had been intercepted after they had 'displayed suspicious behaviour', according to a statement by the US European Command, which added that the ships had been under surveillance for several weeks. Syria summoned the US Chargé d'Affaires in Damascus and lodged a 'strong protest' against the 'act of piracy', according to a Foreign Ministry statement. The US statement confirmed that the searches had come as part of moves 'to deny the Mediterranean to anyone who would wish to use it for any activities associated with terrorism'. At the time navies from ten countries were engaged in world-wide efforts to thwart terrorist operations, especially by Al-Qa'ida.

In an address to the conservative Heritage Foundation in Washington on 6 May, John Bolton, Under-Secretary of State for Arms Control and International Security, attacked Syria, Libya and Cuba as 'rogue states' which were developing weapons of mass destruction and which were only one step removed from the 'axis of evil' comprising Iran, Iraq and North Korea which had been identified by President Bush earlier in the year as major threats to world peace. Syria, said Bolton, was actively pursuing biological and chemical weapons programmes, had acquired 'several hundred' Scud and other medium-range missiles and was trying to develop upgraded versions. Bolton underlined US partisanship by failing entirely to mention that Israel has an arsenal of over 200 nuclear bombs, has a missile capability second to none in the Middle East and a stockpile of chemical weapons.

On 22 May Syria was named for the eighth year running as a state sponsor of terrorism in the State Department's annual report on the subject. Such states are barred from receiving US aid. The previous month a Syria Accountability Act had been introduced in the US Congress by pro-Israeli hawks that urged comprehensive US trade and other sanctions against Damascus. The aim was 'to halt Syrian support for terrorism, end its occupation of Lebanon, stop its development of weapons of mass destruction, cease its illegal importation of Iraqi oil, and by so doing hold Syria accountable for its role in the Middle East'. By mid-September 2002 the draft Act had been endorsed by thirty-six senators and 155 representatives. Despite Washington's considerable irritation at Syria, however, the Bush administration clearly indicated that it would oppose the measure as being counter-productive in terms of other US preoccupations – at that time principally 'regime-change' in Iraq and the war on terrorism.

By April 2002 Bashar himself was questioning key elements of his own reform programme and defiantly affirming that Damascus was not merely one step beyond the 'axis of evil', as Bolton had claimed in his Heritage Foundation address, but was actually part of it. In internal discussions with regime figures he described reform of the administration as his primary aim, rather than a wider economic restructuring; warned that private banks could destabilise the economy;

and ruled out the establishment of private universities – legislation for which had been agreed in late 2000. He criticised Arab states for being too closely aligned with Washington and stressed that while Syria had good relations with Europe it did not depend on European goodwill. Bashar asserted that Syria now formed part of an anti-Western axis with Iran and Iraq. Damascus, he said, was urging its long-standing ally Iran to move closer to Baghdad, its erstwhile 1980–88 Gulf war enemy, because any regime that took power in Iraq with US support would be antagonistic to both Iran and Syria.[25]

Ironically, through its support for an aggressive Israel and through its blundering threats against Iraq and Syria itself, a Western world proclaiming its commitment to democracy, human rights and the rule of law had created conditions in which the most conservative and anti-democratic wing of the Syrian regime had managed to turn back what eighteen months earlier had appeared to be an unstoppable reformist tide. 'Bush and Sharon presented a gift to the hardliners,' commented one Syrian liberal, asking not to be named.[26]

While the Syrian system as a whole looked secure, the distribution of power within did appear to have changed. Hafiz al-Asad was all-powerful. Bashar's failure to carry through his reforms indicated that he had yet to develop fully an effective base of his own and that power had been devolved to some extent to the hardliners. If that trend were to continue, Bashar's future – although not necessarily the regime's – might be in doubt, especially if he were to play into his antagonists' hands, for example by failing to respond sufficiently firmly to US or Israeli provocations or by persisting with reforms opposed by the hardliners. By the time of writing in September 2002 he had shown himself careful not to be left out on any such limb.

Bread and/or Freedom?

Whatever initial hopes Bashar al-Asad might have entertained for a gradual liberalisation of the political system were soon abandoned in the face of stubborn opposition from regime conservatives. Instead, economic reform without political reform became the objective. 'At the start, when Bashar came to power, he just threw a bundle of projects, of issues, on to the table but he soon realised that he could not start immediately by moving on these issues,' said Dr Samir Altaqi of the Syrian Communist Party faction led by Yousef Faisal.[27] Or, as the member of parliament and leading civil society activist Riad Seif told me before he was arrested and imprisoned, the regime had opted in early 2001 for 'bread before freedom' as a pretext for clamping down on a civil society movement whose popularity was worrying the hardliners.[28]

A central issue is whether or to what extent 'bread' can be produced only with 'freedom'. Can a centrally directed, state-dominated economy like Syria's be transformed without parallel changes in the political environment? Many in the country's civil society and wider opposition movement would answer with a resounding 'no'. Riad Seif insists: 'We believe that economic reform without political reform will never succeed and bear fruit if it does not occur within a clear, transparent, parallel political reform programme.'[29] The same position is taken by the influential Syrian Muslim Brotherhood. 'We believe that Bashar will be unable to achieve economic reform without political openness,' said Ali Sadr ad-Din al-Bayanouni, the Brotherhood's superintendent-general.[30]

It has often been asserted – by bodies as powerful as the IMF, the World Bank and the US government – that economic liberalisation leads almost automatically to political liberalisation; that effective private sector economic activity requires accountability and transparency which inexorably will find an echo in the political sphere. 'It's basically nonsense,' said George Joffé, of Cambridge University's Centre for International Studies. 'If you look at Chile just the reverse was true because economic activity in a capitalist mode is fundamentally class activity, and that means that classes will exclude those who don't fit in with their objectives.'[31]

Syria's experience to date suggests that, to an extent at least, economic liberalisation can proceed without democratisation. Syria's private sector was encouraged to expand as a means of compensating for public sector shortfalls, but it was kept on a very tight leash. Private sector activity was confined to certain sectors such as tourism and light industry. Arbitrarily in terms of any market-linked allocation of resources, the regime decided which entrepreneurs should benefit from which opportunities, and it retained the ability to rescind concessions. The result was to fragment the business community and make it dependent on regime goodwill. There is no evidence, meanwhile, that this divide and rule programme is much resented by the entrepreneurs. Most have been happy to get rich as appendages of the regime and there is little clamour for democracy among Syria's business class, whether the traditional Sunni urban merchants or the socially more diverse *nouveaux riches* of younger business people who owe their wealth directly to their links to the regime. Perthes noted:

> While granting a higher degree of autonomy to the private sector and thereby surrendering some economic levers, the regime has not relinquished any of its political powers. Limited and selective pluralism, as granted by the regime, can be regarded as a matter of 'system maintenance' rather than democratisation or substantial political liberalisation. It aims at regaining lost legitimacy and helps to secure the incorporation of indispensable groups into regime structures.[32]

Private entrepreneurs, whether in Syria or elsewhere, may not demand genuine democratisation as a condition of investing. It nevertheless seems probable that there are limits to their tolerance of certain features that characterise despotic rule. This is particularly true of foreign investors who have choices about where to put their money. In particular, investors require predictability, an absence of capriciousness and arbitrariness. They demand a channel not subject to regime manipulation that can mediate their relations with a regime. In practice, this boils down to a reliable legal system. The rule of law may be one of the central demands of the civil society movement, but effective judicial systems can exist without liberal democracy or respect for human rights, at least within the commercial realm. Such a judicial system may not be entirely free from regime interference but it may be sufficiently independent to win investors' confidence. It is very much a question of the degree to which the regime and its key members decide that for the sake of the greater good of increased investment they are prepared to accept occasional adverse rulings which, while perhaps costly to their financial interests, would not threaten their political pre-eminence.

With that in mind, the civil society movement's argument about the rule of law being a prerequisite of economic progress appears only partly correct – although neither does it invalidate the point that a genuinely independent judicial system would be likely to be more acceptable to investors than a partly captive but at least usually predictable system. In Syria, it seems probable that Bashar's 'modernisation' project (assuming that it will not be irretrievably obstructed by the regime's hardliners) will include the establishment of just such a system. Depressing as it may be for lovers of freedom and democracy, it would seem that bread *can* be made without freedom.

Modernisers Will Prevail

The illicit import of Iraqi oil, and an associated mushrooming of other trade with Iraq, may have bought Syria some time – and made it much easier for the hardliners to reassert themselves – but it has done nothing to resolve the country's fundamental economic crisis. The pressing need to avert dangerous economic strains that could translate into political unrest, possibly with a strong Islamist tinge, means that Bashar's technocratic modernisers will very likely prevail in the end. The pace of economic reform may not be sufficiently rapid to satisfy the population's swelling demands but politically this need not matter. Fear of the *mukhabarat* and the rest of the security apparatus will continue to deter protesters from openly challenging the status quo. The primary aim will be to move ahead at a speed and in a manner consistent with regime stability. 'We'll go steady, with the same line towards the future. We'll go as fast as the people and the establishments can absorb,' insisted Ayman 'Abd an-Nur, one of the President's close economic advisers. 'We're not going to make the same mistakes as Eastern Europe made in embarking on a rapid transition from communism to capitalism. We're not going to have a mess here in Syria. We will formulate our own model.'[33]

In reality, Syria looks set to take much the same route as Egypt, Tunisia and Algeria, all of which were centralised, 'socialist', single-party states on the Eastern European model. Under pressure from creditors and the IMF, all three liberalised their economies without more than superficial reforms of their political systems, with different results. Algeria, racked by a violent Islamist insurgency sparked by the military regime's refusal to accept the outcome of a general election in 1991–92, struggles to make economic headway. Egypt, whose economy has been opened since 1974 and which has privatised over 300 state enterprises, suffers from yawning and politically dangerous gulfs between the rich and the very poor and is burdened by as big a trade deficit as it had twenty years ago. In Tunisia a vibrant private sector combined with an efficient bureaucracy and close relations with Europe have resulted in what Joffé termed an economy that 'almost delivers'.[34] In all three states, however, leading regime figures and their families appropriated the best opportunities and retained control of large swathes of the economy. While displaying many of the features of modern economies, these states include an 'occulted, mafia-type system which may enrich the elite but has done little to satisfy the needs of the population at large'.[35]

With the collapse of the Soviet Bloc, Syria found itself relatively isolated beyond its own region. Closer relations with the USA were problematic because of Washington's open-ended support for an Israel which remained in military occupation of Syria's Golan Heights and because Damascus was on the State Department's list of sponsors of international terrorism, a description that Syria has not deserved since the mid-1990s. Accordingly, Syria has increasingly looked to Europe as a trade partner and as a potential source of urgently needed development assistance and political support. In 2000 European Union countries accounted for 34 per cent of Syria's imports and 66 per cent of its exports, including 62 per cent of Syria's oil products exports. Syria's reform efforts will be encouraged (although certainly not determined) by the European Union, with which Damascus started negotiating an association agreement in 2001. Such agreements are wide-ranging economic, political and cultural accords which grant the signatories preferential access to each other's markets and which require signatories to acknowledge the primacy of market forces and to liberalise their economies. The accords are major elements in the Euro-Mediterranean Partnership (often termed the Barcelona Process) that was launched at the first Euro-Mediterranean ministerial summit in Barcelona in November 1995. The ultimate objective is the creation of a Euro-Mediterranean free trade zone by 2010. As of mid-2002 association agreements had been signed and ratified with Tunisia, Israel, Jordan, the Palestinian Authority and Morocco and agreements with Egypt, Algeria and Lebanon had been signed but not yet ratified. For Syria, the implications of an association agreement are far-reaching. The EU's insistence on a liberalised economy does not sit comfortably with Syria's determination to retain centralised control. A compromise is likely, however, with Syria being granted a lengthy transitional period during which it will benefit substantially from Europe's MEDA programme, the development financing arm of the Barcelona Process, and from European Investment Bank funding.

All the association agreements have clauses requiring respect for human rights although *all* the Mediterranean signatories – including Israel – have very poor records in this area. For all its liberal pretensions, however, the EU has done nothing concrete to enforce compliance. Before entering negotiations with Brussels, Syria consulted closely the Arab parties that had already been through the process, and will have taken note of Europe's inaction on human rights. Damascus should not be complacent, however. To many in Europe, human rights matter, and the issue could move up the political agenda. During the 1990s the European Parliament several times blocked financial aid to Syria because of its human rights violations. Although the parliament remains a relatively toothless beast, its powers are likely to grow. On 8 August 2002 the EU declared that it 'deeply regrets' the prison sentences imposed on Syrian civil society activists who had been 'peacefully exercising their legitimate right to freedom of speech' and it called on Syria 'to release all political prisoners'. The statement affirmed the EU's intention to 'continue to monitor the human rights situation in Syria, in particular in the context of a future Association Agreement'.

Human Rights Watch has also taken good note of Syria's potential vulnerability to European pressure. 'The European Union [EU] does a lot of business with Syria, and it has a responsibility to respond to a human rights crisis of this magnitude,' Lotte Leicht, director of the Brussels office of Human Rights Watch, was quoted as saying in a press release on 30 August 2002, responding to the sentencing of the ten pro-democracy activists. Noting that the EU was negotiating an association agreement with Damascus, the statement recalled that all such accords stipulated that relations between the parties 'shall be based on respect of democratic principles and fundamental human rights as set out in the Universal Declaration on Human Rights'. On 18 September Human Rights Watch launched an international campaign to press the EU to act on behalf of the ten prisoners, and it made public a letter it had sent to the European Commission's External Relations Commissioner, Chris Patten; to the EU's High Representative for the Common Foreign and Security Policy, Javier Solana; and to EU foreign ministers. This urged that the EU 'send a clear message to Damascus that further negotiations of the Association Agreement will not proceed until the ten men are released unconditionally'.

US and Israeli policies towards Syria, the Palestinians and the wider region will nevertheless remain the most important external influences on the speed and direction of Bashar al-Asad's reforms. As noted above in relation to 2001–2002, when Syria feels encircled and threatened, regime hardliners come to the fore, insisting that national unity and military preparedness must come first and that possibly destabilising economic and other reforms must wait. Nothing would do more to encourage reform than just and therefore effective Israeli–Palestinian and Syrian–Israeli peace accords and a less belligerent US stance towards Middle Eastern regimes disliked by hawks in Washington.

In asserting that people worry more about their economic welfare than their personal freedoms, Bashar's regime is reiterating the view of the late Hafiz al-Asad. In a private conversation in 1971, Asad expressed the view that the people had 'primarily economic demands' such as the acquisition of a plot of land, a house and a car. Such demands he could satisfy 'in one way or another'. Asad Senior chillingly opined that only 'one or two hundred individuals at most' seriously engaged in politics and would oppose him whatever he did. 'It is for them that the Mezzeh prison was originally intended.'[36]

His and his son's central point – that political freedom is a lesser matter than economics and therefore can wait – may be true up to a point. Someone who is starving plainly needs food more than the vote. Yet it is also self-evident that people do care very much about freedom and are more than mere economic units and that political change can arise independently of economic circumstances. In the short and medium terms there is scant prospect of any serious democratisation in Syria and its civil society movement is likely to remain marginalised and ineffectual. Bashar, however, is not like his father. He appears to have tacitly encouraged the 'Damascus Spring' for as long as he could. It is not unthinkable that, if he can strengthen his position relative to the hardliners, and, given favourable external and economic conditions, Bashar might launch a political reform programme, albeit one that is cautious and limited in scope.

'Repressive systems cause an indefinable destruction of social and moral fibre,' said George Joffé. 'Society loses a sense of cohesion, a sense of itself going somewhere. When someone like Bashar arrives, having had a relatively cosmopolitan set of experiences, he may well feel: this is a mistake. It could be done better than this. I don't want to rule a country where people are becoming torpid, becoming simply clones, without any vitality or sense of purpose. He might decide that, given the right conditions, a degree of freedom can be tolerated.'[37]

Syria's civil society activists are not holding their breath. They understand the political realities. They are not just dreamers. Many have served or are now serving stiff prison terms for expressing views that in a liberal democracy would be considered utterly unexceptional. They understand that Syria is not on the verge of a democratic revolution and that their main impact will be as a lobby group. 'We have to have a certain hope that we can modify the system, even if by 30 per cent, in the direction of more democracy, more respect for human rights and civil liberties,' said one of the movement's thinkers, Sadiq Jalal al-Azm.[38]

To date, Syria's Ba'athist regime, whether under Hafiz al-Asad or his son, has delivered neither bread nor freedom. In future it *might* provide *some* bread and *some* freedom. Sadly, even if it does not the system, sclerotic and dying though it may be, will probably persist. If North Korea – and indeed the Oceania of Orwell's *Nineteen Eighty-Four* – can stagger on for decades, why not Syria too?

Notes

1. Charles Glass, *Tribes with Flags: A Journey Curtailed* (London: Secker and Warburg, 1990), p. 200.

2. E-mail from Albert Aji, proprietor of the Orient Press Centre in Damascus, 14 March 2002. Aji's informant was the Syrian writer Adel Abu Shanab, a long-time Havana customer.

3. Interview with author, Damascus, 5 May 2001.

4. Interview with author, Damascus, 1 December 2001.

5. Hanna Batatu, *Syria's Peasantry, the Descendants of Its Lesser Rural Notables, and Their Politics* (Princeton, NJ: Princeton University Press, 1990), p. 277.

6. Nikolaos Van Dam, *The Struggle for Power in Syria: Politics and Society under Asad and the Ba'th Party* (London: I.B. Tauris, 1996), p. 137.

7. Ibid., p. 142.

8. Volker Perthes, *The Political Economy of Syria under Asad* (London: I.B. Tauris, 1995), p. 253.

9. Eyal Zisser, *Asad's Legacy: Syria in Transition* (London: Hurst and Co., 2001), p. 189.

10. Ibid., p. 184.

11. Interview with author, London, 19 July 2002.

12. Interview with author, Damascus, 17 February 2002.

13. 'Syria Ranks 15 in Economic Performance in the MENA Region', *The Syria Report*, 30 May 2002.

14. World Bank, *World Development Indicators Database* (Washington, DC: World Bank, July 2001).

15. Office of the Prime Minister, *Statistical Abstract 2001*, Central Bureau of Statistics, Syrian Arab Republic.

16. 'CBS Releases Latest Statistics on Syria's Labour Force', *The Syria Report*, 16 September 2002.

17. US Department of State, *Background Note: Syria* (Washington, DC: Bureau of Near Eastern Affairs, February 2002).

18. Volker Perthes, 'The Political Economy of the Syrian Succession', *Survival*, International Institute of Strategic Studies (IISS), 43 (1), Spring 2001.

19. *Middle East Economic Digest*, 13 July 2001, p. 18.

20. *The Syria Report*, 10 January 2002.

21. Office of the Prime Minister, *Statistical Abstract 2001*.

22. World Bank, *Syrian Arab Republic, Country Brief*, October 2001 (updated February 2002).

23. 'An Exclusive Interview with Ghassan ar-Rifai', *Online Briefing*, The Oxford Business Group, 15 January 2002.

24. *The Syria Report*, 29 April 2002.

25. Interviews by author with well-placed sources who requested anonymity, May 2002.

26. Interview with author, Damascus, 1 December 2001.

27. Interview with author, Damascus, 1 December 2001.

28. Interview with author, Damascus, 5 May 2001.

29. Ibid.

30. Interview with author, London, 19 July 2002.

31. Interview with author, London, 16 January 2001.

32. Volker Perthes, 'Stages of Economic and Political Liberalization', in Eberhard Kienle (ed.), *Contemporary Syria: Liberalization between Cold War and Cold Peace* (London: British Academic Press, 1994), p. 70.

33. Interview with author, Damascus, 4 December 2001.

34. Interview with author, London, 26 May 2002.

35. Ibid.

36. Batatu, *Syria's Peasantry*, p. 206.

37. Interview with author, London, 16 January 2001.

38. Interview with author, Damascus, 5 May 2001.

APPENDIX I

The Statement of 99: Published 27 September 2000

§ DEMOCRACY and human rights today constitute a common humanitarian language, gathering peoples and uniting their hopes for a better future. And even if some major countries use these to promote their policies and interests, interaction among peoples need not result in domination and political dictation. It was permitted to our people in the past, and it will be permitted to them in the future, to be influenced by the experiences of others, and to add their own contribution, thereby developing their own distinctiveness without being closed-in on themselves.

Syria today enters the twenty-first century in urgent need for all its citizens to join forces to face the challenges posed by peace, modernisation and the opening-up to the outside world. And for this our people are invited more than ever before to participate in the construction of Syria's present and future.

From this objective need, and from concern for our national unity, believing that the future of our country cannot be built but by its offspring, being citizens in a republican system where everybody has the right to freedom of opinion and of expression, we, the undersigned, call upon the authorities to accede to the following demands:

- an end to the State of Emergency and martial law in effect in Syria since 1963
- an amnesty for all political prisoners and prisoners of conscience and those who are pursued because of their political ideas and allowing the return of all deportees and exiled citizens
- the establishment of a state of law; the granting of public freedoms; the recognition of political and intellectual pluralism, freedom of assembly, the press and of expression

- the liberation of public life from the [restrictive] laws, constraints and [various] forms of censorship imposed on it, such that citizens would be allowed to express their various interests within a framework of social harmony, peaceful competition and an institutional structure that would enable all to participate in the country's development and prosperity

No reform, be it economic, administrative or legal, will achieve tranquillity and stability in the country unless fully accompanied by the desired political reform, which alone can steer our society towards safe shores.

Signatories

1. Abdul Hadi Abbas (lawyer and writer)
2. Abdul Mu'in al-Mallouhi (member of the Arabic Language Academy)
3. Antoun al-Maqdisi (writer and thinker)
4. Burhan Ghalyoun (writer and thinker)
5. Sadiq Jalal al-Azm (writer and thinker)
6. Michel Kilo (writer)
7. Tayeb Tayzini (writer and thinker)
8. Abdul Rahman Mounif (novelist)
9. Adonis (poet)
10. Burhan Bukhari (researcher)
11. Hanna Aboud (writer)
12. Omar Amiralay (cinematographer)
13. Khalid Taja (actor)
14. Bassam Kousa (actor)
15. Naila al-Atrash (theatre producer)
16. Abdullah Hannah (researcher/historian)
17. Samir Suaifan (economist)
18. Faisal Darraj (researcher)
19. Haidar Haidar (novelist)
20. Nazih Abu 'Afsh (poet)
21. Hassan M. Yousef (novelist/journalist)
22. Usama Muhammad (cinematographer)
23. Nabil Suleiman (novelist/critic)
24. Abdul Razzak 'Eid (researcher/critic)
25. Jad al-Karim Jaba'i (writer/researcher)
26. Abdul Latif Abdul Hamid (cinematographer)
27. Samir Zikra (cinematographer)

28. Ahmad Mu'allah (artist)
29. Fares al-Hellou (actor)
30. Ihsan Abbas (researcher)
31. Hanan Kassab Hassan (university professor)
32. Mamdouh Azzam (novelist)
33. Adel Mahmoud (poet)
34. Hazem al-Azmeh (physician and university professor)
35. Burhan Zraik (lawyer)
36. Muhammad Ra'adoun (lawyer)
37. Yasser Sari (lawyer)
38. Yousef Salman (translator)
39. Hind Midani (cinematographer)
40. Munzir Masri (poet/artist)
41. Ahmad Mu'aitah (university professor)
42. Wafiq Slaitin (university professor)
43. Mujab al-Imam (university professor)
44. Munzir Halloum (university professor)
45. Malik Suleiman (university professor)
46. Sarab Jamal al-Atassi (researcher)
47. Toufiq Haroun (lawyer)
48. Issam Suleiman (physician)
49. Joseph Lahham (lawyer)
50. Attiyah Massouh (researcher)
51. Radwan Kadmani (university professor)
52. Nizar Sabour (artist)
53. Shouaib Tlaimat (university professor)
54. Hassan Sami Youssef (cinematographer/writer)
55. Waha ar-Raheb (cinematographer/actress)
56. Hamid Mer'i (economic consultant)
57. Rif'at as-Sioufi (engineer)
58. Muwafaq Nirbiya (writer)
59. Suheil Shabat (university professor)
60. Jamal Shuhaid (university professor)
61. Omar Koch (writer)
62. Raymond Butros (cinematographer)
63. Antoinette Azriyeh (cinematographer)
64. Najib Nussair (critic/writer)
65. May Skaff (actress)
66. Nidal ad-Dibs (cinematographer)
67. Farah Jukhdar (architect)
68. Akram Katreeb (poet)

69. Lukman Dabraki (poet)
70. Hikmat Shatta (architect)
71. Muhammad Najati Tayyara (researcher)
72. Najmeddine as-Samman (novelist)
73. Ali as-Saleh (economist/researcher)
74. Sabah al-Hallak (researcher)
75. Nawal al-Yazji (researcher)
76. Muhammad Karsaly (cinematographer)
77. Sawsan Zakzak (researcher)
78. Shawki Baghdadi (poet)
79. Bashar Zarkan (musician)
80. Fayez Sarah (journalist)
81. Muhammad al-Fahd (journalist/poet)
82. Muhammad Berri La'awani (theatre producer)
83. Najat Amoudi (educator)
84. Adel Zakkar (physician/poet)
85. Mustafa Khodr (poet)
86. Muhammad Sayed Rassas (writer)
87. Kassem Azzawi (poet)
88. Muhammad Hamdan (writer)
89. Nabil al-Yafi (researcher)
90. Tamim Mun'im (lawyer)
91. Ibrahim Hakim (lawyer)
92. Anwar al-Bunni (lawyer)
93. Khalil Ma'atouk (lawyer)
94. Ali al-Jundi (poet)
95. Ali Kanaan (poet)
96. Muhammad Kamal al-Khatib (researcher)
97. Mamdouh Adwan (poet)
98. Muhammad Malass (cinematographer)
99. Muhammad Ali al-Atassi (journalist)

Note

The source for 'The Statement of 99' is *Al-Hayat*, 27 September 2000.

APPENDIX 2

The Statement of 1,000 or Basic Document: Released to the Arab Press 9 January 2001

§ SYRIA needs today, more than ever before, an objective reflection to draw lessons from the last decades and to shape its future, following the deterioration of its social, political, economic and cultural conditions, and in response to the challenges of globalisation and economic integration and the challenges of the Arab–Israeli conflict that our people and nation must confront and whose dangers they must repel.

Arising from a sincere faith in our country, in our people and in their creative capacities and vitality, and keen to interact positively with all serious initiatives for reform, [we assert that] it is vital today to establish a comprehensive dialogue between all citizens and all social classes and political forces, intellectuals and producers and creative people, in order to encourage the development of civil society – a society based on individual freedom, human rights and citizenship; and the establishment of a state of justice and rights, a state for all its people, without favour or exception, in which all can take pride. Our country today needs the efforts of all its citizens to revive civil society, whose weakness, and the attempts to weaken it, over the last decades deprived the country's development and construction process of crucial national capacities that were unable to participate in it actively and positively.

Ambiguity surrounding the meaning of civil society, resulting from the multiple democratic experiments in ancient and modern history, negates neither its existence in our country, as it is a social reality in history and in the world, nor its halting progression into a modern society which produced a vibrant culture, a free press, associations, political parties, trade unions and constitutional legitimacy and a peaceful transfer of power. These made Syria one of the least backward – if not the most advanced – of Arab countries.

This path enhanced our society's national cohesion, until the sudden arrival of that interruption based on 'revolutionary legitimacy' rather than constitutional legitimacy. Marginalising civil society involved disregarding the state, the individual and his position, painting the state with one party, one colour and one opinion. It involved creating a state for one part of society, a part which did not acknowledge its particularity but portrayed itself as representing the people and as 'leading the state and society'. Citizenship was reduced to the narrow concept of belonging to one party and to personal loyalty. This part of society considered the rest of the population as a mere herd. The wealth of the state and of its institutions, the country's resources and those of the institutions of civil society, became like feudal estates that were distributed to followers and loyalists. Patronage replaced law; gifts and favours replaced rights; and personal interests replaced the general interest. Society was desecrated, its wealth plundered and its destiny commandeered by those who became symbols of oppression. Every citizen became a suspect, if not actually considered guilty, to be apprehended at will. The regime treated people not only as a neglected mass, subject to its will, but also as minor, incompetent and under suspicion. The government went so far as to accuse people of treason whenever they took the smallest initiative to express their opinion or demand their rights. It should be mentioned that marginalising civil society led to marginalising the state itself, underlining the organic relationship between them as neither exists without the other. Civil society constitutes the very substance of the modern state, while the state is civil society's political expression. Together, they constitute the democratic system of government.

Our society, with its national revolutions against colonialism and its political movement against political oppression; and which revealed its patriotic and nationalist spirit, eager for liberation and progress; which has been patient and has given many martyrs and sacrifices for freedom and justice, is still capable of rebuilding its social and political life; of rebuilding its economy and culture according to the requirements of modernity and development. It is still capable of joining the march of scientific and technological progress, and can overcome the relationships and structures that produced tyranny and that are intimately linked to the imperialism and national fragmentation that were their cause.

The consequences of coups against political democracy in the name of socialism are now plain. With the collapse of the Soviet model and its East European and Third World extensions, the impossibility of building socialism or establishing social democracy without political democracy became obvious. The Soviet experience also demonstrated the fragility of a state that does not draw its legitimacy from civil society, and of an authority that does not draw its legitimacy from the people. Equally plain is the inadequacy of viewing the people as mere subjects of 'revolutionary will', and of denying the social, cultural and political diversity of society and the different interests of each of its component parts. The Soviet experience underlined the consequences of denying that the rule of law – as a judicial expression of public order and of the essence of the state itself, as well as an expression of all that is common between all citizens and social groups – is an historic compromise between all those interests and diverse groups that should be the basis for genuine national unity.

It is this historic compromise which creates constitutions and laws that are in line with the development of society, which itself is affected by the pace of global development. Constitutions are therefore usually modified, changed and improved according to the needs of that development. The concept of civil society in the world to which we belong – geographically at least – that was revived in the 1970s, represented, and still represents, the reality of societal existence, the latter being defined by the transition of mankind from Nature to society, that is, to human construction and civil politics, to use the expression of [the medieval Arab historian] Ibn Khaldoun. From this concept arose an array of concepts leading to a 'social covenant' as opposed to the 'divine right' claimed by dictators, kings and emperors. The development of this social covenant is nothing more than the political counterpart of the triumph of reason which placed the human being at the centre of human knowledge. Modern societies and modern thinking gave rise to the modern civil state that guarantees freedom of belief and religious practice and unrestrained thought – all within the framework of acknowledging, in practice, a freedom defined by law, conditioned by responsibility and crowned by the creative initiative, love of knowledge and [the spirit of] working with and for the wider group.

For all these reasons there is a great need today to revive societal and social institutions free of domination by the executive authority and by the security apparatus, which usurped full powers. These institutions must also be free of all traditional forms of social ties, relationships and structures, such as those of tribalism and sectarianism, in order to re-establish politics in society as its primary free, conscious and constructive activity, and to achieve the crucial balance between society and state, co-ordinating their activities, and thus achieving liberty, equality and justice. National unity is thus bolstered, as is the dignity and sovereignty of the state. The rule of law becomes the final arbiter for all.

Only in civil society can a comprehensive national dialogue characterised by freedom of expression and speech and respect for diverse opinions be conducted, in order to encourage mass participation for the benefit of all the people. No social or political group has the right to decide by itself where the country's national interests lie, and what means should be pursued to achieve those interests. All groups – including the present ruling power – must make their opinions, ideas and programmes known to the people for discussion and dialogue. No dialogue is possible without freedom of opinion and expression, free political parties and trade unions, a free press, free social organisations and a legislature that genuinely and effectively represents the people.

No reform is possible without a comprehensive national dialogue because dialogue always produces new facts that are relevant to all. The logic of dialogue negates that of holding a monopoly on truth, patriotism, or any other monopoly. That is why we are calling for the adoption of the principle of dialogue, constructive criticism and peaceful development to resolve all disagreements through compromise and understanding. This is one of the most important characteristics and advantages of civil society.

The vitality of civil society is strikingly manifested in the establishment of voluntary, independent, non-governmental organisations based on democratic choice, whose objective is the establishment of justice and the rule of law that ensures civil rights and protects general liberties. That is why we believe that in defending civil society we defend the state and the authority holding power in that state.

For economic reforms and anti-corruption measures to succeed, they must be preceded and accompanied by a comprehensive package of political and constitutional reforms. Otherwise these reforms will not achieve their objectives. The economic and anti-corruption reform process therefore must develop into a permanent legal mechanism that stimulates public participation and encourages a continuous monitoring of state institutions as well as the private sector. All this should be done in an atmosphere of transparency that offers all social groups and forces and political parties the opportunity to participate effectively in the processes of planning, preparation, implementation and correction. It will also enable them to identify mistakes, waste and corruption promptly, as well as enabling the judicial system and supervisory bodies to call miscreants to account. Partial and selective measures will not lead to reform.

Our philosophy and practice consider that:

- human beings are aims unto themselves
- freedom, dignity, welfare and happiness are the purpose of development and progress
- national unity and the general interest are the yardsticks for all policies and practices
- all citizens are equal before the law, since inequality always creates those who are privileged and those who are deprived of all rights, thus sowing the seeds of discrimination and disunity and degrading social relations to sub-political levels

The foundations of our philosophy and practice are that:

- the correct practice of politics is that based on patriotic, national and human interest rather than on private interests
- national achievements are attributable to the people, not to individuals
- social groups and political parties are defined by the entire national social entity
- the people are the source of all powers

We therefore believe that political reform is the necessary and only way out of the current state of stagnation and decline, and the only way of extricating the general administration from its chronic torpor. We believe, furthermore, that the following must be implemented urgently as necessary preludes to political reform:

1. Abrogation of the Emergency Law now in force. Martial law regulations, emergency courts and all similar measures must be cancelled forthwith, and all injustices they caused over the years remedied. Political prisoners must be released, and the situation of those deprived of civil and labour rights by special courts and laws must be rectified. Exiles must be allowed to return.
2. Political freedoms – especially freedom of opinion and expression – must be allowed. Civil and political life must be overseen by democratic legislation regulating the activities of political parties, associations and non-governmental organisations – especially the trade unions which, through their conversion into state institutions, have lost partly or entirely the very reasons for their establishment.

3. Reinstatement of the publications law ensuring freedom of the press that was annulled by the State of Emergency.
4. Enactment of a democratic election law to regulate elections at all levels in a way that ensures that all segments of society are represented fairly, and the electoral process should be subjected to the supervision of an independent judiciary. The parliament elected as the result of this process will be a genuine legislative and supervisory institution, truly representing the will of the people, acting as the highest authoritative reference for all and symbolising the people's membership in the country and their positive participation in deciding how it is governed. The wholeness of the state is never expressed more clearly than by the legislative institution and by the independence and integrity of the judiciary.
5. Independence and integrity of the judiciary, with laws applied equally to rulers and ruled.
6. Ensuring that citizens are accorded their full economic rights, most of which are stated in the Constitution. The most important of these constitutionally guaranteed rights are (i) a fair share of national wealth and income; (ii) suitable employment and a life of dignity; and (iii) protecting the right of future generations to their fair share of the country's wealth and to a clean environment. Economic and social development are senseless if they are not aimed at erasing social injustice, humanising conditions of work and life and countering unemployment and poverty.
7. Insisting that the parties affiliated to the Progressive National Front (PNF) truly represent the most vibrant of forces in Syrian society; that they by themselves totally fill the vacuum of Syrian politics; and that the country needs nothing more than the reinvigoration of the PNF will serve only to perpetuate further the social and economic stagnation and political paralysis. It is imperative to review the relationship of the PNF with the government, to reconsider the concept of 'the leading party in society and the state', and to review any other concept that excludes the people from political life.
8. Abolition of legal discrimination against women.

Stemming from a desire to participate constructively in the process of social development and reform, we call for the establishment of committees for reviving civil society in all sectors of Syrian life as a continuation and development of the concept of the 'friends of civil society'. From a sense of national responsibility and independence, we hope that these committees will play their part in overcoming the negativity and demoralisation, and [enabling Syria to] emerge from the stagnation that doubles our backwardness in relation to the pace of international development. Through these committees, we hope to take the step to a free, independent and democratic society that takes part in laying the foundations for a renaissance that will ensure a better future for the Arab nation.

Note

The source for 'The Statement of 1,000' is *Al-Watha'iq as-Sadirat 'an al-Hiy'at at-Ta'sisia, Lijan Ihya' al-Mujtama' al-Madani fi Suria*, Damascus, undated.

APPENDIX 3

Towards a National Social Contract in Syria: Issued 14 April 2001[1]

§ THE Constituent Board of the Committees for the Revival of Civil Society in Syria wishes to propose this National Social Contract to all social and political forces in the country as a basis for a new social, political and moral covenant grounded in the honour and freedom of the individual, human rights linked to the law and a sense of responsibility, equality of opportunity, social justice and equality before the law. This contract is intended to provide broad guidelines that will apply in word and deed, and in the light of which we can define our positions regarding various social, economic, cultural and political issues. We intend this contract to become a foundation for a comprehensive national dialogue that will open new opportunities for positive participation in the process of reform, development and modernisation on which the future of our country depends. The contract outlines the most effective means of carrying out the reform process and provides it with the most appropriate balances of power in all fields as a means of attaining the desired democratic and just system.

We affirm that the Committees for the Revival of Civil Society are independent social and societal committees with no party affiliation, which aim to revitalise public life and enable citizens to return to public life and positive participation. A further aim is to reform culture and politics in society, as these two domains are vital for progress and building democracy, as well as for consolidating national unity on the bases of citizenship and the rule of law, in order to cement the nation's independence and sovereignty, liberate our occupied lands and strengthen Syria's position and its role in the rebirth of democracy.

After issuing its Basic Document, which was the result of intense discussions amongst intellectuals and concerned parties, and which won the support and acceptance of a broad segment of Syrian citizens, both inside the country and abroad, as well as the support of not a small number of Arab intellectuals, of whose solidarity we are proud, as we value the opinions of those who criticise from a stance of desiring the best and the ideal, the Constituent Board, with a sense of shared responsibility and congruence, presents the following:

1. Citizens shall be treated as free subjects whose liberties and rights must be guaranteed constitutionally, legally and practically. All measures necessary should be undertaken to enable them to participate positively in public affairs. Free citizens should be the building blocks for our social and political system, and the cornerstones of its stability and progress. Citizens must not be apprehended, arrested or tortured, whether physically or mentally. They must not be treated in ways inconsistent with human dignity. Their homes, correspondence and communications must not be violated, nor must any of their civil rights, and there should be no punishment except through the law. There should be no violation of any of the social, economic, political or cultural rights outlined in those international agreements and conventions mentioned in the country's Constitution. Citizenship entails a number of rights and duties, lack of respect for which is an absolute and consistent yardstick of civilisation and progress.
2. The people shall be treated only as a unitary entity of free citizens and not as a body of diverse religious and economic groups and sects. No effort should be spared to consolidate the people's national identity and to counter all those who try to undermine their unity and damage their interests. National unity must be enhanced on a daily basis through policies and practices based on the public interest, in all spheres of social life; and stemming from the need to consolidate and fortify the unity of our people, public life must be built on contractual obligations which together comprise a social, economic and moral contract that defines all national and human interests, policies and principles, for the state and society, provided that such a contract is always entered into through a frank and open national dialogue in which all social and political forces participate on an equal basis.
3. The independence, freedom, dignity, strength and unity of our country are common goals in a continuing battle that also targets domestic greed and, abroad, the Zionist enemy and forces of

plunder and hegemony. Democracy is our most potent weapon for winning this battle.

4. The state shall be based on justice and the rule of law; a state that belongs to all its citizens without exception or discrimination as to ethnic, political or religious affiliation.
5. The Syrian economic system is in need of profound reform based on the following guidelines:

   (a) Both public and private property are sacrosanct. It is the duty of legislation and government to protect property. The government is responsible to the people and the legislature with regard to conditions for developing properties, and must report regularly on any changes which may occur in those conditions;
   (b) Democracy, which embraces transparency, political and media pluralism, civil society, the rule of law, separation of authorities and free elections held under independent supervision, is a necessary condition for the success of economic reform that replaces monopolising, corruption and greed with the national interest and the rights of citizens;
   (c) Economic, legislative and administrative reform should aim at increasing economic growth, enhancing scientific and technological progress, accelerating human development, reducing the prosperity gap, strengthening national unity, ending emigration, fighting unemployment and poverty, helping the poor and those with special needs, enabling the nation and citizens to rely on themselves, providing the means necessary for maintaining steadfastness and liberating the occupied territories, and turning Syria into a preferred destination for working, living and investment, a socially and economically developing country which attracts inward investment;
   (d) Increasing citizens' share of the national income and increasing individual incomes in line with responsibility and authority, on the one hand, and with a dignified standard of living, on the other, with these increases in income arising from the reform process;
   (e) Enabling citizens, whether producers or consumers, to pursue their legitimate affairs, and defending their rights against blackmail and exploitation, cheating in specifications and pricing, and unjust policies and measures. Incentives for innovation and initiative should be encouraged and conditions for women, children and families improved. All the above cannot be achieved without publicised reform plans and programmes that are debated and supported by society.

6. Occupied Arab lands cannot be liberated without an Arab democratic system that can activate the necessary potential and effort. The current peace process is not, and should not be, the end of the struggle against the racist Israeli Zionist enemy. Linking patriotism to pan-Arabism, and linking both to democracy, is the condition for establishing true nationalism; nationalism that can successfully counter Zionist and imperialist designs and lead the struggle with the national enemy in a way that includes recovering all the nation's rights.
7. Work should be undertaken towards rebuilding Arab solidarity and strengthening ties between Arab states to a level where they can face the threats confronting the Arab nation. Steps should be taken to facilitate Arab unity, which we consider to be the essential condition for our nation's renaissance and progress, and we see its establishment as a vital requirement for us: societies, states and citizens. We see Arab unity as possible and necessary. The task should be started by building up all social, economic, political and cultural spheres of life with unity in mind. Arab unity cannot be separated from the democratic project, the latter being the matrix that will bind Arab states together into a stable union. The essential and possible step today towards unity is the opening of borders between all Arab countries, ensuring free movement of persons, goods and capital between them; and the creation of an Arab common market to confront the threats posed by global capitalism and economic mergers and the connected system of major economic blocs.
8. The people shall not be held in trusteeship. The people's right to choose the social, political and economic system they want for themselves shall not be usurped, since they are the source of all authority and the sole font of legitimacy. Citizens are adult and responsible individuals who should be enabled to practise their right to choose who represents them at all levels. Our country shall not revert to the days of chaos and military coups. The continuation of the state of unemployment and stagnation threatens us all with serious ramifications and can only be reversed through an enlargement of democracy and through liberating civil society from the tyranny of political and ideological exclusivity.
9. The adoption of dialogue and consensus as a way to settle problems in our country, and the rejection of violence in all shapes and forms. Oppression and coercion should be abandoned as a way to

run our national life and as a means to regulate the relationship between the people and government.

Historical experience shows that reforms cannot achieve their objectives without the involvement of all governmental, state and societal forces. We, the Committees for the Revival of Civil Society, are optimistic that we can persuade our society to adopt this programme, which must be based on our country's realities and potentials, in order to place our people and our country firmly on the road of progress and advancement.

Note

1. Based with permission on a translation in *MidEast Mirror* (19 April 2001, p. 18) of the text published in *An-Nahar*.

Select Bibliography

Amnesty International, *Torture, Despair and Dehumanisation in Tadmur Military Prison* (London: Amnesty International, September 2001).

Article 19, *Walls of Silence: Media and Censorship in Syria* (London: Article 19, June 1998).

Batatu, Hanna, *Syria's Peasantry, the Descendants of Its Lesser Rural Notables, and Their Politics* (Princeton, NJ: Princeton University Press, 1990).

Campagna, Joel, *Syria Briefing* (New York: Committee to Protect Journalists, September 2001).

Daguerre, Violette (ed.), *Democracy and Human Rights in Syria*, Arab Commission for Human Rights in co-operation with the European Commission (Paris: Eurabe Publishers, 2002).

Ehrenberg, John, *Civil Society: The Critical History of an Idea* (New York and London: New York University Press, 1999).

European Commission, *Euro-Med Partnership, Syria: Country Strategy Paper 2002–2006 & National Indicative Programme 2002–2004* (Brussels: European Commission, n.d.).

Glass, Charles, *Tribes with Flags: A Journey Curtailed* (London: Secker and Warburg, 1990).

Hinnebusch, Raymond, *Syria: Revolution from Above* (New York and London: Routledge, 2001).

Human Rights Watch, *The Silenced Kurds* (New York: Human Rights Watch, October 1996).

International Press Instiute (IPI), *2001 World Press Freedom Review: Syria* (Vienna: IPI, 2002).

Jeffreys, Andrew (ed.), *Emerging Syria 2002* (London: Oxford Business Group, 2002).

Khoury, Philip S., *Syria and the French Mandate: The Politics of Arab Nationalism, 1920–1945* (Princeton, NJ: Princeton University Press.

Kienle, Eberhard, *Ba'th v. Ba'ath*, (London and New York: I.B.Tauris, 1990).

— (ed.), *Contemporary Syria: Liberalization between Cold War and Cold Peace* (London: British Academic Press, 1994).

Lieve, Joris, *The Gates of Damascus* (Hawthorn, Australia: Lonely Planet Publications, 1996).

Ma'oz, Moshe, *Asad: The Sphinx of Damascus* (New York: Weidenfeld and Nicolson, 1988).

Middle East Watch, *Syria Unmasked: The Suppression of Human Rights by the Asad Regime* (New Haven, CT and London: Yale University Press, 1991).

Perthes, Volker, *The Political Economy of Syria under Asad* (London and New York: I.B.Tauris, 1995).

— 'The Political Economy of the Syrian Succession', *Survival*, International Institute of Strategic Studies (IISS), 43 (1), Spring 2001.

Seale, Patrick, *The Struggle for Syria* (Oxford University Press, 1965); new edn with an Introduction by Albert Hourani (London: I.B.Tauris, 1986).

— *Asad: The Struggle for Power in the Middle East* (London: I.B.Tauris, 1988; Berkeley and Los Angeles: University of California Press, 1995).

UNDP, *The Arab Human Development Report 2002* (New York: UNDP, July 2002).

UN Human Rights Committee, *Consideration of Reports Submitted by States Parties under Article 40 of the Covenant. Second Periodic Report of States Parties Due in 1984. Syrian Arab Republic*, Geneva, 25 August 2000.

US Central Intelligence Agency, *The World Factbook: Syria* (Washington, DC: CIA, 2001).

US Department of State, Bureau of Democracy, Human Rights, and Labor, *Syria: International Religious Freedom Report*, 26 October 2001.

US Department of State, Bureau of Near Eastern Affairs, *Background Note: Syria,* Washington, DC, February 2002.

US Library of Congress, Federal Research Division, *Syria: A Country Study*, (Washington, DC: Library of Congress, 1987).

Van Dam, Nikolaos, *The Struggle for Power in Syria: Politics and Society under Asad and the Ba'th Party* (London: I.B.Tauris, 1996).

Zisser, Eyal, *Asad's Legacy: Syria in Transition* (London: Hurst & Co., 2001).

Index